For Mr. Justice Michael Hanna,

In appreciation of your unfailing courtesy, and your contribution, as a Member of the bench of the High Court,

PATRICK

Medical Negligence Litigation in Ireland

Current Issues and Approaches

Medical Negligence Litigation in Ireland

Current Issues and Approaches

Editors
Caoimhe Daly
Patrick Treacy

Published by

Clarus Press Ltd,
Griffith Campus,
South Circular Road,
Dublin 8
www.claruspress.ie

Typeset by
Deanta Global Publishing Services

Printed by
SprintPrint Ltd,
Dublin

ISBN
978-1-911611-66-0 (Paperback)
978-1-911611-82-0 (Hardback)

A catalogue record for this book is available from the British Library

All rights reserved.

No part of this publication may be reproduced, or transmitted in any form or by any means, including recording and photocopying or any digital means, without the written permission of the copyright holder, application for which should be addressed to the publisher. Written permission should also be obtained before any part of the publication is stored in a retrieval system of any nature.

Disclaimer

Whilst every effort has been made to ensure that the contents of this book are accurate, neither the publisher, editors or contributors can accept responsibility for any errors or omissions or loss occasioned to any person acting or refraining from acting as result of any material in this publication.

Joint Copyright © Contributors and Clarus Press 2022

CONTENTS

A festschrift in honour of Mr Justice Kevin Cross   vii
Foreword   ix
The Chair of the Council of The Bar of Ireland   xv
Introduction   xvii

PART A – THE DUTY OF CARE   1

I. Has the duty of care for medical professionals been changed by the introduction of the test of 'the standard of approach' into the duty of care?   3
Julia Best and Oisín Quinn SC

PART B – CAUSES OF ACTION   17

II. Informed Consent: What five might find in *Lanarkshire*?   19
Eoghan Quinn and Luán ó Braonáin SC

III. Does a cause of action arise for nervous shock through witnessing the harm caused to a family member by reason of medical negligence and if so, in what circumstances does it arise?   49
Hugh O'Leary and Adrienne Egan SC

IV. What is the extent of the causes of action for wrongful conception and wrongful birth in the Republic of Ireland?   75
Sophie Treacy and Timothy O'Leary SC

PART C – CAUSATION   89

V. Has causation in medical negligence litigation now moved from the 'but for' test to one of 'material contribution'?   91
Anne Spillane and Eoin McCullough SC

PART D – TIME LIMITS   105

VI. Are the time limits for medical negligence litigation essentially different to those which apply in personal injuries litigation?   107
Hugh Kelly and Rónán Dolan SC

VII. Issuing proceedings but not serving them – is there a wider tolerance and justification for this practice in medical negligence litigation?   121
Trinity Geddis and Richard Kean SC

PART E – PRACTICE AND PROCEDURE   139

VIII. Forward to the past: Are the concepts of hindsight bias, blind reviews and inter-observer variability now established in medical negligence litigation practice?   141
Ashling Gallagher and Conor Halpin SC

IX. Open disclosure in Ireland: How will the proposed legislation impact upon medical practitioners, patients and medical negligence litigation?   159
Sadhbh Brennan and Declan Buckley SC

X. Is mediation preferable to negotiation as a means of alternative dispute resolution in ways that are specific to the nature of medical negligence litigation?   173
Fionn O'Callaghan and Sara Moorhead SC

PART F – DAMAGES   187

XI. Post-*Morrissey*: Hobson's choice for terminally ill plaintiffs and their statutory dependants?   189
Kate McCullough and Oonah McCrann SC

XII. Do the Personal Injuries Guidelines of the Judicial Council establish a statutory cap upon general damages and if so, are they constitutionally suspect in doing so?   203
Lauren Keane and Derry O'Donovan SC

Index   219

A *FESTSCHRIFT* IN HONOUR OF MR JUSTICE KEVIN CROSS

Mr Justice Kevin Cross was a Judge of the High Court of Ireland between 2011 and 2021. All of the Senior Counsel and members of the Inner Bar of Ireland who have contributed to this publication did so in the knowledge that it is a *festschrift* in his honour and in appreciation of the contribution which he made while he held this office.

During that decade, Mr Justice Cross made an immense contribution to the development of the legal principles which apply to personal injuries claims founded upon an allegation of negligence and breach of duty in the provision of a healthcare service. His contribution is self-evident from the content of the articles comprised in this publication as they constantly reference judgments of his.

Mr Justice Cross was not just greatly respected as a Judge by the members of the Bar of Ireland. He was also immensely popular. On one level, this arose from the obvious trust which he had in the integrity of the legal practitioners who appeared before him. At a deeper level, however, this widespread and enduring affection for him arose from observing how he treated all parties who appeared in the Court in which he presided. He had a style, a way of proceeding, formed in kindness, courtesy and humour which was unique. The Senior Counsel who contributed to this publication appeared regularly before him. It was this unique style of his as a Judge which they wish to honour in contributing to this publication.

> *Of Courtesy, it is much less*
> *Than Courage of Heart or Holiness,*
> *Yet in my Walks it seems to me*
> *That the Grace of God is in Courtesy.*

From the poem '*Courtesy*' by Hilaire Belloc

FOREWORD

I would like to say what an honour it is to be asked to write the foreword for this unique and wonderful venture in legal scholarship and that it is a *festschrift* in the manner as described. I am truly touched by this honour for judges, like everyone else, are just passing through. Whatever we might like to think, our judgments have little impact apart from the parties involved in the cases from which they arise. The notion that any decision has 'settled the law' is, if believed by the judge, almost always strong evidence of the onset of the dreaded 'judges' disease'. Written judgments usually do not long survive being altered and revised as circumstances dictate. Only those lawyers who might be described as 'affidavit readers' and 'submission drafters' will look at the store of law described in this publication as being the last word on anything. The Common Law is far more subtle than a perusal of the written word in judgments might suggest.

This is, as I said, a unique and wonderful publication, being twelve chapters jointly written by twelve leading Senior Counsel from the Round Hall, specialising in medical negligence litigation, together with twelve of the best and the brightest law students. Such welcome collaboration has never previously been attempted and in this volume, the result is extraordinary. All contributors and, in particular, the hard-working editors, Caoimhe Daly BL and Patrick Treacy SC, are to be congratulated.

The Round Hall is the beating heart of the civil Bar of Ireland where barristers are required to display a dexterity of the mind and of footwork to a much higher degree and at much more rapid a pace than is needed by their colleagues who practice in the more fashionable courts. The developing field of medical negligence litigation is, in many ways, the cutting edge of the Round Hall, so this publication is most timely and welcome. A swift glance at any of the chapters in this publication will rapidly demolish the myth that personal injuries litigation is devoid of law. Indeed, a criticism I would make is that there is now too much law in the practice and procedure involved in personal injuries litigation, too many traps for the unwary. This increasing complication may make more work for barristers, but the fear is that what was essentially a fairly simple system, designed to bring cases to trial as early as possible, is creating barriers to swift trials by unnecessary procedural motions which have the effect of aiding the big battalions at the expense of the ordinary litigant.

Friedrich Nietzsche, not a philosopher with whom I am in much agreement by the way, once said that one should philosophise with hammers in order to test theories and see if they are hollow. If I have any criticism of this publication and, overall it is a small one, it is that the authors, whom I suspect are the barristers and not the students, are sometimes too deferential when speaking of the various judgments upon which they comment and, in particular, of some of my utterances.

Kate McCullough and Oonah McCrann SC, in their chapter, refer to the 'Hobson's Choice' faced by terminally ill plaintiffs and their statutory dependents following the decision of the the Supreme Court in *Morrissey and another v Health Service Executive and others*.[1] It would be more accurate to refer to it as 'Sophie's Choice'. While, as their chapter makes clear, Clarke CJ did say the issue required 'a final determination', the tenor of that judgment is that once a claim is resolved during the lifetime of a plaintiff, that plaintiff's statutory dependents are barred from bringing any claim pursuant to the provisions of Part IV of the Civil Liability Act, 1961 even though the Supreme Court's judgment excluded from the plaintiffs' claim the damages the dependents would suffer after the death of the first named plaintiff. In other words, terminally ill plaintiffs must choose to vindicate their rights and establish the negligence which caused their terminal illness during their lifetime, or choose to die, without that vindication, so that their statutory dependents, including minor dependents, can recover their separate damages for their losses.

It is surely the obligation of judges to try to solve and not create problems. The idea that a mother, like the late Mrs Morrissey, in future could, by recovering her own damages, have the effect of depriving her minor children from recovering their entirely separate damages, is not just cruel but illogical and, dare I say it, could not be constitutional. This issue is admirably dealt with in the article by McCullough and McCrann. I do not agree that lawyers or judges who create problems should be allowed to demand that the legislature solve the problem that we have created. Courts should recognise that the legislature has many other priorities, rather than sorting out the mess we make. I fully accept that the solution I suggested in the High Court (through a loss of consortium and/or the 'lost years' approach) was not acceptable to the Supreme Court. By leaving the situation as it now seems to be, however, until the constitutionality of the rule is tested, a real injustice has been created. I am pleased to hear that already the ingenuity of the Round Hall is beginning to address the issue.

The issue of the 'cap' on general damages in catastrophic cases is dealt with in the final chapter written by Lauren Keane and Derry O'Donovan SC. They rightly draw attention to the Supreme Court decision of *Gough v Neary*[2] in which Mr Justice Geoghegan stated:

---

[1] [2020] IESC 6.
[2] [2003] IESC 39.

In my view there is no compulsory "cap" if there is no "omnibus sum" or in other words if the special damages are low. On the other hand, that does not mean that the "cap" figure cannot be taken into account in a general way in assessing the appropriate general damages in a non-cap case.

Gough has never been overturned and has been relied upon in numerous High Court cases. The Law Reform Commission's report on this subject, and in particular chapter two thereof, confirms that the decision of the Supreme Court in *Morrissey* does not alter the legal principles which apply to the status of the 'cap' (as opposed to the amount of it) on general damages.[3] As that is clearly the case, any suggestion that the decision of the Supreme Court in *Morrissey* has clarified or altered the legal status of the 'cap' on general damages is, I suggest, suspect, as are a number of judgments of the Court of Appeal which did not refer to the decision of the Supreme Court in *Gough*.

As Keane and O'Donovan make clear, assuming the Personal Injuries Guidelines, which were adopted by the Judicial Council on the 6 March 2021, are ultimately deemed to be constitutional, the obligation for judges, when assessing damages, is not to first consult these guidelines in order to mathematically fix the damages to be awarded. Rather, judges should first proceed to assess the damages, as before, in terms of whether they are fair and reasonable compensation to the wronged party for the injuries suffered and whether they are proportional, taking into account factors such as economic and social conditions. It is only then that judges should proceed to consider the appropriate range of figures specified in these guidelines. If the result is not acceptable, the court can (and should) depart from the range of figures specified in the guidelines, while giving rational, cogent and justifiable reasons for so doing.

In the opening chapter, Julia Best and Oisín Quinn SC dispel the fear that the judgments, both at first instance and on appeal, given in *Morrissey*, somehow opened 'the floodgates' or created a different standard of care. They helpfully set out the clear statement of the law in the relation of the duty of care as enunciated by the Supreme Court in that case and subsequently by Hyland J in her judgment in *Freeney v Health Service Executive*.[4]

Eoghan Quinn and Luán ó Braonáin SC deal with the subject of 'informed consent' in their chapter. They set out, in a most useful manner, Irish and United Kingdom cases in relation to this subject. Anyone wishing for a statement of the law in this area could hardly do better than consulting this article. I note that the latest Irish case which they cite is that of the Supreme Court in

---

[3] *'Capping Damages in Personal Injuries Actions'* Law Reform Commission Report, 2020 (LRC 126-2022).
[4] [2020] IEHC 115.

Fitzpatrick v White[5] in 2008. In my experience, trying medical negligence cases, 'informed consent' was never a serious issue. Doctors and hospitals are now fully alive to the need for 'informed consent' and this is a good example of lessons in patient safety having been learnt from past litigation.

Hugh O'Leary and Adrienne Egan SC deal with the issue of nervous shock through witnessing harm caused to family members by reason of clinical negligence. The authors set out the law in relation to 'nervous shock' as defined by the Supreme Court in *Kelly v. Hennessy*[6] in 1995. They proceed to refer to my decision on the issue in *Morrissey* and the Court of Appeal in *Harford v Electricity Supply Board*.[7] The authors also give a comprehensive analysis of the position in the United Kingdom which is based on somewhat different reasoning but also seeks to put limits on recoverability.

A most interesting chapter, concerning the possibility of actions for wrongful conception/wrongful birth, is written by Sophie Treacy and Timothy O'Leary SC. The authors deal with the position in the United Kingdom as to the wrongful conception of a healthy child and the wrongful conception and birth of a disabled child. The authors correctly state that such cases may now arise after the repeal of the Eight Amendment of the Constitution of Ireland and conclude that these cases 'provide challenging moral and legal dilemmas for the courts'. On reading this article I am indeed glad to no longer have responsibility to decide such cases.

Anne Spillane and Eoin McCullough SC deal with the fascinating issue of causation and whether the test is still 'but for' or whether it has moved to one of 'material contribution'. Frequently, in medical negligence cases, the real issue is not the alleged negligence on the part of a defendant, but whether any negligence admitted, or so found, caused the plaintiff's injuries. The authors note that in Ireland the 'but for' test is still dominant. They argue that the 'but for' test ought be adjusted to avoid unfairness or illogical results in cases of multiple causality.

Two important chapters concern time limits. Hugh Kelly and Rónán Dolan SC consider whether time limits for medical negligence litigation are essentially different from other personal injuries actions. In the following chapter, Trinity Geddis and Richard Kean SC then consider the practice and procedure of issuing proceedings but not serving them. Kelly and Dolan deal with ss 2 and 3 of the Statute of Limitations (Amendment) Act 1991 and emphasise the judgment of Charlton J in *O'Sullivan v Ireland, The Attorney General & others*[8] who said:

---

[5] [2008] 3 IR 551.
[6] [1995] 3 IR 253.
[7] [2021] IECA 112.
[8] [2019] IESC 33.

Foreword

> The core issue is always at what stage such a plaintiff had such broad knowledge from facts which he or she either had, or might reasonably have been expected to acquire, from observable or ascertainable facts, or only on the basis of consulting an expert to ascertain such fact or facts.[9]

Geddis and Kean deal with the extension of time to serve issued proceedings given the prohibition upon counsel signing professional negligence proceedings absent a supportive expert report and they address, in particular, the decision of the Court of Appeal in *Murphy v Health Service Executive*.[10] The authors conclude that the failure to serve proceedings within the one year time frame is a practice which 'enjoys a wider tolerance and justification in clinical negligence litigation.'

Ashling Gallagher and Conor Halpin SC deal with the issue of hindsight bias and blind reviews of slides. This is an issue which was first ventilated in the course of the hearings in *Morrissey*. Courts must always be aware of the possibility of bias — old age pensioners may possibly speed. In the case of the subsequent review of cytology slides, arising in the course of cervical cancer screening, which are deemed to contain cancerous cells, the issue of hindsight bias must be addressed. The authors discuss the advisability of a 'blind review' as possibly the best way of ensuring as little bias as possible. They note that both of the judgments given by the High Court and the Supreme Court in *Morrissey* were neutral in relation to the issue of blind reviews. From my point of view, no subsequent analysis can reproduce the original screener's position. When considering the value of a 'blind review', the question is whether or not the reviewer is aware that there is a problem with at least one of the slides under review. The court's function is to then assess the evidence bearing in mind hindsight bias.

Sadhbh Brennan and Declan Buckley SC discuss the issue of 'open disclosure' and proposed legislation in relation to it. It is proposed that existing voluntary 'open disclosure' be replaced by mandatory disclosure. The authors rightly welcome this development and stress the need for constant review and to have a robust policy plan and supports in place to complement the legislation in order to guarantee success from it. I have no doubt that prompt and sincere apology for errors, whether they be negligent or not, would not only reduce anger but would help to reduce litigation. Many plaintiffs, initially at least, primarily want to be given an explanation as to what went wrong.

Fionn O'Callaghan and Sara Moorhead SC write about whether mediation is preferable to negotiation in the resolution of medical negligence litigation. As someone who grew as a barrister witnessing the success of the force of senior colleagues, such as Colm Condon SC or Jim O'Driscoll SC, in effecting settlements, my starting position was one of suspicion of mediation. I saw

---

[9] ibid at para 35.
[10] [2021] IECA 3.

it as creating an extra layer of lawyering which, while good for lawyers, was, I felt, unnecessary. As a judge, I found, however, especially in medical negligence litigation, that mediation, in some instances, achieved a settlement that negotiation could not achieve. Whether this is because present day practitioners do not possess so hard a boot as some of my former and more senior colleagues or, as I think to be the case, the raw issues which often arise in medical negligence cases require someone who is neutral, I cannot be sure. The authors are clear as to the benefits of mediation in such cases and rightly refer to the stress of medical negligence litigation, not just upon plaintiffs but also upon defendants.

So, we see in this one volume a magnificent collaboration between law students and barristers. The rule of law is essential for a free society. The independence of the judiciary is essential for the rule of law. An independent Bar is essential for the independence of the judiciary. Judges need to know when counsel address them that they are not being misled and barristers need to be sufficiently independent that they can robustly call Judges to account if they stray in their judgments or conduct. The independent Bar needs a regular refreshment from the best and the brightest amongst law students. All twelve students here have demonstrated their excellence. I hope all of them join the Bar in due course and if they do, I am confident they will have great success. They deserve it, as does this work. I thoroughly recommend it.

Kevin Cross
December 2022

CHAIR OF THE COUNCIL OF THE BAR OF IRELAND

It gives me great pleasure as Chair of the Council of The Bar of Ireland to introduce this valuable publication.

Firstly, the educational value that may be attributed to having a group of undergraduate law students work with a group of senior counsel in order to prepare a legal textbook, particularly one which is primarily aimed at practitioners in the field in question, cannot be underestimated. This endeavour neatly underpins one of the objectives of The Bar of Ireland's Equality Action Plan, launched on 1 June 2022, which is to enhance access to the profession. This publication is but one example of how The Bar of Ireland can connect with third level law schools and faculties so as to provide experience to undergraduate law students of what is involved in being a barrister-at-law and to inform them about a career at the Bar.

A second theme is that the collaborative engagement by barristers in writing this text enhances knowledge of the area of legal practice under consideration. It is consistent with the increasing emphasis by the Council on promoting continuing professional development. Those involved with this publication have a further aim of providing continuing professional development seminars in the future, based upon sections of this text, with the engagement of the students and the barristers who wrote the articles. These seminars will provide an excellent opportunity for continuing professional development while also providing further experience and mentoring for the students in question. A further purpose of these intended seminars is to use them as a means by which to raise funds for the Bar Benevolent Society.

An adjacent theme arising from the initiative of The Bar of Ireland in producing a legal textbook, through the collaboration of its members and law students, is that it is a visible and tangible example of the accessibility of the independent referral bar in providing legal expertise for the benefit of the wider community.

Finally, and related to the last theme, the approach of preparing a text in this manner, through bringing undergraduate students in a law school or faculty together with practising barristers, is a model that could be adopted in any area of legal practice in which members of the Irish Bar are engaged. Thus, this initiative may serve as a template for future collaboration between the Bar and third level law schools and faculties, so as to continue to promote the Bar and enhance knowledge of, and access to, the Bar amongst all third level students, and to advance inclusion and diversity at the Bar in the years to come.

I congratulate everyone involved with the initiative which has led to this publication and the intended manner in which it will be used to support the invaluable work of the Bar Benevolent Society. Indeed, I look forward to seeing the students mentioned within these pages, and future pages, one day appearing beside us as colleagues at the Bar.

Sara Phelan SC
Chair
Council of The Bar of Ireland
December 2022

INTRODUCTION

Anyone who suffers a significant injury learns how every aspect of one's life is negatively impacted upon by what has occurred. When this injury has resulted from the negligence of another person, the physical and psychological harm one suffers is compounded by the wrong which has given rise to it. When this personal harm has further resulted from negligence and breach of duty in the provision of a healthcare service, the negative consequences are exacerbated further by the failure of professional standards which this entails. It is in this context that every legitimate claim of medical negligence arises. It is to be expected, therefore, that plaintiffs who have been wronged in this manner will have strong feelings in relation to how they have been harmed, both in relation to their physical person but also in terms of their personal dignity.

It is also difficult to conceive of any career which is as demanding and challenging as that of a medical professional. The academic study and professional training required to become a registered medical practitioner is difficult and protracted. Once qualified, junior doctors are regularly required to endure long working hours. Often, a medical practitioner, who provides invaluable service, can rightly feel aggrieved at being the subject of an allegation of negligence and breach of duty, in the course of medical practice, which is in the public domain and which may serve to undermine years, if not even a professional lifetime, of exemplary service to patients.

All of these legitimate and often conflicting concerns come to the fore in the course of medical negligence litigation. It is of little surprise then that these claims can often be keenly contested. In so doing, the judgments that arise in this area of legal practice can be dynamic and provide significant insights into our understanding of the legal principles which apply not just in this specific field of litigation but also in relation to tort and practice and procedure before the Superior Courts.

It is entirely facile, however, to present medical negligence litigation as a binary battle between patients and healthcare providers. To begin with, at the commencement of the provision of any medical care, patients and their healthcare providers have the same goal of restoration of the health of the patient as far as is possible. Invariably, when proceedings arise from the provision of this care and when the action of a plaintiff is not contested in relation to liability and causation or ultimately compromised, it is because another independent medical practitioner has advised the defending party that the standard of care in the provision of the healthcare in question was not at the level which was reasonably required.

This publication is not intended to give an overview of every aspect of practice that arises in medical negligence litigation. There are existing and excellent textbooks prepared by legal practitioners in this field in this country which provide such a comprehensive understanding of this subject. Rather, the purpose of the chapters of this publication is to reflect upon the key contemporary areas of practice in medical negligence litigation which are at the frontier of our understanding of it. Accordingly, this publication seeks to address and reflect upon the most current and recurring issues which arise for legal practitioners and the judiciary in the course of medical negligence litigation, so that this analysis may hopefully be of assistance when a case is being prepared for trial or during the course thereof.

The twelve chapters of this publication are arranged in six sections. The first section addresses the foundational subject of the duty of care which applies in medical negligence litigation. Sometimes, it can be wrongly perceived that a claim of medical negligence can be easily established in evidence before the Superior Courts. As the first chapter of Julia Best and Oisín Quinn SC explains, the test to establish negligence and breach of duty on the part of a medical professional remains that as enunciated by the Supreme Court in *Dunne v National Maternity Hospital and another*.[1] A successful plaintiff must establish in evidence that the medical professional in question was guilty of such failure or omission as no medical professional of equal specialist or general status and skill would be guilty of if acting with ordinary care. Following the decision of the Supreme Court in *Morrissey and another v Health Service Executive and others*,[2] this article discusses the significance of that judgment in clarifying that it is the medical profession itself which dictates the standard of approach which is to be adopted and which is then applied by the Superior Courts within the framework of the principles for determining if there has been a breach of duty as defined by the Supreme Court in *Dunne*.

The second section of this publication addresses two causes of action which are particularly controversial at this time. In their chapter, Eoghan Quinn and Luán ó Braonáin SC consider the subject of a cause of action based upon a lack of informed consent. While this is the longest chapter in this publication, their detailed analysis of this topic warrants the extensive treatment which they give it. The issue of informed consent is a cause of action which is hovering in the background of so much medical negligence litigation but which rarely comes before the Irish Superior Courts for the clarification and elucidation which it deserves.

---

[1] [1989] IR 1.
[2] [2020] IESC 6.

Introduction xix

This section also comprises a chapter by Hugh O'Leary and Adrienne Egan SC which addresses, in an equally comprehensive manner, the controversial subject as to whether a cause of action for nervous shock arises from witnessing the deterioration of the health of a family relative by reason of negligence in the provision of healthcare to that relative. This issue came before Mr Justice Kevin Cross in *Morrissey and another v Health Service Executive and others*[3] during the hearing of this action, at first instance, in the High Court. Cross J refused to grant the damages for nervous shock to the second named plaintiff, the husband of the plaintiff who was terminally ill with cervical cancer. This aspect of the judgment was not part of the appeal to the Supreme Court as the plaintiffs did not appeal any of that judgment when responding to the varied appeals of the other Defendants in those proceedings. The significance and implications of this judgment is addressed in this chapter within the context of the relevant caselaw both in the United Kingdom and in this jurisdiction.

The next chapter of this section of this publication, by Sophie Treacy and Timothy O'Leary SC, addresses the controversial subject of causes of action which are advanced based upon wrongful conception and wrongful birth. This chapter captures how the causes of action which arise in medical negligence litigation are often at the frontier, not just of the evolution of legal principles, but also of where cultural and societal values currently stand in terms of defining what is or is not acceptable in the making of a claim before the Superior Courts.

The third section of this publication is comprised of one chapter by Anne Spillane and Eoin McCullough SC on the critical subject of causation. The law in relation to causation in the area of medical negligence litigation rests on a precipice at the moment in relation to whether the 'but for' test holds or whether a more nuanced and sophisticated understanding of causation prevails in terms of whether the alleged wrong has materially contributed to the injuries sustained by a plaintiff. This chapter compares both understandings of causation and also delves into the complex area of claims which advance a claim for damages based upon having lost a chance of making a full or proper recovery from an illness or injury for which medical treatment had been sought.

The fourth section of this publication addresses the issue of time limits in relation to the commencement and prosecution of medical negligence proceedings. Hugh Kelly and Rónán Dolan SC provide an overview in their chapter of two key judgments of the Supreme Court in 2019 which wrestle with the question of the application of the limitation period of two years to the particular nature and circumstances of medical negligence litigation. Their article underlines how difficult it can be to apply the provisions of s 2 of the Statute of Limitations (Amendment) Act 1991 to the particular facts and circumstances which give rise to a claim for medical negligence. They underline that these

---

[3] [2019] IEHC 268.

cases are invariably highly fact specific and are not easily amenable to a broad application of the provisions of the Statutes of Limitations.

Trinity Geddis and Richard Kean SC then address in their chapter the additional complex question of the renewal of a personal injuries summons which has commenced a claim alleging medical negligence but which was not served within twelve months of the date of its issue because experts' reports had not been obtained, within that time, to establish the claim in terms of liability and causation. As Order 8 of the Rules of the Superior Courts 1986 was substantially amended in 2018, this article provides a detailed analysis of the consideration by the Superior Courts of the new formulation of this Order since then and particularly as it applies to the commencement of actions claiming damages arising from alleged negligence in the provision of healthcare.

The penultimate section of this publication then contains three chapters considering specific issues of practice and procedure which arise in medical negligence litigation. In their chapter, Ashling Gallagher and Conor Halpin SC identify and consider new approaches which have entered into the consideration of evidence in cases which involve the retrospective evaluation of the healthcare provided and particularly in the context of cancer screening. They address how the Superior Courts have approached the recent presentation of the concepts of hindsight bias, 'blind reviews' and inter-observer variability in the defence of medical negligence claims.

Sadhbh Brennan and Declan Buckley SC address in their chapter another issue which forms a significant backdrop to the conduct of medical negligence litigation, namely the relatively recent legislative requirements for open disclosure to patients of errors which may have arisen in the provision of healthcare to them and how this impacts upon the conduct of litigation arising thereafter. This is a particularly sensitive subject which goes to the heart of the relationship between patients and healthcare providers and receives welcome attention in this chapter in terms of its integration with the adversarial nature of medical negligence litigation.

Fionn O'Callaghan and Sara Moorhead SC then consider in their chapter a constantly recurring question which arises when medical negligence proceedings come to be resolved, which is whether a mediator should be engaged. The essential question which practitioners have to address, when seeking to resolve the proceedings, is what does a mediation offer in terms of the satisfactory resolution of the proceedings which a straight-forward negotiation between the parties does not. Hopefully, this article will assist practitioners in making a more discerned decision in this regard when contemplating which avenue of dispute resolution to proceed with as a medical negligence claim approaches its trial date.

The final section of this publication addresses the area of damages and in so doing concentrates upon two of the most controversial subjects which have arisen in the conduct of medical negligence litigation in recent times. The chapter by Kate McCullough and Oonah McCrann SC addresses one highly significant outcome from the judgment of the Supreme Court in *Morrissey and another v Health Service Executive and others*.[4] This is the awful choice which is now faced by a terminally ill parent, in particular, who is considering commencing proceedings claiming damages arising from an allegation that he or she is facing imminent death by reason of a failure in the healthcare provided. As the law currently stands, such a parent, for instance, now faces the dilemma of suing for general damages for personal injury, which are likely to be at the highest level, but then potentially barring a claim of the surviving dependants pursuant to Part IV of the Civil Liability Act 1961. Alternatively, this dying parent could forego the claim for general damages, at the highest level, so as to preserve one sole claim for his or her children or other dependants pursuant to this statutory provision, arising after this person has died. This chapter explains why a statutory amendment is essential and urgent so as to end this terrible dilemma which is being currently presented to terminally ill claimants, with statutory dependants, who have well-founded claims alleging that medical negligence has given rise to the loss of their lives.

Lauren Keane and Derry O'Donovan SC conclude this publication by considering whether the Personal Injuries Guidelines of the Judicial Council of Ireland establish a statutory cap upon general damages and if so, whether they are constitutionally suspect in doing so. The consideration of this question is particularly germane to medical negligence litigation as claims are regularly advanced by plaintiffs who have suffered catastrophic injuries or who are terminally ill by reason of alleged negligence in the provision of healthcare to them. In this context, the consideration of the 'cap' on general damages in these guidelines of €550,000 is particularly apposite both in terms of its constitutional status and as to how legal practitioners can best approach it in the conduct of such litigation.

Separate to the content of this publication, it is also an attempt to forge a new way of conducting legal research and education between the Bar of Ireland and law faculties and schools within this jurisdiction. It is the first collaborative publication between a group of practising barristers and law students. It is a way of proceeding in legal research and publishing which could be formally adopted by the Bar of Ireland in future, through connecting with the heads of different law faculties and schools in Ireland. In this way, it provides a real opportunity for law students to gain insight into the professional career of a barrister-at-law. It also greatly assists barristers in continuing to develop an expertise in a particular area of legal practice. The views expressed by Sara Phelan SC, the Chair of the Council of the Bar of Ireland, at the beginning of this publication are particularly welcome in this regard.

---

[4] [2020] IEHC 6.

A further objective of this publication is to explore how a legal publication, produced by members of the Bar of Ireland, can raise the profile, and support the work, of the Bar Benevolent Society, which largely goes unnoticed. The Bar Benevolent Society adopts the strictest levels of confidentiality in its work but, in so doing, the Bar does not learn of the profound difficulties which some of its members have to encounter, nor of the great work which the society does. It is intended that this publication will be used, in whatever manner possible, to raise funds for the work of the society, commencing with its launch in December 2022 by Mr Justice Paul Coffey.

This publication is also novel in the sense that the members of the Inner Bar of Ireland, who worked with law students in contributing chapters to it, did so as part of a *festschrift* in appreciation of the judicial career of Mr Justice Kevin Cross as a Judge of the High Court of Ireland. All of these contributors had regular and direct contact with him during his decade as a Judge from 2011 to 2021. They were unanimous, if not even at times bordering on unrestrained, in their approval that they would contribute to this publication once it was being written in appreciation of all that he did for others when he served in this capacity.

As can be seen from the contents of this publication, this is a collaborative work involving considerable time and effort by a whole range of people. There are some people, however, who have significantly contributed to this publication and which is not apparent from reading the chapters within it. Professor Gerard Whyte of the School of Law, Trinity College Dublin, offered many helpful insights in relation to the publication of this text, both in terms of its substantive content and also in relation to how the Bar of Ireland and law schools and faculties could collaborate in the future in a manner which is mutually beneficial to law students and to legal practitioners alike. Similarly, Ciara McGoldrick BL was a constant source of guidance in bringing this publication to fruition. Indeed, a number of emerging legal principles in this area of legal practice, which this publication elucidates, arise from legal submissions and arguments which she crafted in her practice and which she educated Senior Counsel in how to present to the Superior Courts.

Eric Rainsberry designed the front cover of this publication. Without having ever frequented the Round Hall in the Four Courts, let alone stand there on a busy morning after the call-over of cases listed in Court One, he was able to capture the dynamism of what occurs there in the beautiful cover which he designed.

Sara Phelan SC and Denise Brett SC, Chair and Vice-Chair respectively of the Council of the Bar of Ireland, were both continuously supportive of the evolution of this publication and have done everything possible to support and promote it. Denise Brett SC was formerly the Chair of the Education Committee of the Council of the Bar of Ireland when the idea of this publication was first presented to her and she did everything she could to encourage its emergence thereafter.

Finally, particular appreciation is due to David McCartney of Clarus Press. From the very outset, he was entirely supportive and enthusiastic about this publication. He understood from the beginning how this publication is seeking to pilot a new way in which the Bar of Ireland can work with third level law faculties and schools so as to facilitate legal scholarship and mentoring in the future. Hopefully, the collaborative approach of writing this publication, between law students and members of the Bar of Ireland, will arise continually in the future and lead to many more legal publications which are of the same standard as the excellent legal publications which these publishers have already produced.

Caoimhe Daly BL
Patrick Treacy SC
December 2022

PART A
THE DUTY OF CARE

Chapter I

HAS THE DUTY OF CARE FOR MEDICAL PROFESSIONALS BEEN CHANGED BY THE INTRODUCTION OF THE TEST OF 'THE STANDARD OF APPROACH' INTO THE DUTY OF CARE?

Julia Best and Oisín Quinn SC[1]

Introduction

The standard of care for medical professionals has recently been the subject of particular focus in the Irish courts. On 19 March 2020, during the height of the early days of the COVID-19 pandemic, the Supreme Court delivered a seminal judgment in *Morrissey and another v Health Service Executive and others*.[2] Clarke CJ, on behalf of the Court, restated the legal test for medical negligence, describing the standard of care as 'the standard of approach'. The clinical activity in *Morrissey* involved screening of cervical smear tests taken as part of the National Cervical Screening Programme. The description by the courts of the application of an 'absolute confidence' test gave rise to some 'doomsday' public commentary predicting that the application of such a test would make screening systems unworkable.[3] This chapter will explore whether *Morrissey* has refined the long-settled enunciation of the duty of care in medical negligence litigation, as notably summarised by the judgment of the Supreme Court in *Dunne v National Maternity Hospital and another*,[4] and whether there is any credibility to such concerns.

The first section of this chapter will set out the long-established test for determining medical negligence, summarised succinctly by Finlay CJ in *Dunne*.[5] The second section of this chapter will then review the case of *Morrissey* and the judgments in the High Court of Cross J[6] and then in the

---

[1] Julia Best prepared this chapter as a final year undergraduate student at the School of Law at Trinity College Dublin. Oisín Quinn SC is a member of the Inner Bar of Ireland.
[2] *Morrissey and another v Health Service Executive and others* [2020] IESC 6.
[3] See para 6.29 of the judgment of Clarke CJ *in Morrissey*.
[4] *Dunne v National Maternity Hospital and another* [1989] IR 91.
[5] ibid.
[6] *Morrissey and another v Health Service Executive and others* [2019] IEHC 268.

Supreme Court, and discuss both the apparent restatement of the law on medical negligence and the debate which has arisen regarding that restatement and the claims made by some on behalf of the medical profession that a potentially onerous or unworkable standard has been placed upon medical practitioners. Finally, this chapter will then assess those concerns in light of the High Court's more recent application of the 'standard of approach' test in *Freeney v Health Service Executive*.[7]

It will be argued that in fact Cross J in the High Court merely applied the well-established principles set out in *Dunne*, and that although the phrase the 'standard of approach' introduced by the Supreme Court is unfamiliar, in reality the Supreme Court, in upholding Cross J's findings as to the standard of care, did not change the law but rather has helpfully restated the *Dunne* principles in a way that brings additional clarity to their application and a new focus on their underlying logic.

The chapter will conclude by drawing attention to the clear demonstration by the Supreme Court[8] that when applied, this legal approach does no more than involve an initial factual search by the Court – by reference to the evidence of the relevant professionals themselves – for the standard of the profession, so that it is the evidence of the professionals themselves that determines the standard to be applied by the Court to another expert against whom an allegation of clinical negligence is made.

THE WELL-ESTABLISHED TEST FOR THE DUTY OF CARE IN MEDICAL NEGLIGENCE CASES: *DUNNE V NATIONAL MATERNITY HOSPITAL AND ANOTHER*

In the earlier seminal case of the Supreme Court, *Dunne v National Maternity Hospital and another*, Finlay CJ summarised the well-settled principles to be applied in cases involving allegations of professional negligence by medical practitioners. *Dunne* involved an infant plaintiff who had sustained irreversible brain damage during birth. His mother, on his behalf, took a negligence action for damages. In the Supreme Court, Finlay CJ succinctly stated the principles which have since dominated medical negligence judicial rulings in the succeeding four decades to their establishment.[9] Although it has been observed that the principles essentially reiterate the decision of a preceding case, *O'Donovan v Cork County Council*,[10] the way in which the principles were presented as a clear and succinct set of rules, characteristic of their author's style, led to the case being widely cited in contemporary litigation rather than its predecessor.

---

[7] *Freeney v Health Service Executive* [2020] IEHC 115.
[8] See paras 6.14–6.16 of Clarke CJ in *Morrissey* in particular.
[9] Annual Review of Irish Law 2019, Tort (Thomson Reuters (Professional) Ireland Limited) 1(1), 665–712 at p 8.
[10] *O'Donovan v Cork County Council* [1967] IR 173.

The Duty of Care

In considering how to formulate a comprehensive statement of the principles that underpin the law on medical negligence in terms of the duty of care, Finlay CJ held that the authorities established six key principles to be considered, which can be summarised as follows.

Firstly, the true test for establishing negligence in diagnosis or treatment on the part of a medical practitioner is whether they have been proved to be guilty of such failure as no medical practitioner of equal specialist or general status and skill would be guilty of if acting with ordinary care.

Secondly, if the allegation of negligence against a medical practitioner is based on proof that they deviated from a general and approved practice, that will not be sufficient to establish negligence unless it is also proved that the medical course they did take was one which no medical practitioner of like specialisation and skill would have followed had they been taking the ordinary care required from a person of their qualifications.

The third principle establishes that a medical practitioner charged with negligence may not avoid liability by establishing that their conduct was approved of by their colleagues of similar specialisation and skill, if the practice has been shown by the plaintiff to have inherent defects which ought to have been obvious to any person giving the matter due consideration. Similarly, the fourth principle states that an honest difference of opinion between medical practitioners as to which treatment plan is best for the patient will not provide grounds for a finding of negligence.

Notably, the penultimate *Dunne* principle declares that it is not for a judge to decide which of two alternative courses of treatment is preferable; their function is to decide whether the course of treatment followed by the defendant practitioner, on the evidence, complied with the careful conduct of a medical practitioner of like specialisation and skill. This principle essentially abdicates the role of the court, in part, allowing the standard of negligence to be established by medical practitioners alike.

The final *Dunne* principle highlights that if there is an issue of fact, the determination of which is necessary for the decision as to whether a particular medical practice is or is not general and approved within the meaning of these principles, that issue must in a trial held with a jury be left to the determination of the jury.

Furthermore, Finlay CJ highlighted two competing 'broad parameters', which he explained the courts must always seek to give equal regard to. The first of these parameters he described thus:

> The development of medical science and the supreme importance of that development to humanity makes it particularly undesirable and inconsistent with the common good that doctors should be obliged to

carry out their professional duties under frequent threat of unsustainable legal claims.

The second he explained as follows:

> The complete dependence of patients on the skill and care of their medical attendants and the gravity from their point of view of a failure in such care, makes it undesirable and unjustifiable to accept as a matter of law a lax or permissive standard of care for the purpose of assessing what is and is not medical negligence.

Finlay CJ then stated, 'In developing the legal principles outlined and in applying them to the facts of each individual case, the courts must constantly seek to give equal regard to both of these considerations'. Throughout the judgment delivered by Finlay CJ, there is an obvious consideration afforded to the importance of balancing a number of competing policies in order to avoid a chilling effect which professional legal liability can create. Thus, the *Dunne* principles were undoubtedly developed with the partial goal of ensuring that doctors are not unduly burdened by litigation claims.

In many ways, the last three *Dunne* principles may be viewed together as they share a clear recognition that inconsistency is a reality of clinical medicine, as medical practitioners will not always be unanimous on the correct approach to be taken.[11] Furthermore, these principles recognise the court's lack of competence and expertise in judging the merits of medical approaches and the subsequent limited role which the court should have.[12] Accordingly, the final three *Dunne* principles give the first two real evidential effect, allowing the standard of negligence to be set by medical practitioners with the expertise to do so.

THE NEXT STEP: *MORRISSEY AND ANOTHER V HEALTH SERVICE EXECUTIVE AND OTHERS*

In the recent case of *Morrissey and another v Health Service Executive and others*, the standard of the duty of care traditionally laid out by the *Dunne* principles became of particular focus in both the High Court and the Supreme Court. This section will provide an outline of the facts of the case before exploring the judgments of both courts.

The factual background to the Morrisseys' case

The claims of the Morrissey family, as acknowledged by Clarke CJ in the Supreme Court, arose from very tragic circumstances. Mrs Morrissey (first

---

[11] Ciarán Craven, 'Medical Negligence and the *Dunne* Principles: The Third and Later Principles' (2006) 1 Q Rev Tort L 12 17.
[12] ibid.

The Duty of Care 7

plaintiff), who is sadly now deceased, was married to Paul Morrissey (second plaintiff) and who together have one young daughter. Mrs Morrissey had undergone two smear tests in August 2009 and August 2012 in accordance with the National Screening Programme (CervicalCheck). The first smear test was analysed by a laboratory owned by Quest Diagnostics Incorporated (the second defendant) in Michigan, USA. The second smear test was examined by MedLab Pathology Limited (the third defendant) at a laboratory in Dublin. In both instances, the results of the smear tests were provided as negative. Following a subsequent biopsy and MRI scan in 2014, however, performance of which was prompted by symptomatic bleeding, Mrs Morrissey was diagnosed with cervical cancer. A subsequent audit of these two smear tests, arising by reason of Mrs Morrissey having been diagnosed with the cervical cancer, revealed that the results of both tests were incorrectly determined as negative. This was not disclosed to Mrs Morrissey until May 2018, in the immediate aftermath of the disclosure of the audit results of a cohort of women arising from the resolution of proceedings brought by the late Mrs Vicky Phelan in late April of that year. In fact, this information was only disclosed to Mrs Morrissey when she learnt what had unfolded in Mrs Phelan's case and intuited that she was one of those women whose audit results of prior smear tests had not been disclosed to her, thereby prompting her to enquire as to whether an error had been made in the reading of her tests. Mrs Morrissey and her husband subsequently commenced proceedings against the defendants, the Health Service Executive (HSE), Quest Diagnostics Incorporated and MedLab Pathology Limited for negligence and breach of duty.

THE EMERGENCE OF THE 'ABSOLUTE CONFIDENCE' TEST IN THE HIGH COURT

Following an urgent hearing of this case, which began in July 2018 and which was expedited at every stage by Cross J, by reason of interim applications and adjournments that arose after the trial commenced, judgment was delivered on 3 May 2019 in the High Court. The trial had proceeded over more than 35 days in court. Although Cross J identified that there were numerous issues identified in the case, this chapter is concerned primarily with the first issue, 'the standard of care'. In determining this issue, Cross J highlighted that a number of legal principles and guidelines may be of relevance. In his judgment, Cross J begins by laying out the *Dunne* principles,[13] emphasising that they 'remain the standard test in relation to professional negligence'.[14] Cross J then goes on to note the guidelines for the review of cytology samples in the context of litigation or potential litigation issued by the American Society of Cytopathology, highlighting that these guidelines do not 'in any way' set a legal standard which the court is obliged to follow.[15]

---

[13] At para 52.
[14] At para 54.
[15] See paras 57–64.

Notably, Cross J found that the test of the English Court of Appeal laid out in *Penney, Palmer and Cannon v East Kent Health Authority*[16] was of the 'greatest importance'.[17] The case of *Penney, Palmer* also concerned the alleged negligent misreading of smear tests by cytology screeners. A number of similarities can be drawn between the judgment delivered in *Penney, Palmer* by Lord Woolf MR and by Cross J in *Morrissey*. Thus, it could reasonably be said that Cross J was rightly influenced by the rationale of this judgment of the English Court of Appeal when delivering his own judgment in the Irish High Court.

In the judgment of Lord Woolf, as cited by Cross J, it is formally established that there are three questions which are to be considered when determining medical negligence in cytology screening. Lord Woolf further notes, however, that these questions are not intended to replace the traditional legal test for the standard of care in medical screening cases as stated in *Bolam v Friern Hospital Management Committee*.[18] Cross J highlights in his judgment that *Bolam*, together with *Bolitho v City and Hackney Health Authority*,[19] can be understood as the English equivalent of *Dunne v National Maternity Hospital*. In doing so, Cross J is implicit in his suggestion that the *Dunne* principles remain the legal standard in Irish law.

Furthermore, as noted by Cross J in his judgment in the High Court, the English Court of Appeal in *Penney, Palmer* endorsed the standard of the duty of care set by the opinions of the experts in the particular case. This standard was 'absolute confidence'. In the *Morrissey* trial, a number of experts for the plaintiffs also supported the standard of 'absolute confidence' for screeners, although it must be noted that the experts for the defendants were not 'entirely happy' with this standard. Accordingly, Cross J, drawing from the persuasive precedent of the English Court of Appeal, held that the overall assessment of negligence in the context of medical screening was as follows:

> the legal standard to be applied on the issue of the liability of the defendants is the Dunne test. Questions of fact, however, are for my decision on the balance of probabilities. The questions of fact include what was to be seen on the individual slides. Accordingly, as in *Penney, Palmer*, the correct approach is to determine:
>
> (I) what was to be seen on each slide;
> (II) whether a reasonably competent screener at the relevant time could have failed to see what was on the slide; and
> (III) whether a reasonably competent screener in the light of what he or she should have observed, could have treated the slide as negative.

---

[16] *Penney, Palmer and Cannon v East Kent Health Authority* [2000] Lloyd's Rep Med 41.
[17] See para 66.
[18] *Bolam v Friern Hospital Management Committee* [1957] 1 WLR 583.
[19] *Bolitho v City and Hackney Health Authority* [1988] AC 232.

> Questions (ii) and (iii) above and any issues as to adequacy are to be decided in the light of the 'absolute confidence' test and thereafter, the test for negligence is as stated in Dunne.[20]

Notably, Cross J stated that the standard of the duty of care to be applied to the cytology screeners is '"absolute confidence" ... in relation to their analysis of what is on the slide and indeed the adequacy of the sample', as established by the expert evident presented in the case.[21] Furthermore, Cross J reiterated that the legal issue is grounded in 'whether or not they have carried out that duty in accordance with the *Dunne* principles'. At paragraph 71 of his judgment, Cross J concluded:

> These extra tests set out in *Penney, Palmer* are combinations of factual and legal matters, but I accept that a screening programme especially one such as in Ireland which does not have annual retesting, is inherently deficient if screeners ascribe as normal, results in which they are in any doubt. Accordingly, to ascribe as normal, a slide which the screener has any doubt of that fact even if he legitimately believes it to be normal on the balance of probabilities, is to fall below the Dunne standards required of that screener. Whether the screeners were right not to have any doubt is a matter to be assessed at law in accordance with the Dunne principles.

Applying this test, Cross J found that the liquid-based cytology slide of Mrs Morrissey, which had been screened by Quest Diagnostics Incorporated, had abnormalities upon it which its screening process should have detected. It is critical to note, however, that while Cross J also found that the other slide of Mrs Morrissey, which had been screened by MedLab Pathology Limited, had certain abnormalities upon it, they were not of such a significance as to constitute negligence or a breach of duty in reporting the slide as not showing any such abnormality. This defendant was found liable for negligence and breach of duty for an entirely different reason, namely that the slide did not meet the prescribed test of adequacy for assessment and should not, therefore, have been assessed at all. This finding of the High Court in relation to MedLab Pathology Limited demonstrates the court's acknowledgement that abnormalities can exist on a cervical smear slide which can fail to be detected and this may not amount to negligence and breach of duty on the part of the screening laboratory.

The judgment, having been delivered on 3 May 2019 with written copies circulated to all interested parties, including the media, was then formally published five days later on 8 May 2019. In the five days prior to the publication of the judgment, a considerable amount of criticism from both the medical and legal community had already emerged. In what can only be described as a 'media frenzy', numerous Irish media outlets declared their disapproval of the

---

[20] See para 74.
[21] See para 71.

judgment. In particular, controversy arose regarding the standard of 'absolute confidence', a phrase which has often been misquoted as 'absolute certainty', which Cross J had 'imposed' upon medical practitioners. Dr Cliona Murphy, Chair of the Institute of Obstetricians and Gynaecologists (IOG), RCPI, speaking to the *Medical Independent*, stated that the judgment 'perpetuates the myth of medical certainty',[22] further stating that the phrase 'absolute confidence' is not one which sits well within scientific matters, rather the evidence supports a conclusion, or it does not.[23] Notably, neither the test laid out by the English case *Penney, Palmer* nor the words of Cross J in *Morrissey* suggested that the *Dunne* principles should be departed from. In fact, the detailed judgment of Cross J is almost repetitive in its assurance that the *Dunne* principles remain the legal standard. Instead, Cross J simply restated the standard that had been established by the medical experts throughout the trial.

Furthermore, there is no indication in the High Court judgment that the court had taken upon itself the role of setting the standard of professional negligence for medical practitioners. In fact, Cross J highlights this point as he cites Lord Woolf in *Penney, Palmer*, who quoted with approval from the judgment of the original court: 'The standard which I have to apply is that of a reasonably competent screener exercising reasonable care at the time when the screening took place'. Indeed, Cross J stated that this acts as a careful and 'important' reminder to a court that they do not themselves define the legal standard for medical negligence.

THE SUPREME COURT JUDGMENT AND 'THE STANDARD OF APPROACH'

It was in the wake of this media frenzy that Clarke CJ was tasked with providing clarity to the law of medical negligence. Both counsel for the Health Service Executive and Quest Diagnostics Incorporated critically analysed the judgment of Cross J before the Supreme Court. In particular, counsel disagreed with the reliance by Cross J upon *Penney, Palmer*. Counsel for the Health Service Executive highlighted that the standard of 'absolute confidence' in *Penney, Palmer* was never intended to change the application of the standard 'the reasonably competent screener exercising reasonable care at the time when screen process took place'.[24] Furthermore, counsel for Quest Diagnostics Incorporated put forth the argument that 'absolute confidence' was never a legal standard of care in England, noting that this has been confirmed through subsequent case law.[25]

---

[22] Catherine Reilly, 'In pursuit of absolute confidence' *Medical Independent*, 29 April 2020.
[23] ibid.
[24] *Ruth Morrissey and Paul Morrissey v Health Service Executive and Quest Diagnostics Ireland Ltd and MedLab Pathology Limited*, submissions of the first appellant (the Health Service Executive).
[25] *Ruth Morrissey and Paul Morrissey Health Service Executive and Quest Diagnostics Ireland Ltd and MedLab Pathology Limited*, submissions of the second appellant (Quest Diagnostics Incorporated).

Counsel for both of these defendants and the appellants also presented arguments relating to the onerous standard of 'absolute confidence'. Counsel for the Health Service Executive argued that confidence in the medical profession would, in no circumstances, be absolute, as even in the strict application of criminal or environmental law, language of reasonable doubt is used. Furthermore, counsel lamented that this was an impossible standard which is incompatible with utterances accepted by the court that non-negligent errors can occur in medicine, especially in the highly subjective work of a screener. Similarly, counsel for Quest Diagnostics Incorporated contended that the standard of absolute confidence is utterly incompatible with the work of a cytology screener.

Acknowledging that the case had been granted a rare 'leapfrog appeal' to the Supreme Court, Clarke CJ began his judgment, which was the sole and unanimous judgment of the Supreme Court, noting the importance of bringing certainty to this area of law. To do so, Clarke CJ suggested that the use of the phrase 'the standard of approach' was more suitable in such medical cases, rather than 'the standard of care'.[26] He attributed some of the misunderstanding of the judgment at first instance of Cross J to the confusion between 'the standard of care', which has a precise legal meaning, and 'the standard of care', which colloquially would be used to describe the standard of care for a patient in a medical case. Accordingly, throughout the judgment, Clarke CJ uses 'the standard of approach' to mean the standard which has been 'shown to be required of a particular professional in particular circumstances'.[27] This change of language must be seen as very helpful as it provides a more universal phrase which can more easily be understood by those unfamiliar with legalistic language.

Following this, Clarke CJ clarifies a further point of confusion regarding the relevance of the English cases of *Bolam* and *Bolitho*, cited by Cross J in the High Court. Clarke CJ notes that the *Bolam* test 'has no application where the judge is required to make findings of fact'.[28] It can be likened, however, to the fourth *Dunne* principle and, thus, it is consistent with Irish law.

Clarke CJ then goes to clarify the position of medical negligence in Irish law. For the purposes of providing clarity, he suggests that the *Dunne* test can be reduced to 'one overarching principle with a number of subsidiary considerations which impact on the application of that overarching principle in particular circumstances'.[29] Accordingly, it is the first point, which states that the standard of approach of a medical professional is to apply a standard appropriate to a person of equal specialist or general status acting with ordinary care. Clarke CJ states that 'the starting point in any professional negligence case requires the identification of the standard of approach which would have

---

[26] See para 6.3.
[27] ibid.
[28] See para 6.4.
[29] See para 6.7.

been applied by a professional of the appropriate standing or skill as the person against whom the allegation of negligence is made'.[30] A failure to act in that way will amount to negligence, which is the overarching principle governing medical negligence.[31] Thus, it is the medical profession which dictates the standard of approach in a particular case. Clarke CJ then proceeds to carefully explain how the further *Dunne* principles (two–six) can all be seen as flowing from this 'overarching' principle as he states that each 'of the other points made by Finlay CJ derive from that overall obligation'.[32]

In passing, it may be worth noting that in relation to the third principle enunciated in *Dunne*, Clarke CJ does use the descriptor 'professional', which may seem narrower than the words in *Dunne*, namely 'any person'. It does not appear likely, however, that this was intended to convey any alteration to the meaning of the principle and, importantly, no issue arose in *Morrissey* concerning the adoption of a common practice which had inherent defects that ought to have been obvious to 'any person giving the matter due consideration'.[33] This impression is reinforced by the observation made by Clarke CJ at paragraph 6.13 of his judgment, which does suggest that there may be some cases, but not 'many', where the court will be willing to apply an objective scrutiny to the medical profession's standards where he states:

> It follows that, at least in many cases, the court has no role in determining the standard to be applied other than to assess the evidence given by professionals as to the standard to which they themselves regard as being appropriate to someone of the standing and skill of the defendant. There may be some scope for the court reaching a further assessment in those limited cases where it is said that a professional did comply with an accepted practice but where there were also said to be inherent defects in the practice concerned. As already noted, no such issues arise in this case.

Clarke CJ then proceeds to highlight the standard presented by the medical experts in the *Morrissey* trial, noting that Dr McKenna, a Consultant Cellular Pathologist based in Northern Ireland, who gave evidence on behalf of the Morrisseys, stated that 'unless you are absolutely – and that is 100% – convinced that the slide is negative, do not call it negative … in other words, no doubt'.[34] Furthermore, Ms Tan, a cytotechnologist based in New York, who also gave evidence on behalf of the Morrisseys, 'stated that there is no tolerance for any doubt in the assessment of the normality of the cells' and that 'the cytotechnologist should be confident if a slide is negative or if it is possibly abnormal to refer it to the pathologist'.[35] Clarke CJ likens this to the *Penney*,

---

[30] See para 6.6.
[31] See para 6.7.
[32] See paras 6.8–6.11.
[33] See para 6.12.
[34] See para 6.22.
[35] See para 6.24.

Palmer case, emphasising that the adoption of the 'absolute confidence' test for cytology screeners in England and Wales stemmed from evidence given by medical experts on both sides of the *Penney, Palmer* case. It was not the court in this case who developed this standard, rather it was endorsed by the court upon hearing the evidence of such experts on the 'agreed position of experts in the field'.[36]

Upon reviewing the evidence, Clarke CJ succinctly highlights that the standard of 'absolute confidence' was 'no more than a synopsis of the evidence given', likening the scenario to the case of *Penney, Palmer*. The judgment goes on to acknowledge the criticisms of this standard. In response to such criticisms, Clarke CJ highlights that 'the more extreme comments are very hard to reconcile with the fact that there was clear evidence that such a standard is actually applied in the United Kingdom' and, furthermore, 'the evidence of an expert witness from Northern Ireland'.[37] The screening systems in both those countries have not become unworkable as some of the 'doomsday' predictions suggested.[38] Thus, Clarke CJ dismissed the appeal relating to the standard of care, reaffirming that the *Dunne* principles remain the central precedent in Irish professional negligence.

At the conclusion of the judgment, at paragraph 16.2 thereof, Clarke CJ provides a summary of the unanimous finding of the Supreme Court in relation to this critical issue of the duty of care. It is, perhaps, useful to review this statement in full because of the clear manner in which it encapsulates the determination of the court:

> The first question concerns the proper standard of approach to be adopted by a screener involved in a scheme such as CervicalCheck. I have set out the reasons why I consider that the Dunne test remains the basis for identifying the legal standard of care by reference to which a claim in clinical negligence is to be assessed. To avoid any lack of clarity, I have made a number of observations in respect of that test. In substance, the legal standard of care applied in any clinical negligence claims, or indeed other professional negligence claims, requires the court to assess whether no reasonable professional of the type concerned could have carried out their task in the manner which occurred in the case in question. That overall test requires a court to determine what standard a reasonable professional would apply. For the reasons set out earlier in this judgment, I have used the phrase 'standard of approach' to describe the standard that a reasonable screener would be expected to apply in order to avoid any confusion with the term 'standard of care', because that latter term has a precise legal meaning. As noted earlier, I consider

---

[36] See para 6.20.
[37] See para 6.29.
[38] ibid.

that the use of the term 'absolute confidence' may have created more confusion than clarity.

However, it is clear that all of the relevant witnesses agreed that a screener should not give a clear result in respect of a slide unless they had no doubt but that the sample was adequate and did not contain any suspicious material. That standard is not one imposed by the court but rather one which stems from the profession itself. The determination of that standard requires either agreement between the parties or, in the event of disagreement, an assessment by the court of expert evidence.

THE FALSE FEAR OF FLOODGATES: *FREENEY V HEALTH SERVICE EXECUTIVE*

Despite this clear explanation of the legal test concerning the standard of care in medical negligence cases, a concern remained that *Morrissey* had opened a metaphorical 'floodgate' to medical negligence claims, due to the high standard of 'absolute confidence' established in the case. The recent case of *Freeney v Health Service Executive*, however, suggests that this fear is ill-founded. It is the first case in the Irish Superior Courts to apply the principles set out by the Supreme Court in *Morrissey* in terms of what is the duty of care in medical negligence litigation.

The case of *Freeney* concerned the breast screening of the plaintiff, Mrs Freeney, in 2015. The screening was conducted by the national screening service BreastCheck, provided and managed by the defendant, the Health Executive Service. Mrs Freeney asserted that her screen was conducted negligently, claiming that it should have been recalled for further examination. The plaintiff argued that if this had been done, the cancer would have been detected on the earlier date of 2015, meaning she would have avoided chemotherapy and radiotherapy and had her lifespan significantly less shortened.

In the High Court, Hyland J dismissed the plaintiff's claim, holding that the law in Ireland in respect of professional negligence had recently been 'restated' in *Morrissey*. Hyland J, following the 'clear road map' laid out in *Morrissey*, noted that the starting point of a negligence case is to determine the 'standard of approach' or, as stated by Clarke CJ, '[W]hat would an ordinary competent professional of the type and skill of the individual concerned have done, and did the professional who is sued meet that standard?' Hyland J gives clear recognition, therefore, to the need to allow medical professionals to guide the court in establishing the standard of approach and, subsequently, the level of negligence or lack thereof.

Again, this judgment of the High Court is a model of clarity in relation to the approach which the Superior Courts now take in relation to the determination of the duty of care in medical negligence proceedings. Hyland J, at the commencement of her judgment, in paragraphs 5 and 6 thereof, stated the position, in the clearest possible terms, as follows:

> Legal Standard
>
> 5. The law in this jurisdiction in respect of professional negligence, including in the context of screening decisions, has been recently restated by the Supreme Court in the case of *Morrissey v HSE* [2020] IESC 6. Clarke C.J., giving the decision on behalf of the Supreme Court, summarised the legal standard of care in a clinical negligence claim, or indeed any professional negligence claim, as requiring 'the court to assess whether no reasonable professional of the type concerned could have carried out their task in the manner which occurred in the case in question. That overall test requires a court to determine what standard a reasonable professional would apply' (paragraph 16.2). He observed that the test in *Dunne (an Infant) v National Maternity Hospital* [1989] I.R. 91 remains the basis for identifying the legal standard of care by reference to which a claim in clinical negligence is to be assessed.
>
> 6. Helpfully, the case of *Morrissey* sets out a clear road map in a case of alleged professional negligence. The starting point is the identification by the court of the standard of approach that would have been applied by a professional of the appropriate standing or skill as the person against whom the allegation of negligence is made (paragraph 6.6). Or, as restated at paragraph 6.12 of the judgment of the Chief Justice, 'what would an ordinary competent professional of the type and skill of the individual concerned have done, and did the professional who is sued meet that standard?'

The practical working out of this judicial deference to what the medical profession states as the standard of approach meant that Hyland J applied 'a standard operating procedure' or set of guidelines which BreastCheck had itself formulated and used in the course of the assessment of women in its breast cancer screening programme. Accordingly, when applying the terms of the particular standard operating procedure which applied in this case, Hyland J proceeded to dismiss the plaintiff's claim because she found that the plaintiff had not established that the defendant had failed to act in accordance with the standard of approach as specified in its own guidelines.

The dismissal of the plaintiff's claim in *Freeney* makes evident that neither the judgment of the High Court nor the judgment of the Supreme Court in the case of *Morrissey* has placed a 'catch all' standard of 'absolute confidence' on medical professionals. Rather the restatement of the well-established legal principles and their underlying rationale under the description of the 'standard of approach' provides a clear road map as to how the courts should determine what the reasonable professional in any given case concerned ought to have done, and thus, determine the question as to what is the standard required and assist the court in determining whether or not there has been a breach of that standard.

On a final note, while it is clear that the courts have set out a 'standard of approach' that is based on a test that allows medical professionals to guide the court in establishing the standard of approach, it is less clear that all of the professionals themselves have grasped this. Somewhat surprisingly, the *Interval Cancer Report* of CervicalCheck, produced by an Expert Reference Group in October 2020, seven months after the decision of the Supreme Court in *Morrissey* and five months after the decision of the High Court in *Freeney*, appears to reiterate unfounded fears about the legal duty of care expected by the Irish Superior Courts in relation to the National Screening Service. For example, on page eight of the Report, the assertion is made that 'since the cytology smear test is prone to significant observer variability, it cannot be considered a diagnostic test, nor can it provide absolute certainty that it rules out precancerous changes'. It is perhaps surprising that the Report chose to employ the term 'absolute certainty' in making this assertion, given that it has not been used in the judgments of the courts and is inconsistent with the acknowledgement in those judgments that a false negative can arise in a non-negligent context. A similar misunderstanding appears on page 43 of the Report, which states:

> Furthermore, the Supreme Court Ruling of 'Absolute Confidence' in the Morrissey case will inadvertently create the erroneous impression that all cytology must be 100% accurate. This is unachievable.

As can be seen above, the Chief Justice in *Morrissey* was careful not to use the phrase 'absolute confidence' for the reasons explained by him. Accordingly, it should be reassuring to members of the public and medical professionals that the courts have made a clear restatement of the well-established legal principles, using the description of 'the standard of approach' and, to those who read the judgments carefully, they provide a clear road map as to how the courts should determine what the reasonable professional in any given case concerned ought to have done.

PART B
CAUSES OF ACTION

Chapter II

INFORMED CONSENT: WHAT FIVE MIGHT FIND IN *LANARKSHIRE*

Eoghan Quinn and Luán ó Braonáin SC[1]

This chapter considers the potential implications for the law in Ireland concerning informed consent arising from the decision of the United Kingdom Supreme Court in *Montgomery v Lanarkshire Health Board*.[2]

Introduction

The presence of a patient's informed consent to medical treatment has long been a requirement of fundamental importance. Judicial consideration of this requirement has arisen in medical negligence litigation, where patients have complained of deficits in the advice given to them in anticipation of treatment carrying with it risks of harm. Accepting that they consented to the treatment at issue, such that it did not amount to a trespass to their person, these patients nonetheless contend that the medical advice neglected to properly appraise them of the risks and options arising, such that they would not have consented to the treatment undergone had they only been given the requisite information. It is in this sense that their consent is claimed to have been less than a properly informed consent.

The courts, reflecting changing attitudes regarding patient rights, have moved from a paternalistic 'doctor knows best' approach towards a more patient centred one that puts personal autonomy and individual rights closer to centre-stage.

The jurisprudential refinements by which this move has been made have been many, crafted over decades by different judges approaching the issues in different ways. The routes taken by the courts in Ireland, on the one hand, and those in England and Wales, Scotland, Canada, Australia and the United States, on the other, have been distinct – and have presented to the Irish courts opportunities to digest on the developments devised by their Common Law

---

[1] Eoghan Quinn prepared this chapter as a final year undergraduate student at the School of Law at Trinity College Dublin. Luán ó Braonáin SC is a member of the Inner Bar of Ireland.
[2] *Montgomery v Lanarkshire Health Board* [2015] UKSC 11.

cousins. While the routes we speak of have been distinct, they have shared some common landmarks, upon which we mean to touch as we explore the milestones, potholes and signposts of their respective journeys.

STANDARD OF PROFESSIONAL CARE FOR MEDICAL PRACTITIONERS

It is well established in Irish law that the case of *Dunne v National Maternity Hospital*[3] describes the appropriate standard of care in medical negligence cases. Since 1989, *Dunne*'s description of this standard of professional care has been held to apply to allegations of negligence against every form of medical practitioner,[4] architect, engineer, solicitor, mechanic, receiver and veterinary surgeon, among others.

Central to *Dunne* is the concept of reasonable care, also described in this context as ordinary care. The obligation of the professional is to apply the ordinary care expected of someone with their level of skill. Inherently, this allows for some degree of variation in practice and difference in conclusion as between professionals. It contemplates, of course, a category of professional judgments that are 'reasonable' as opposed to 'perfect'.

THE *DUNNE* PRINCIPLES

In *Dunne*, Finlay CJ (affirming the general test for professional negligence set down in *Roche v Peilow*[5]) summarised the applicable principles in the following classic statement:

1. The true test for establishing negligence in diagnosis or treatment on the part of a medical practitioner is whether he has been proved to be guilty of such failure as no medical practitioner of equal specialist or general status and skill would be guilty of if acting with ordinary care.
2. If the allegation of negligence against a medical practitioner is based on proof that he deviated from a general and approved practice, that will not establish negligence unless it is also proved that the course he did take was one which no medical practitioner of like specialisation and skill would have followed had he been taking the ordinary care required from a person of his qualifications.
3. If a medical practitioner charged with negligence defends his conduct by establishing that he followed a practice which was general and which was approved by his colleagues of similar specialisation and skill, he cannot escape liability if in reply the plaintiff establishes

---

[3] *Dunne v National Maternity Hospital* [1989] IR 91.
[4] *Kiernan v Health Service Executive* [2015] IEHC 141, where Cross J confirmed that the *Dunne* test applied to public health nurses.
[5] *Roche v Peilow* [1989] IR 232.

that such practice had inherent defects which ought to be obvious to any person giving the matter due consideration.
4. An honest difference of opinion between the doctors as to which is the better of two ways of treating a patient does not provide any ground for leaving a question to the jury as to whether a person who has followed one course rather than the other has been negligent.
5. It is not for a jury (or for a judge) to decide which of two alternative courses of treatment is in their (or his) opinion preferable, but their (or his) function is merely to decide whether the course of treatment followed, on the evidence, complied with the careful conduct of a medical practitioner of like specialisation and skill to that professed by the defendant.

To make the general principles applicable to the facts of the *Dunne* case, Finlay CJ provided the following further guidance:

(a) 'General and approved practice' need not be universal but must be approved of and adhered to by a substantial number of reputable practitioners holding the relevant specialist or general qualifications.
(b) Though treatment only is referred to in some of the statements of principle, they must apply in identical fashion to questions of diagnosis.
(c) In an action against a hospital, where allegations are made of negligence against the medical administrators on the basis of a claim that practices and procedures laid down by them for the carrying out of treatment or diagnosis by medical or nursing staff were defective, their conduct is to be tested in accordance with the legal principles which would apply if they had personally carried out such treatment or diagnosis in accordance with such practice or procedure.

The *Dunne* principles, guiding standards of medical care and treatment in general, came to influence at least one judicial perspective on the assessment and formulation of standards of medical advice around treatment risks and options.

We seek to provide below, as best we can, the factual background against which judicial statements of principle have been expressed. This is done to allow, where possible, for a practical understanding of factors influencing the development of those judicial perspectives.

APPLICATION OF THE *DUNNE* PRINCIPLES TO INFORMED CONSENT

In 1992, Finlay CJ, in *Walsh v Family Planning Services Ltd*,[6] emphasised the duty on a medical practitioner, where possible, to inform their patient of the

---
[6] *Walsh v Family Planning Services Ltd* [1992] 1 IR 496.

potential risks associated with any given procedure. The case concerned a vasectomy – an elective procedure. The plaintiff complained that he had been told that the operation would not disimprove his sex life and could improve it; that there might be some discomfort in the immediate aftermath; and that in about one in forty cases a more severe swelling might occur that could result in time off work. He and his wife signed the consent forms and the operation was later performed by the surgeon, assisted by a trainee.

In the event, the plaintiff suffered post-operatively from a variety of complaints with his testicles. A year later, his left testicle had contracted. In subsequent years, different treatments were attempted, including removal of the left testicle. Three years after the operation, the plaintiff continued to suffer. Expert evidence indicated that he was suffering from orchialgia, a known but exceptionally rare consequence of vasectomy.

The plaintiff sued, contending that there had been negligence in the performance of the surgery; and that the procedure had constituted an assault and battery (a) because of a failure to advise him of the potential consequences of the operation and (b) where he had not consented to the trainee's surgery. The High Court rejected his contentions that the surgery had been performed negligently and that the warning given had been insufficient. Nonetheless, the High Court found there to have been a technical assault and battery, where the plaintiff had not consented to surgery by the trainee. The defendants appealed and the plaintiff cross-appealed.

The Supreme Court declined to disturb the finding that the operation had been performed without negligence. The Supreme Court held by a majority that where the gist of a plaintiff's plea is a lack of informed consent to a surgical procedure, then their claim should be determined on ordinary negligence principles – rather than upon an identification of a vitiated consent transforming the treatment into an assault and battery. Consequently, the defendants' appeal against the finding of a technical assault and battery was allowed. The Supreme Court also declined by a majority to disturb the High Court's determination that a sufficient warning had been given.

Of particular interest to us are the different approaches adopted by the members of the Supreme Court in their assessments of the informed consent claim.

Finlay CJ said:

> I am satisfied that there is, of course, where it is possible to do so, a clear obligation on a medical practitioner carrying out or arranging for the carrying out of an operation, to inform the patient of any possible harmful consequence arising from the operation, so as to permit the patient to give an informed consent to subjecting himself to the operation concerned. I am also satisfied that the extent of this obligation must, as

a matter of common sense, vary with what might be described as the elective nature of the surgery concerned.[7]

Finlay CJ drew a distinction between instances of surgical procedures necessary to the maintenance of life or health, including but not limited to emergency surgery, and surgical procedures at the other end of the elective scale, such as a vasectomy. The distinction drawn was as to the extent of discussion or warning required concerning possible side effects – where limited discussion might be appropriate in the 'necessary' cases, with the obligation to give a warning of possible harmful consequences being more stringent and onerous in the 'elective' cases. Having so identified a scale of electivity, by which the information required for an informed consent might be measured, Finlay CJ determined that the standard of care to be exercised in giving warnings as to the risks of surgical procedures was not in principle any different from the standard of care to be exercised by medical practitioners in giving treatment or advice.

Finlay CJ held, therefore, that the *Dunne* principles applied to the standards of care applicable to the giving of such warnings. Notably, however, Finlay CJ further held that medical practitioners defending the sufficiency of their warnings by establishing that they had followed general practice might, 'certainly in relation to very clearly elective surgery', find that the court could more readily reach a conclusion that the extent of the warning given or omitted in general practice contained inherent defects.

APPLICATION OF NEGLIGENCE PRINCIPLES TO THE OBLIGATION TO OBTAIN INFORMED CONSENT

Disagreeing with Finlay CJ, O'Flaherty J (with whom Hederman J concurred) did not accept that the question of the sufficiency of warnings fell to be determined by reference to general and approved practice, in accordance with the criteria established in *Dunne*. Rather, O'Flaherty J thought it a matter for the court to assess, applying established principles of negligence, whether there had been a breach of duty in failing to give a particular warning to a particular plaintiff. This, noted O'Flaherty J, had been the approach of the Supreme Court of Canada in 1980 in *Reibl v Hughes*.[8]

In adopting this approach, O'Flaherty J made clear that he was leaving aside the requirements that might come into play in cases of emergency or essential surgery, where questions of life and death arise, as well as questions of possible emotional upset to patients with whom warnings of surgical risks are shared. He was dealing only with the case at hand. In that context, O'Flaherty J said:

---

[7] ibid 510.
[8] *Reibl v Hughes* (1980) 114 DLR (3d) 1.

> I have no hesitation in saying that where there is a question of elective surgery which is not essential to health or bodily well-being, if there is a risk – however exceptional or remote – of grave consequences involving severe pain stretching for an appreciable time into the future and involving the possibility of further operative procedures, the exercise of the duty of care owed by the defendants requires that such possible consequences should be explained in the clearest language to the plaintiff.

We consider it fair to say that the bar was set high by O'Flaherty J, with the concurrence of Hederman J, in requiring explanation of all and any risks, regardless of their rarity or remoteness, where elective surgery of a kind not essential to health or bodily well-being was at play. The 'ordinary' standard of care in negligence, so expressed, applies a weighty burden upon the medical practitioner. It is notable, however, that this requirement was identified in *Walsh* as applying only where such risks were of grave consequences involving severe pain stretching for an appreciable time into the future and involving the possibility of further operative procedures. O'Flaherty J was clear in so delineating the scope of his finding. It appears to us then that O'Flaherty J considered the weight of the burden imposed on the practitioner to be commensurate with the weight of the potential consequences at issue for the patient.

A practical question arises as to what quality of evidence could satisfy this weighty burden in the minds of O'Flaherty and Hederman JJ. O'Flaherty J believed that the warning stated by the advising doctor to have been given was 'sufficient in the light of the prevailing medical knowledge and experience'. This he did while noting the plaintiff's contention that he had been given no warning and identifying reasons for affording little weight to that claim. It is notable that in *Walsh* the doctor had no recollection of the session she had with the plaintiff and his wife, such that her evidence was about what she always did by way of counselling in relation to vasectomies. She explained the finality of the operation, the mechanics thereof and then possible complications. These complications included that the operation might fail to achieve sterilisation. Then she explained that swelling could be expected, with bruising of the scrotum for several days. This could in some cases take longer than a week to settle. She explained that the plaintiff should contact the clinic if discomfort lasted more than two weeks. The doctor explained that occasionally there were minor medical complications such as inflammation of the testes and epididymis and the formation of haematomas and granulomas. Sometimes they needed medical treatment but they generally resolved themselves with time. Importantly, the doctor pointed out that very rarely, for no known reason, some patients experienced pain for some years after the operation. In response to a question by the trial judge, the doctor quantified the potential duration of such pain as 'ongoing, indefinitely', but said that this was very rare. While the consent form acknowledged that no assurance had been given that the operation would be '100% safe or successful', it did not contain the kind of detailed advice outlined by the doctor in evidence.

It can be seen, therefore, that oral evidence of the individual doctor's custom and practice was sufficient to satisfy O'Flaherty J in his assessment of whether the high standard identified by him had been satisfied, even absent direct recollection of the actual advice given. So it was that the majority of the Supreme Court, Finlay CJ, Hederman and O'Flaherty JJ, came to the conclusion that the defendants' appeal should be allowed and the plaintiff's cross-appeal dismissed. On the issue of informed consent, of the three judges forming the majority, only Finlay CJ relied upon and sought to apply the *Dunne* principles. The others preferred an application of the established principles of negligence.

'PATIENT CHOICE'

A different conclusion was reached by McCarthy and Egan JJ as to what they believed ought to have been the outcome in *Walsh*. The difference hinged on the sufficiency of the pre-operative warning given not only as to the risk of ongoing pain, but also as to the potential consequences for the plaintiff's capacity for sexual intercourse after the vasectomy. An information leaflet had been given by the clinic to the plaintiff and his wife, answering the question 'Does it affect your sex life?' with 'No'. Quite apart from the plaintiff's complaints of ongoing pain, however, the plaintiff had also complained that his sex life had come to a halt by reason of the pain. Indeed, his case had been that considerable concern had been shared with the advising doctor around the issue of potential adverse impacts upon his sexual capacity and his 'masculinity'. The leaflet's answer on this issue was, in the views of the members of the dissenting minority, inadequate.

McCarthy and O'Flaherty JJ agreed on many aspects of the case, a feature emphasised expressly by Egan J. While McCarthy J adverted to the *Dunne* principles, this appears to have been primarily with a view to assessing the merits of the plaintiff's cross-appeal against the dismissal of his complaint that the vasectomy had been performed negligently. On the issue of informed consent, however, McCarthy J addressed the elective nature of the procedure at hand and turned then to the judgments of the Supreme Court in an older case from 1953, *Daniels and anor v Heskin*,[9] describing it as 'the only case cited in respect of patient choice'. *Daniels* was a case in which a doctor that attended to the suturing of a perineal tear after labour had not informed the patient that the first needle used by him had broken, leaving a part of it in her flesh.

It is interesting to consider the straightforward terms in which Maguire CJ, delivering his dissenting judgment in *Daniels*, recognised the 'prerogative of the patient' to decide whether they would accept or reject advice given. This, of course, required the advice to be given rather than omitted. It is perhaps equally interesting to consider the reasons offered by the majority in *Daniels* for finding that the decision not to inform the patient was acceptable. These

---

[9] *Daniels and anor v Heskin* [1954] IR 73.

included disregarding the requirement for a subsequent retrieval operation as 'damage'; the character of the patient; her social position; her intelligence; the fact that the patient was passing through a post-partum period during which 'the possibility of nervous or mental disturbance is notorious'; and that the 'husband and wife were of a class and standard of education which would incline them to exaggerate the seriousness of the occurrence and to suffer needless alarm'.

McCarthy J in *Walsh*, reflecting on *Daniels*, found the observations made on matters such as social position or class or standard of education 'difficult to understand as relevant criteria'. The passage of time has not imbued these matters with any greater relevance. He then turned to the treatment of the duty of disclosure in *Irish Law of Torts* (McMahon and Binchy, 2nd edn, Bloomsbury Professional), which had been published in 1990. This analysis brought McCarthy J to two decisions of the courts of England and Wales that remain the subject of judicial attention there. Three principal solutions were identified by the authors in determining the 'proper test for deciding whether the doctor has given sufficient instruction to the patient'.

The first of these solutions addressed the question by reference to what was referred to then as the *Bolam* test. The judgment of 1957 of the Queen's Bench Division in *Bolam v Friern HMC*[10] found, as was subsequently determined in Ireland in the *Dunne* case, that a doctor acting in accordance with a practice accepted as proper by a responsible body of medical opinion skilled in the form of treatment in question was not negligent merely because there was a body of competent professional opinion that might have adopted a different technique. Unlike *Dunne*, which had not considered expressly the issue of informed consent, the court in *Bolam* considered the consent issue and established the following test – first, whether or not the doctor, in not warning of risks involved in the treatment, had fallen below a standard of practice recognised as proper by a competent body of professional opinion and, if good medical practice did require a warning, and second, whether the plaintiff, if warned, would have refused to undergo the treatment (in respect of which the burden of proof lay on the plaintiff). The authors of *Irish Law of Torts* considered that the *Bolam* test treated the decision as to the information to be given as being primarily a matter of medical judgment and discretion.

The second of the principal solutions considered in *Irish Law of Torts* was described by its authors as lying at 'the other end of the spectrum'. This concentrated on the patient's right of self-determination with regard to what was done to their body. It required full disclosure of all material risks incident to the proposed treatment, so that the patient, rather than the doctor, made the real choice as to whether treatment was to be carried out.[11]

---

[10] *Bolam v Friern HMC* [1957] 1 WLR 582.
[11] *Miller v Kennedy* (1975) 85 Wash 2d 151.

The third of the principal solutions was described by the authors of *Irish Law of Torts* as being an approach lying between the foregoing two extremes, where medical judgment and discretion lay at one end and patient choice and self-determination lay at the other, and was attributed to the judgments delivered in 1985 by the members of the House of Lords in *Sidaway v Governors of the Bethlehem Royal Hospital*.[12] This mid-way approach, according to the authors of *Irish Law of Torts*, applied the *Bolam* test

> save where disclosure of a particular risk 'was so obviously necessary to an informed choice on the part of the patient that no reasonably prudent medical man would fail to make it ...'

While McCarthy J in *Walsh* considered the second and third of the principal solutions enunciated as 'essentially the same' for the purposes of the case in hand, the authors of *Irish Law of Torts* have, in subsequent editions, emphasised that the two are evidently not the same – even if they may lead to the same result in some cases. McCarthy J ultimately held in *Walsh* that 'in determining whether or not to have an operation in which sexual capacity was concerned, it [seemed to him] that to supply the patient with the material facts was so obviously necessary to an informed choice that no reasonably prudent medical doctor would fail to make it'. While the language adopted by McCarthy J was what he had identified as the language of *Sidaway*, it is appropriate to note that he himself had seen no distinction between that test and the language of self-determination advanced under the heading of the second solution. There is some ambiguity, therefore, as to which solution would have been adopted by McCarthy J in a wider discussion.

Some hint as to the wider school of informed consent for which McCarthy J might have plumbed may be detected in his consideration of what constituted 'material facts' requiring disclosure by the doctor in *Walsh*. On this issue, McCarthy J said:

> What then is material? Apart from the success ratio of the operation, what could be more material than sexual capacity after the operation and its immediate sequalae? Whatever about temporary or protracted pain or discomfort, the only information given to the plaintiff and his wife on the score of sexual capacity, upon which they placed so much emphasis, was that contained in the brief paragraph headed 'Does it affect your sex-life? No.' This is not a question of merely determining that a particular outcome is so rare as not to warrant such disclosure that might upset a patient but, rather, that those concerned, and this includes the authors of this information sheet, if they knew of such a risk, however remote, had a duty to inform those so critically concerned with that risk. Remote percentages of risk lose their significance to those unfortunate enough to be 100% involved.

---

[12] *Sidaway v Governors of the Bethlehem Royal Hospital* [1985] AC 871.

It appears to us significant that McCarthy J emphasised:

- the overwhelming objective materiality of sexual capacity,
- the fact that the plaintiff and his wife had themselves placed great emphasis upon sexual capacity,
- that the plaintiff was critically concerned with the risk to sexual capacity,
- that the remoteness of the risk was secondary to its materiality.

In dealing with the issue of causation of damage, McCarthy J considered it sufficient to establish a failure to warn of sexual impotence in order to establish the plaintiff's right to damages. Contrary, then, to the *Bolam* test, McCarthy J did not consider it necessary for the plaintiff to prove that he would have foregone the vasectomy if he had been properly warned of the risk of sexual impotence. Viewing these features against the background of the only judgment in *Walsh* to have considered the law under the heading of 'patient choice', it appears to us that McCarthy J shone a particular judicial light upon the matters of special concern to the plaintiff and his wife.

That the issue of sexual capacity, and the risk thereto, found no expression in the judgment of O'Flaherty J, despite being at the forefront of the judgment of McCarthy J, illustrates, it seems to us, the extent to which the materiality of issues and risks requiring disclosure can be subjective, even in as rigorous a judicial setting as the Supreme Court. This being so, it seems appropriate to consider whether the discussion between practitioners and patients of issues and risks in treatment should be encouraged to be more exploratory of, and attendant to, the subjective wants of the patient, as well as informative of medical practice and experience, enabling them to make their own decisions around their treatment.

Finlay CJ, in his judgment, was satisfied that the evidence did not establish that consequences including a loss of sexual capacity were known complications of a carefully carried out vasectomy. The evidence, in his view, extended only to establishing a known risk of indefinite pain or orchialgia, of which the plaintiff had been warned.

It is fair to observe that the various judgments in *Walsh* did not combine so as to present a clear resolution of the issues around informed consent. As it has been put by the authors of *Irish Law of Torts* (McMahon and Binchy, 4th edn, Bloomsbury Professional 2013), at paragraph 14.102, 'it cannot be said that Walsh left the law in a clear or satisfactory state' and, at paragraph 14.118, '*Walsh* left the law on informed consent in an unsatisfactory and confused state'.

The route to the 'reasonable patient' test

The state of Ireland's law on informed consent after *Walsh* left it somewhat challenging to steer a course through the issue. In *Bolton v Blackrock Clinic*[13] the High Court was concerned in 1994 with a patient who had undergone bronchial and lung surgery on two occasions, with permanent, distressing and incapacitating consequences. She complained, amongst other things, of a failure to obtain her informed consent to a sleeve resection of her left main bronchus. In dismissing the plaintiff's claim, Geoghegan J 'noted the view' of O'Flaherty J in *Walsh* and applied his test to the facts of the case, finding the information given around risks to have been adequate. Geoghegan J made no reference to the other approaches to informed consent offered in *Walsh*. The plaintiff appealed to the Supreme Court.

On appeal[14] in 1997, Hamilton CJ agreed with the conclusion reached by Geoghegan J in the High Court and dismissed the appeal. Hamilton CJ based his assessment of the case on the approach advanced by Finlay CJ in *Walsh*, making no reference to the test stated by O'Flaherty J upon which the High Court had relied and making no reference either to the judgments of McCarthy and Egan JJ. Perhaps an opportunity to bring clarity was missed.

Geoghegan v Harris – a closely reasoned discussion of informed consent in 2000

In *Geoghegan v Harris*[15] a dental patient, left with chronic neuropathic pain after a jaw graft performed with a view to dental implant surgery, claimed damages against a specialist dentist. The plaintiff contended that the dentist had assured him prior to the operation that the procedure would involve no pain whatsoever and had also failed to warn him that the procedure could result in the development of chronic pain. The plaintiff claimed that he would not have undergone the surgery had he been properly warned.

The authors of *Irish Law of Torts* (McMahon and Binchy, 4th edn, 2013) describe the High Court judgment by Kearns J in *Geoghegan* as providing 'for the first time in Ireland a sophisticated and closely-reasoned discussion of the subject'. Kearns J contrasted the 'reputable school of medical opinion' test applied by Finlay CJ, based on the *Dunne* principles, with the test adopted by O'Flaherty J, based on *Reibl v Hughes*. Kearns J described the latter as

---

[13] *Bolton v Blackrock Clinic* (Unreported, High Court, Geoghegan J, 20 December 1994).
[14] *Bolton v Blackrock Clinic* (Unreported, Supreme Court, 23 January 1997) [1997] JIC 2306.
[15] *Geoghegan v Harris* [2000] 3 IR 536.

being 'at the other end of the spectrum', concentrating on the patient's right to determine what is to be done to their body. The latter required, Kearns J observed, disclosure of all material risks incident to the proposed treatment, so that the patient, thus informed, rather than the doctor, makes the real choice as to whether treatment is to be carried out.

The close analysis performed by Kearns J in *Geoghegan* served to clarify, in so far as a judgment of the High Court might achieve, the tests to be applied under *Walsh*. Kearns J identified two critical questions, to which an analysis of the judgments in *Walsh* yielded the same answers, arrived at by the application of the different principles expressed, that is to say:

a. The requirement on a medical practitioner is to give a warning of any material risk which is a '*known complication*' of an operative procedure properly carried out;
b. The test of materiality in elective surgery is to inquire only if there is any risk, however exceptional or remote, of grave consequences involving severe pain stretching for an appreciable time into the future.

Kearns J found that Finlay CJ had, while applying the *Dunne* principles in the case, come to essentially the same conclusion as that 'so trenchantly stated' by O'Flaherty J. Finlay CJ had clearly felt that the 'exception for inherent defects' provision in *Dunne* could be invoked in the circumstances of the case, so that there was a requirement to give a warning of a remote risk with grave consequences.

Kearns J emphasised that the duty to warn extended only to 'known complications' of a 'carefully carried out operation', such as to confine the duty to such complications or to consequences that might be described as foreseeable or predictable consequences arising from such complications. Coincidental or unrelated risks could not properly fall within the compass of any duty.

The Supreme Court in *Bolton* had not varied or altered the requirement for the type of warning necessary in elective surgery. Kearns J held that the risk of intractable neuropathic pain was, while itself in the order of one in thousands, but a subset of the risk of nerve damage intrinsic to the placement of dental implants. It was not, therefore, a different species of risk or an unrelated risk. Kearns J also held that the condition of which the plaintiff complained merited characterisation as severe. Consequently, even though the views of the medical experts had been to the effect that no warning was necessary of the remote risk of neuropathic pain, Kearns J found that the decision in *Walsh* bound him to hold that there was an obligation to warn. The judgment in *Geoghegan* then took an interesting turn.

Under the heading 'Is the "Reasonable Patient" test the preferable option?', Kearns J addressed what he considered to be the inappropriate deployment of the *Dunne* principles in addressing issues of informed consent. He noted the statement made by Finlay CJ regarding the application of the third *Dunne* principle, the 'inherent defects' exception to the 'general and approved practice' line of defence, where Finlay CJ said:

> it may be, certainly in relation to very clearly elective surgery, that the court might more readily reach a conclusion that the extent of warning given or omitted contained inherent defects which ought to have been obvious to any person giving the matter due consideration that it could do in a case of complicated medical or surgical procedure.

Having noted this statement and having clearly reflected on it and its ramifications, Kearns J had a considerable deal to say about it:

> With considerable diffidence, I venture to suggest that this statement really only highlights the unreality of relating or contrasting the duty of disclosure to or with complicated medical treatment which is a separate and quite different function. Beyond indicating that a lower threshold may be sufficient for the court to intervene, the criteria for doing so are not further elaborated. The ease or otherwise of the courts' task is hardly an appropriate marker for intervention. Where the medical professional standard is adopted, subject to a caveat or saver, then, to me at least, it makes no great sense to oust from any meaningful role the views of the self-same medical practitioners as to the materiality of a risk or the need for a warning. Their views are received and relied upon in ordinary medical negligence cases. Who else can supply evidence on inherent defects? To substitute its own view, effectively in opposition to the experts on whose views, at least in the first instance, it purports to rely, the court sets at nought the professional standard test and the result in the instant case is that the defendant must be found to be in breach of duty when not a single expert from either side believes a warning to be necessary.

Kearns J recognised the power of the court to override expert opinion in matters of professional standards. Ultimately, the rule of law applies to doctors as equally as it applies to solicitors or engineers and the courts are entitled to hold liable a defendant whose adherence to general practice has been 'blind, lax or inherently negligent'. Kearns J identified these latter criteria for applying the exception to general practice as being clear from the Supreme Court decision in *Roche v Peilow*,[16] a solicitors' negligence case that had itself informed the

---

[16] *Roche v Peilow* [1985] IR 232.

development of the *Dunne* principles. Kearns J quoted extensively from *Roche*; some of its findings we paraphrase here:

- that neglect of duty does not cease by repetition to be neglect of duty,
- the duty imposed by law rests on the standard to be expected from a reasonably careful member of a profession, not one automatically and mindlessly following the practice of others where taking thought would enable realisation that the practice at issue was fraught with peril,
- that it is the professional's duty to guard against clear and present dangers known to inhere in a general practice,
- that the consequences of the risk materialising were well-known and that the consequences were obvious.

Having highlighted the foregoing 'criteria', Kearns J suggested that the exception provided by the third *Dunne* principle was, on the topic of informed consent, an inappropriate mechanism to find fault with medical practitioners for failing to warn of very remote risks which, for that very quality of remoteness could not be regarded as obvious or 'clear and present' dangers, even on due consideration. Kearns J said:

> It is yet another reason to think that the third principle in Dunne, though suitable for medical treatment, is perhaps inappropriate in the distinctly different context of disclosure. One must surely conclude that the more remote the risk, the harder it is to judge any practice of not disclosing it to be 'blind, lax or inherently negligent'. The converse approach adopted in Walsh was justified by reference to the elective nature of the surgery, but that consideration, discussed later, is more appropriate to the issue of causation than any duty of disclosure, where the seriousness of the consequences and the frequency of the risk are the real concern.

Having so analysed and criticised the application of the third *Dunne* principle to the issue of disclosure of risks, Kearns J proposed the application of a reasonable patient test, saying that it seemed 'more logical in respect of disclosure'. This would establish the proposition that the patient, as a general principle, has the right to know and the practitioner a duty to advise of all material risks associated with a proposed form of treatment.

Kearns J recognised that the courts would ultimately have to decide what was material. He considered 'materiality' to include consideration of *both* (a) the severity of the consequences *and* (b) the statistical frequency of the risk. He considered it obvious that both are critical because a risk with serious consequences could be so rare as not to be regarded as significant by many. Furthermore, Kearns J was of the view that the reasonable person, entitled as they were to full information of material risks, does not have impossible expectations nor seeks to impose impossible standards. The reasonable person 'must be taken as needing medical practitioners to deliver on their medical expertise without excessive restraint or gross limitation on their ability to do so'.

By this analysis, Kearns J homed in on a central problem with the *Walsh* judgments – that they confined the test of materiality to the severity of consequences only, regardless of the remoteness of the risks at play. This could result in advice being given in respect of risks so remote that it could needlessly deter patients from undergoing operations that are in their best interests.

Kearns J concluded his analysis of the obligation to warn by proposing the following 'reasonable patient' test:

> Each case it seems to me should be considered in the light of its own particular facts, evidence and circumstances to see if the reasonable patient in the plaintiff's position would have required a warning of the particular risk.

The judgment in *Geoghegan* then turned to the important issue of causation. Kearns J commenced his analysis by stating:

> It is not sufficient to establish that a warning should have been given but was not given to entitle a plaintiff to recover damages. He must also establish that, had he been given a proper warning, he would have opted to forego the procedure.

Given the majority finding in *Walsh* that an adequate warning had been given, there was only a limited call in that case for analysis of the causation question. Of course, greater consideration of the issue had to be given by the authors of the dissenting judgments, McCarthy and Egan JJ. After all, they concluded that the warning given had not been adequate and that the question of damage caused by that deficit fell to be decided. McCarthy J said that it did not automatically follow that the plaintiff would not have undergone the procedure but identified and accepted the plaintiff's evidence that he would not. Egan J considered that evidence of causation of damage was not required at all, where breach of duty was established. His opinion in this regard, it might be said, did not accord with established principles on causation of damage by negligence.

Accepting that causation of damage falls to be established by a plaintiff where a want of care is established, Kearns J considered in detail whether the issue of causation ought to be determined on an objective or subjective basis. There are evident difficulties in determining the issue solely by reference to the evidence of the patient – they will hardly have sued unless prepared to swear that they would have foregone the procedure if only they had been warned differently.

Kearns J observed that such concerns prompted the US Court of Appeals for the District of Columbia in *Canterbury v Spence*[17] and the Supreme Court of Canada in *Reibl*[18] to require that the issue of causation be determined upon an objective basis – by showing that a reasonable patient in the plaintiff's position would have declined the treatment by reason of the risks involved, but not advised.

Kearns J also considered how the subjective approach had been adopted in Australia in *Ellis v Wallsend District Hospital*[19] and in other cases. These cases emphasised the capacity of a court to disbelieve evidence found to be tainted with hindsight. He remarked that the subjective test catered also for the idiosyncratic patient who does not conveniently fit into the box that contains 'the reasonable patient' for reasons peculiar or particular to that individual patient. In the United Kingdom, Kearns J observed, the subjective approach had also been preferred in certain cases, while others described well the problems in dealing with causation on such a subjective basis.

Having examined closely the approaches adopted in the various jurisdictions mentioned, it seemed to Kearns J that both objective and subjective approaches were valuable in different ways and that *both* should be considered. In the first instance, the court should consider the problem from an objective point of view – asking what a reasonable person, properly informed, would have done in the plaintiff's position. This would provide what Kearns J termed 'the yardstick against which the particular plaintiff's assertion must be tested'. As the criteria constituting 'the plaintiff's position', Kearns J instanced the following:

- the plaintiff's age,
- pre-existing health,
- family and financial circumstances,
- the nature of the surgery,
- anything that can be objectively assessed, although personal to the plaintiff.

It strikes us that the foregoing criteria have the capacity to lay the ground for applications for discovery of documentation evidencing a plaintiff's family and financial circumstances, that might not otherwise arise but for an allegation of a failure to obtain informed consent.

While Kearns J held that consideration of the causation question should start with an objective assessment, he also held that any objective test must sometimes yield to a subjective test when, but only when, credible evidence, and not necessarily that of the plaintiff, in the particular case so demands. While the court was required to accord due deference to the testimony of both

---

[17] *Canterbury v Spence* (1972) 464 F 2d 772.
[18] op cit.
[19] *Ellis v Wallsend District Hospital* [1990] 2 Med LR 103.

patient and medical practitioner, the jurisprudence highlighted the challenges that each might have in providing a reliable account. For this reason, Kearns J stated that the court should, where possible, look elsewhere for credible information.

Kearns J recognised that the dual approach suggested by him might 'smack of pragmatism'. He had no hesitation in suggesting it all the same. It was, he said, an exercise in 'fact construction' that was more about methodology of judicial assessment than any legal principle.

Notably, the 'reasonable patient' was held by Kearns J to be a patient to whom the statistical likelihood of a risk occurring was a matter of significance – in respect of which the views of medical practitioners were extremely important. If a risk was 'virtually off the spectrum', as Kearns J put it, he believed that a reasonable patient might accept or even disregard that risk where it was not in the more serious category of risks.

Kearns J doubted the relevance of the elective nature of a surgical procedure in determining the nature and extent of the duty to inform the patient of risks. He saw this factor as being of particular significance on the issue of causation. It was common sense to hold that a person might be more likely to forego surgery when they had a real choice in the matter.

Ultimately, the application by Kearns J of the objective test led him to conclude that the reasonable patient was more likely to have proceeded with the operation. He felt compelled, however, to resolve the causation issue in the case before him by reference to the subjective test, given that a 'credible and reliable picture' had emerged overall on his analysis of the evidence. The plaintiff had been given a video and brochure, at which he had not looked until the defendant insisted on it. The plaintiff had not adhered to the protocol that the defendant followed prior to surgery. The defendant had to chase down the plaintiff for a second consultation, threatening to cancel the operation if the plaintiff did not attend. The defendant had presented to the plaintiff a letter detailing possible complications, including nerve damage, but the plaintiff had never read it. Taking particular note of the apparent hostility with which the plaintiff had responded to his complication post-operatively, contrasted with the relative nonchalance with which he had approached matters pre-operatively, Kearns J was satisfied to find that the plaintiff was not going to be put off having his operation because of some very remote risk, when balanced against what he saw as the benefits of the procedure.

THE INQUISITIVE PATIENT

In *Geoghegan*, the court concluded by addressing the plaintiff's complaint that specific questions raised by the patient had not been answered.

Kearns J considered the judgment of the House of Lords in *Sidaway*[20] and the conclusion that if a patient does ask specific questions he is entitled to accurate answers, so far as the doctor is able to give them. The impetus for development of the 'inquisitive patient' doctrine in England and Wales, as identified in *Sidaway*, was the limited nature of the duty of disclosure imposed on medical practitioners by *Bolam*.

Having addressed the evidence and found that there was no substance to the plaintiff's complaints in this regard, Kearns J observed that any real consideration of the 'inquisitive patient' in Irish law was subsumed by the onerous obligation of disclosure set down by the Supreme Court in *Walsh*. The obligation in Ireland is to inform the patient of any material risk, whether he inquires or not, regardless of its infrequency.

THE SUPREME COURT REVISITS INFORMED CONSENT – *FITZPATRICK V WHITE*

By 2007, Kearns J had been elevated to the Supreme Court. The dismissal by the High Court of an informed consent case in *Fitzpatrick v White*[21] presented him with an opportunity to revisit *Walsh* and *Geoghegan*, from a higher bench. As the Supreme Court panel hearing *Fitzpatrick* comprised of three judges, however, as distinct from the panel of five judges that had heard *Walsh*, a wholesale recalibration of the principles expressed in *Walsh* was not on the cards. Nonetheless, *Fitzpatrick* presented an opportunity for further exploration of the themes and tests explored by Kearns J in *Geoghegan*, from the Supreme Court's position. Kearns J delivered the court's judgment, with which Macken and Finnegan JJ agreed.

The plaintiff, a Dublin musician with a squint, claimed the defendant had failed to warn him of a risk of diplopia, or double vision, in a corrective procedure he underwent. The plaintiff claimed that during the consenting discussion, had very shortly prior to the surgery, while the plaintiff was in a gown on a ward in hospital, there had been no mention of complications, side effects or adverse consequences. He stated that if he had been told of a risk of muscle loss or slippage resulting in double vision he would have remembered it and 'walked straight out of the hospital'.

The defendant hospital's doctor could not specifically recall meeting the plaintiff on the date of surgery but gave evidence of his general practice. It was his standard practice to warn patients of the complication of diplopia associated with under or over correction. He also warned, he said, of rare complications, such as slippage of muscle, that could also lead to double vision. This was an extremely unusual condition. Unfortunately, the latter complication manifested itself in the months following the surgery.

---

[20] op cit.
[21] *Fitzpatrick v White* [2008] 3 IR 551.

The trial judge in the High Court, White J, held that the plaintiff was not a credible witness and found him to have been exaggerating the extent and effect of his double vision. The trial judge found that the plaintiff's sole concern was cosmetic effect and that irrespective of whether a warning had or had not been given, the plaintiff's attitude towards surgery would not have altered.

Kearns J considered afresh the authorities – Irish, American, Canadian, Australian and English – that had been considered in *Geoghegan*. Kearns J, in *Fitzpatrick*, reiterated the two critical conclusions reached in *Walsh*, albeit by reference to different principles, as he had stated them in *Geoghegan*. He repeated his preference for the 'reasonable patient' test formulated by O'Flaherty J in *Walsh*.

Kearns J observed that a 'doctor centred' approach had been the law for many years in England and Wales, established in cases such as *Bolam* and *Sidaway* (albeit that Lord Scarman in *Sidaway* had opted for the 'prudent patient' test). Kearns J detected in more recent cases, however, a move by the courts in England from the *Bolam* test to a version of the 'reasonable patient' test. He quoted, in particular, Lord Woolf MR in *Pearce v United Bristol Healthcare NHS Trust*,[22] whose judgment emphasised the responsibility of doctors to inform patients of significant risks that would affect the judgment of a reasonable patient, if the information is needed, so that the patient could determine for him or herself as to what course they should adopt.

Kearns J noted that the language of self-determination adopted by Lord Woolf in *Pearce* had since been referred to with approval by Lord Steyn, who formed a part of the majority in the House of Lords in *Chester v Afshar*.[23] Similar language had been used by other judges in *Chester*. Moreover, Kearns J observed that the 'patient centred' approach had been adopted in virtually every major common law jurisdiction, including Australia (*Rogers v Whitaker*[24]), Canada (*Reibl*[25]), and the United States (*Canterbury*[26]).

Kearns J had particular regard to the close analysis of the topic in which the High Court of Australia had engaged in *Rosenburg v Percival*.[27] Kirby J in *Rosenburg* had set out detailed arguments for confining the rule by reference to practical considerations – and also detailed reasons of principle and policy underpinning the validity of the patient centred approach. Kearns J found that the analysis undertaken by Kirby J in *Rosenburg*

> supported the argument that the giving of an adequate warning, far from being a source of nuisance to doctors, should be seen as an opportunity

---

[22] *Pearce v United Bristol Healthcare NHS Trust* (1999) 48 BMLR 118.
[23] *Chester v Afshar* [2005] 1 AC 134.
[24] *Rogers v Whitaker* (1992) 175 CLR 479.
[25] op cit.
[26] op cit.
[27] *Rosenburg v Percival* [2001] HCA 18.

to ensure they are protected from subsequent litigation at the suit of disappointed patients.

Kearns J said:

> I am thus fortified to express, in rather more vigorous terms than I did in *Geoghegan v Harris* my view that the patient centred test is preferable, and ultimately more satisfactory from the point of view of both doctor and patient alike, than any 'doctor centred' approach favoured by part of this court in *Walsh v Family Planning Services Ltd*.

CONTENT OF THE WARNING TO A REASONABLE PATIENT

Kearns J recognised that the court in *Fitzpatrick* was not free to depart from the views expressed by a Supreme Court of five members in *Walsh*, to the effect that a warning must in every case be given of a risk, however remote, of grave consequences involving severe pain continuing into the future and involving further operative intervention. In so far as the court in *Fitzpatrick* was so confined, however, Kearns J highlighted that *Walsh* addressed only that limited category of cases where such consequences were the downside risk. On that basis, he felt free to distinguish *Fitzpatrick* from *Walsh*, to offer what he described as a 'somewhat less extreme view of the scope of the duty in cases where ongoing severe pain involving further operations is not one of the known complications'.

Having so loosened the shackles of *Walsh*, Kearns J said:

> I would see as more reasonable for those cases the test outlined by Lord Woolf MR, namely, that if there is a significant risk which would affect the judgement of a reasonable patient, then in the normal course it is the responsibility of a doctor to inform the patient of that significant risk. This is still an onerous test and not dissimilar from the requirement enunciated in *Rogers v Whitaker* and in this context I would regard the words 'significant risk' and 'material risk' as interchangeable. In *Geoghegan v Harris* I suggested that any consideration of 'materiality' would involve consideration of both (a) the severity of the consequences and (b) the statistical frequency of the risk. Putting it another way, a risk may be seen as material if, in the circumstances of a particular case, a reasonable person in the patient's position, if warned of the risk, would be likely to attach significance to it. I am leaving to one side here consideration of those cases where the medical practitioner may be aware that the particular patient, if warned of the risk, would be likely to attach significance to it where another patient might not.

Timing of the warning to a reasonable patient

For the purpose of his appeal, recognising the principles for the adjudication of an appeal as prescribed by the Supreme Court in *Hay v O'Grady*,[28] the plaintiff did not seek to challenge on appeal the findings of fact reached as to the giving of a relevant warning on the morning of surgery. The plaintiff nonetheless challenged the validity of the warning given by reference to its proximity to the surgical procedure itself.

Kearns J recognised that there were obvious reasons why, in the context of elective surgery, a warning given only shortly before an operation is undesirable. While Kearns J noted the views of a number of the experts in the case to the effect that this practice of warning day patients on the day of their operation had its advantages, he was clearly of the view that the disadvantages were far greater – including the possibility of an embittered patient later asserting that they were too stressed or in too much pain to understand what was said or to make a free decision and that they were, effectively, deprived of any choice. In the instant case, where the plaintiff had testified under cross-examination that he would have walked straight out of the hospital had he been warned on the day, the plaintiff could not credibly maintain that his capacity to appreciate or act on the warning found to have been given was hampered in any way. The appeal on this point, therefore, failed.

Kearns J wished, nonetheless, to 'make the point strongly ... that in other cases where a warning is given late in the day, particularly where the surgery is elective surgery, the outcome might well be different'. Earlier advice and warnings, leaving an opportunity for discussion and reflection, are therefore clearly advisable.

More recent developments in Ireland

In *Healy v Buckley*[29] the High Court had dismissed the plaintiff's claim for negligent prescription of medication in 2000 and for failing to obtain the plaintiff's informed consent to the course of medication at that time. The Court of Appeal in 2015 identified as the leading judgments on the issue of informed consent those of Kearns J in the High Court in *Geoghegan* and in the Supreme Court in *Fitzpatrick*. The court identified the test to be applied as the 'reasonable patient test', with a view to ensuring that it was the patient, thus informed, rather than the doctor, who made the real choice as to whether the treatment was to be carried out. In deciding whether or not a warning would cause a patient to forego an operation, the Court of Appeal found that

---

[28] *Hay v O'Grady* [1992] 1 IR 210.
[29] *Healy v Buckley* [2015] IECA 251.

the appropriate course was to adopt first an objective test, which was to yield to a subjective test where there was clear evidence from which a court could reliably infer what a particular patient would have decided.

We are struck by the clarity of the language adopted by the Court of Appeal in identifying the applicable test as the 'reasonable patient test' and the simplicity with which its judgment attributed to that test the purpose of ensuring that it was the patient, and not the doctor, who made the real choice as to whether the treatment was to be carried out.

The Court of Appeal in *Healy* noted the approval by the Supreme Court in *Fitzpatrick* of the *Geoghegan* test and approach on causation. Applying the law on informed consent in Ireland, thus stated, to the facts of the *Healy* case, the Court of Appeal found that the defendant's behaviour did not fall foul of the decision on consent in *Geoghegan*.

The Court of Appeal noted that the law on consent to medical treatment had been continuing to develop and that the latest decision in the United Kingdom Supreme Court had been delivered only some months previously in *Montgomery v Lanarkshire Health Board*.[30] The Court of Appeal characterised the judgment in *Montgomery* as reflecting an enhanced status of the patient as the chooser of the treatment and remarked that the law on consent in Ireland might require reconsideration in light of what it described as the patient's capacity under *Montgomery* to choose between treatment and no treatment. Recognising that the judgment in *Montgomery* was delivered on 11 March 2015, however, the Court of Appeal was satisfied that it would be quite unjust to the defendant to apply any new standard identified therein to a course of treatment in respect of which advice had been given in 2000.

It is not immediately apparent, having regard to the terms in which the Court of Appeal had stated the 'reasonable patient test' and the simplicity of the language with which it had identified its purpose, how the court might have considered the judgment in *Montgomery* to have reflected a further enhanced status of the patient as the chooser of the treatment. It is necessary, therefore, to consider the decision in *Montgomery* in some detail below.

The plaintiff in *Healy* applied to the Supreme Court for leave to appeal. The Supreme Court's determination to refuse leave to appeal[31] held that the Court of Appeal's decision did not mark 'a new departure' in the law in Ireland on informed consent. The Supreme Court described both the High Court and the Court of Appeal as having applied 'well-settled legal principles'. The Supreme Court determined that the Court of Appeal's judgment not to consider evolving jurisprudence in other jurisdictions was rational and just – and did not lay the ground for an appeal on a matter of general public importance in the case.

---

[30] *Montgomery v Lanarkshire Health Board* [2015] UKSC 11.
[31] *Healy v Buckley* [2016] IESCDET 18.

MONTGOMERY V LANARKSHIRE HEALTH BOARD[32] – THE DISAPPLICATION OF BOLAM AND THE END OF SIDAWAY?

While the Court of Appeal in *Healy v Buckley*[33] did not consider in detail the potential implications in Ireland of adopting some or all of the *ratio* and conclusions reached by the UK Supreme Court in *Montgomery v Lanarkshire Health Board*,[34] and with the Supreme Court in the circumstances of the *Healy* case declining to do so, it remains to be seen what a Supreme Court of Five – freer to revisit the issue of informed consent than the Court of Three in *Fitzpatrick v White* – might find of interest in *Montgomery*.

The decision of the UK Supreme Court in *Montgomery* has been described as a landmark decision. The plaintiff claimed damages on behalf of her son, who was born with severe disabilities due to complications at delivery. The plaintiff attributed these injuries to the negligence of a consultant obstetrician and gynaecologist employed by the defendant, who was responsible for the plaintiff's care during her pregnancy and labour. The plaintiff advanced two distinct grounds of negligence. The first, and the only ground of relevance to this chapter, concerned her antenatal care and related to the issue of informed consent. The plaintiff complained that she should have been made aware of the risk of shoulder dystocia (the inability of the baby's shoulders to pass through the pelvis) and of the alternative possibility of electing for a caesarean section. The occurrence of shoulder dystocia was described by an expert witness, Dr Philip Owen, as 'a major obstetric emergency associated with a short and long term neonatal and maternal morbidity [and] an associated neonatal mortality'.

The plaintiff had diabetes and for that reason had a higher chance of giving birth to a baby that was larger than normal. This, in turn, increased the risk of her baby experiencing shoulder dystocia during labour. The evidence was that there is about a 10% risk of shoulder dystocia in babies born to diabetic mothers. The obstetrician told the plaintiff that the baby would be larger than normal – but not about the risks. The plaintiff expressed concerns about the baby's size, but the obstetrician advised her to deliver the baby vaginally. Had she requested a caesarean, however, she would have been given one. Notably, the plaintiff's evidence had been that she would have elected for a caesarean if she had been told about the risk of shoulder dystocia.

The obstetrician felt the risk of shoulder dystocia 'was low' and did not, therefore, raise the issue. Significantly, the obstetrician acknowledged that had she raised the risk with the plaintiff, 'she would have no doubt requested a caesarean section, as would any diabetic today'. It was for this reason that the obstetrician had determined not to inform the plaintiff of the risk of shoulder dystocia, being of the opinion that a vaginal delivery was more appropriate.

---

[32] *Montgomery v Lanarkshire Health Board* [2015] UKSC 11.
[33] *Healy v Buckley* [2015] IECA 251.
[34] *Montgomery v Lanarkshire Health Board* [2015] UKSC 11.

At trial before the outer house of the Scottish Court of Session, the Lord Ordinary was invited by counsel for the plaintiff to accept that the plaintiff should have been advised of the risks of shoulder dystocia and the alternative of delivery by caesarean section. He rejected this contention, on the basis that the *Bolam* test[35] had not been met, where the evidence established that the absence of advice as to this risk was accepted as proper by a responsible body of medical opinion. The Lord Ordinary also considered the approach determined in *Sidaway*,[36] holding that the plaintiff's claim did not fall within the exception of a substantial risk of grave circumstances arising in respect of which a judge could conclude, notwithstanding any medical practice to the contrary, that a patient's right to decide whether to consent to the treatment was so obvious that no prudent medical practitioner could fail to warn of the risk. While the risk of shoulder dystocia was significant, in the vast majority of cases 'shoulder dystocia was dealt with by simple procedures and the chance of a severe injury to the baby was tiny'. The risk at issue, as determined by the Lord Ordinary, was not the possibility of shoulder dystocia occurring, but the much smaller risk of a grave adverse outcome.

The Lord Ordinary accepted that the plaintiff had stated concerns but held that the mere expression of such concerns did not result in a duty to explain the risks involved. The Lord Ordinary held that in order for a duty to explain particular risks to arise 'questions of specific risks' needed to be raised.

On appeal to the Inner House of the Scottish Court of Session, the plaintiff again argued that the obstetrician should have informed her of the risk of shoulder dystocia. Lord Eassie rejected this argument and applied *Sidaway*. Lord Eassie held that in advising a patient of medical risks, the law on informed consent was understood to follow the practice of a responsible body of medical practitioners. He also accepted, however, the opinion of Lord Bridge in *Sidaway* that there may be exceptional cases where the risk involved was so obviously substantial that the court could say no practitioner could reasonably omit to warn the patient. Lord Eassie agreed with the Lord Ordinary's conclusion that this was not such a case, for the reasons given. Lord Eassie also rejected the plaintiff's further contention, that her expressions of concern were such as to trigger the duty described by Lord Bridge in *Sidaway*, where a doctor questioned specifically by a patient is to answer as truthfully and as fully as the questioner requires. He found the plaintiff's concerns to have been of a general nature only and therefore to have fallen short of Lord Bridge's observation.

On causation, the plaintiff advanced an alternative argument based on the decision in *Chester v Afshar*.[37] In *Chester*, a back operation had resulted in the occurrence of an undisclosed risk. The patient claimed she would not have had

---

[35] *Bolam v Friern Hospital Management Committee* [1957] 1 WLR 582, 587.
[36] *Sidaway v Governors of the Bethlehem Royal Hospital* [1985] 1 AC 871.
[37] *Chester v Afshar* [2005] 1 AC 134.

the operation had she known about the risk. Both the Lord Ordinary and Lord Eassie distinguished *Chester* as the birth of a baby was not an operation that could be deferred.

THE JUDGMENT OF THE UK SUPREME COURT

The UK Supreme Court unanimously allowed the appeal. Lord Kerr and Lord Reed together gave the lead judgment, with which the other five members of the court agreed. Lady Hale's agreement with, and deferment to, the lead judgment was expressed by her delivery of a short concurring judgment.

The judgment of Lord Kerr and Lord Reed offers a comprehensive review of the law relating to informed consent in the United Kingdom, as informed in part by Canadian and Australian jurisprudence. The individual judgments in *Sidaway*, especially, are considered each in striking detail in highlighting the *ratio* thereof and in assessing their respective merits.

Lord Kerr and Lord Reed found that in the 20 years since *Sidaway* the paradigm of the doctor–patient relationship implicit in the speeches in that case had 'ceased to reflect reality'. It was a mistake to view patients as uninformed, incapable of understanding medical matters or wholly dependent on information from doctors. Courts had also become increasingly conscious of fundamental values such as self-determination.

Lord Kerr and Lord Reed found that the majority's analysis in *Sidaway* was unsatisfactory and that it was no surprise that courts had difficulty applying what was effectively the *Bolam* test subject to two qualifications. Furthermore, they found that courts had, in reality, adopted *Chester v Afshar* as the authority in this area. Application of the *Bolam* test was liable to result in sanctioning differences in practice not attributable to divergent schools of thought in medicine, but to divergent attitudes among doctors as to the degree of respect owed to their patients.

The court concluded that the correct position was to be found in the approach adopted by Lord Scarman in *Sidaway* and by Lord Woolf in *Pearce*, subject to the refinement made by the High Court of Australia in *Rogers v Whitaker*. At paragraph 87 of their judgment, Lord Kerr and Lord Reed say:

> An adult person of sound mind is entitled to decide which, if any, of the available forms of treatment to undergo, and her consent must be obtained before treatment interfering with her bodily integrity is undertaken. The doctor is therefore under a duty to take reasonable care to ensure that the patient is aware of any material risks involved in any recommended treatment, and of any reasonable alternative or variant treatments. The test of materiality is whether, in the circumstances of the particular case, a reasonable person in the patient's position would be likely to attach

significance to the risk, or the doctor is or should reasonably be aware that the particular patient would be likely to attach significance to it.

Lord Kerr and Lord Reed mention circumstances where it may be reasonable for a doctor to withhold information from a patient. These circumstances include where a patient is unconscious, and emergency surgery is required. A doctor would also be entitled to withhold information from a patient if they believed the disclosure of such information would be detrimental to the patient's health.

Three further points are made by the court: First, assessing the significance of a risk is fact-sensitive and cannot be reduced to percentages. Second, in order to advise, the doctor must engage in dialogue with her patient. Third, the therapeutic exception is limited and should not be abused.

Ultimately, the Court concluded that the obstetrician should have advised the plaintiff of the substantial risk of shoulder dystocia. In so finding, the court emphasised the evidence that the occurrence of shoulder dystocia is, in and of itself, a 'major obstetric emergency'. For this reason, the focus of the Outer and Inner Houses of the Scottish Court of Sessions upon the tiny risk of grave harm to the baby had been misplaced. The Lower Courts should have focused upon the plaintiff's likely reaction had she been fully informed of the risk of shoulder dystocia itself. On this issue, the obstetrician's unequivocal evidence had been that the plaintiff would have opted for a caesarean section had she been so advised – and, moreover, that it had been to avoid that consequence that the obstetrician had withheld the information.

Lady Hale, in her concurring judgment, reasoned that it was impossible to consider a particular procedure without regard to its alternatives. Pregnancy was, in her view, a 'particularly powerful illustration'. Where either mother or child is at heightened risk from vaginal delivery, Lady Hale found that doctors should volunteer the pros and cons of that option compared to a caesarean. Lady Hale observed that one is concerned not only with risks to the baby, but also with risks to the mother. She considered the obstetrician's view that caesarean sections are not generally in maternal interests to be a value judgment. Once the argument departed from purely medical considerations, as in this case, the *Bolam* test was inapposite. Lady Hale stated that a patient is entitled to take into account her own values, and that her choices must be respected, unless she lacks capacity. She is at least entitled to information enabling her to take part in the decision.

IMPLICATIONS FOR INFORMED CONSENT IN IRELAND

It goes without saying, perhaps, that the decision of the UK Supreme Court in *Montgomery v Lanarkshire Health Board* has no direct implications for the law regarding informed consent in Ireland. That law is to be found in the decisions of the Irish courts. This is not to say, as the Court of Appeal in *Healy v Buckley* observed, that the enhanced status of the patient as described in *Montgomery* might not commend itself to the Irish Supreme Court in any recalibration of the law on informed consent. That said, it seems appropriate to note that the Irish law on informed consent already:

- prefers a patient centred test to a doctor centred test,
- identifies the test to be applied as the 'reasonable patient test',
- aims to ensure that it is the patient, properly informed, rather than the doctor, who makes the real choice as to whether treatment is to be carried out,
- and thereby recognises the autonomy of the patient and their right to self-determination,
- and in deciding whether or not a warning would cause a patient to forego an operation, adopts first an objective test, which is to yield to a subjective test where there is clear evidence from which a court could reliably infer what a particular patient would have decided.

Against that background, it may appear to the Supreme Court that the Irish law on informed consent already reflects the enhanced status of patients in determining the rights and duties at play when determining whether a properly informed consent was given.

Montgomery demonstrates that the English courts have now moved beyond even the reasonably prudent patient approach proposed by Lord Scarman in his patient centred judgment in *Sidaway*. The comments of Lord Kerr and Lord Reid on the test of materiality go further than a duty measured by reference to an objectively reasonable patient and provide for a *subjective approach* when assessing the materiality of the known facts to individual patients.[38] Consequently, not only do facts fall to be checked for general significance, but they also require assessment as to whether a particular fact is important to a particular patient. The criteria by which such an evaluation is to be performed by medical practitioners are not clear and a comparative assessment of the reasonableness of different doctors' approaches in respect of their different patients looks set to be a challenge in litigation.

The approach of the UK Supreme Court in *Montgomery* can be distinguished from the approach of the Irish Supreme Court in *Fitzpatrick v White*, where the determination of material information to be given falls to be assessed on an objective basis by reference to the 'reasonable patient' in the plaintiff's position. In Ireland, it is only when embarking upon its analysis of the question of causation of damage that a subjective element may arise for a court's consideration, where compelling evidence exists as to the plaintiff's likely response to the absent information.

---

[38] R Heywood 'RIP *Sidaway*: Patient – Oriented Disclosure – A Standard Worth Waiting For?' (2015) 23 Medical Law Review 455–66.

The UK Supreme Court in *Montgomery* determined that the medical practitioner's duty of care is not confined to the disclosure of material risks, but that the disclosure of *alternative or variant treatments* is also included. One of the key issues in *Montgomery* was that the obstetrician had failed to disclose to the plaintiff the availability of alternative treatment, namely a caesarean section. Of course, in the case of pregnancy, there are a finite number of ways in which its end will come to pass – of which a caesarean section is an obvious example. In other cases, however, it is less clear how a medical practitioner is to identify what alternative or variant treatments are reasonable. The judgments in *Montgomery* do not answer this question. It would seem to go beyond any standard of reasonableness to require medical practitioners to disclose every conceivable alternative or variant treatment. On this issue of objective identification of what alternative or variant treatments are considered reasonable, the implications of *Montgomery* are not clear.

Irish law on informed consent does not, as matters stand, expressly require discussion of alternative or variant treatments. A discussion of material risks may well include a discussion of alternatives in any event, but it remains to be determined whether such is required before a properly informed consent may be given.

Another important finding of the judgments in *Montgomery* is that for consent to be truly informed, patients must *understand* the risks that are being disclosed. Without such understanding, the patient will not truly be put in a position to make an informed decision as to their treatment, if any. The UK Supreme Court cautioned against overloading patients with information – of 'bombarding' them with technical information that they cannot reasonably be expected to grasp, as the court put it. Understanding is, however, a subjective concept that changes from patient to patient, and in that regard, the judgment leaves one with some uncertainty.[39]

It can be difficult for a medical practitioner to effectively gauge a particular patient's understanding – and difficult for a judge to set standards of what reasonable steps should have been taken for a patient to understand the material risks of surgery. The court in *Montgomery* urged medical practitioners to use 'dialogue' rather than technical information when disclosing material risks to patients. We suggest that a dialogue that takes as its starting point the option to do nothing can present a helpful foundation for a discussion of reasonable alternatives and their attendant material risks.

It merits recognition that notwithstanding the foregoing difficulties, the Medical Council of Ireland's 'Good Medical Practice in Seeking Informed Consent to Treatment', approved on 27 February 2008, advises that disclosures are to be made to patients 'in a way that they can understand' and offers advice

---

[39] Kevin Williams, 'Comprehending Disclosure: Must Patients Understand the Risks They Run?' (2000) 4 Med L Intl 97.

as to measures to be taken with a view to ensuring comprehension. Avoiding complex medical terminology, adopting lay language, deploying common everyday analogies and the use of pictorial representations, are all advised.

Conclusion

What, then, might an Irish Supreme Court comprised of five judges, in a position amongst other things to revisit, recalibrate and overturn that court's decision in *Walsh v Family Planning Services Ltd* find in *Montgomery v Lanarkshire Health Board* to assist? Irish law on informed consent already recognised the right of the patients to material information, so as to enable them to make their own autonomous decisions with regard to their medical treatment. The addition of a subjective test in the determination of what constitutes material information, above and beyond the reasonable patient test, appears to bring with it potential challenges to the patient–doctor relationship, without evident benefit for the standards of reasonable dialogue required between patients and doctors. A requirement for a discussion around options for treatment or management, including the option not to treat, would do no more than reflect the Medical Council of Ireland's Guidelines in being since February 2008.

Ultimately, it may well be that the priority for the Irish Supreme Court when it next takes the opportunity to revisit the law on informed consent in Ireland should be to reflect less on the UK Supreme Court's judgments in *Montgomery v Lanarkshire Health Board*, when it had adopted a patient centred approach before that court ever did, and instead revisit the remnants of its own decision in *Walsh v Family Planning Services Ltd*, left as yet undisturbed by its judgment in *Fitzpatrick v White*. The opportunity to review the value of requiring disclosure of *all* risks, however remote, of grave long-term consequences involving severe pain, with the benefit of the close analysis applied in *Fitzpatrick v White*, would be a welcome one, whatever the result.

Chapter III

DOES A CAUSE OF ACTION ARISE FOR NERVOUS SHOCK THROUGH WITNESSING THE HARM CAUSED TO A FAMILY MEMBER BY REASON OF MEDICAL NEGLIGENCE AND, IF SO, IN WHAT CIRCUMSTANCES DOES IT ARISE?

Hugh O'Leary and Adrienne Egan SC[1]

To date, there have only been two reported cases where damages for nervous shock have been sought, in the context of a claim for medical negligence. Accordingly, we propose to outline the general principles of law relating to the recovery of damages for nervous shock, both in this jurisdiction and in the United Kingdom, before discussing the circumstances in which we believe a cause of action might arise through witnessing the harm caused to a family member by reason of medical negligence.

General principles of law relating to nervous shock

The first decided High Court case on nervous shock in modern times is that of *Mullaly v Bus Éireann*[2] where the plaintiff was informed that her husband and three sons had been involved in a serious bus accident and were critically ill or dying. She immediately went to the two hospitals where her family members were being treated. The evidence established that the plaintiff's ordeal in witnessing the aftermath of this accident caused her to suffer post-traumatic stress disorder, from which she continued to suffer at the date of the trial.

In awarding €75,000 in respect of general damages, Denham J (as she then was) stated that in the circumstances of the case, the plaintiff's post-traumatic stress disorder had been a reasonably foreseeable injury caused by the negligence of the defendant. She was of the view that it would be unjust and contrary to

---

[1] Hugh O'Leary prepared this chapter as a final year undergraduate student at the School of Law and of Political Science at Trinity College Dublin. Adrienne Egan SC is a member of the Inner Bar of Ireland.
[2] *Mullaly v Bus Éireann* [1992] ILRM 722.

the fundamental principles of negligence not to find a legal nexus between the negligence of the defendant and its resultant aftermath, including the appalling hospital scenes and injuries to the plaintiff's immediate family.[3]

The issue of recovery for nervous shock was then examined by the Supreme Court in the seminal case of *Kelly v Hennessy*.[4] Again, in this case, the plaintiff had not been present at the scene of the accident concerned but had witnessed its immediate aftermath in a hospital, where her husband and two daughters were being treated for very significant injuries. Hamilton CJ, with whom Egan J agreed, held that in order to recover damages for nervous shock a plaintiff must prove:

(i) that he suffered a recognisable psychiatric illness;
(ii) that such illness was shock-induced;
(iii) that the nervous shock was caused by the defendant's act or omission;
(iv) that the nervous shock sustained was by reason of actual or apprehended physical injury to the plaintiff or a person other than the plaintiff;
(v) that the defendant owed him or her a duty of care not to cause him or her a reasonably foreseeable injury in the form of nervous shock, as opposed to a personal injury in general.[5]

It was held that the law permits the recovery of damages for nervous shock and psychiatric illness induced thereby where a plaintiff comes on the immediate aftermath of an accident.[6] The relationship between the plaintiff and the person injured must be close. In the instant case it was considered that the relationship between the plaintiff and those injured could not be closer.

In the same case, Denham J stated that where a person with a close proximate relationship to an injured person, while not a participant in an accident, heard of it very soon afterwards and visited the injured person as soon as practicable and was exposed to the serious injuries of the primary victim, that person became a secondary victim to the accident. In the course of her judgment, Denham J stated that there were three elements in the requirement of proximity:

(i) proximity of relationship between persons;
(ii) proximity in a spatial context (i.e. the person must perceive the aftermath of the accident); and
(iii) proximity in a temporal sense (i.e. that 'shock' must be the cause of the illness).[7]

---

[3] ibid 731.
[4] *Kelly v Hennessy* [1995] 3 IR 253.
[5] ibid 258–259.
[6] ibid 264.
[7] ibid 270.

The next case in this area is that of *Fletcher v Commissioners of Public Works*.[8] This is not, strictly speaking, a 'nervous shock' case but is important as an illustration of the willingness of the courts to exclude certain categories of claim where it is considered necessary to do so for reasons of public policy. In *Fletcher* the plaintiff worked as a general operative from 1985 to 1989, during which time, due to the negligence of his employer, he was brought into contact with significant amounts of asbestos. A consultant respiratory physician gave evidence that while the plaintiff had been exposed to the risk of developing asbestosis and an increased risk of lung cancer, he had not contracted either and it was very unlikely that he would do so in the future. He was also at risk of contracting mesothelioma, which might not manifest for 20 years or more from the first exposure, but this risk was very remote.

On the facts of the case, Keane CJ determined that the matter was not a 'nervous shock' case in the sense that that term had been used in cases such as *Kelly v Hennessy*, as there had been no 'sudden perception of a frightening event or its immediate aftermath'.[9] In the circumstances, if the plaintiff was to be entitled to recover damages it must be because such damages could be recovered in respect of a psychiatric disorder brought about otherwise than by 'nervous shock' (in that case by a combination of anger and anxiety which was the result of the plaintiff having been informed of his exposure to the risk of contracting mesothelioma because of his employer's negligence). Both Keane CJ and Geoghegan J, who delivered the other judgment of the court, described this as 'uncharted territory',[10] and ultimately concluded that as the claim arose from an irrational fear of disease it should be refused on the grounds of public policy. In this regard Keane CJ stated:

> I would have no hesitation in rejecting the proposition that, in considering whether particular categories of negligence which have not hitherto been recognised by judicial decision should be so recognised, policy decisions should play no part.[11]

Geoghegan J, having reviewed the relevant case law, observed:

> Reasonable foreseeability is not the only determining factor in establishing a duty of care. 'Proximity', which is given an elastic definition in the decided cases, the reasonableness of the imposition of a duty of care and questions of public policy can be additional determining factors.[12]

The next relevant case is that of *Cuddy v Mays*,[13] where the High Court considered the type of relationship which was required to be established

---

[8] *Fletcher v Commissioners of Public Works* [2003] 1 IR 465.
[9] ibid 481.
[10] ibid 482.
[11] ibid 482.
[12] ibid 519.
[13] *Cuddy v Mays* [2003] IEHC 103.

between the plaintiff and the primary victim in the context of nervous shock claims. Here the plaintiff was working as a porter in a hospital, to which a number of young people were brought after a horrific car accident. Among the dead was the plaintiff's own brother. His sister was also admitted with serious, life-threatening injuries. The plaintiff claimed damages for nervous shock. The defendants accepted that the first four conditions in *Kelly* had been satisfied but argued that the fifth condition had not. Specifically, it was argued that it was not reasonably foreseeable to a negligent defendant that a brother of one person killed and another person injured in the same accident would happen to be present at the nearby hospital when the victims were admitted. Kearns J stated that there could be no possible basis for excluding the plaintiff on this ground. He found that had the plaintiff not been present in his capacity as a porter, he would almost certainly have come to the hospital in any event and would, as a matter of probability, have been exposed to most, if not all, of what he did actually see and experience.[14] It was also argued that, in any event, the category of persons entitled to maintain claims as aftermath or secondary victims for nervous shock should not be extended or deemed to include a brother or more distant relative of the person injured or killed in the accident. In this regard Kearns J stated:

> This court would certainly support the proposition that policy considerations would dictate that the ambit of recoverability and the category of relationships entitled to successfully claim damages for nervous shock should be tightly restricted. However, to recognise such a principle is not in any way to resolve the problems that arise in deciding who may recover in these cases ...
>
> One of the ways is, of course, to exclude certain categories of relationships, invoking policy grounds to do so. But which relationships are included and which are excluded when such policy grounds are invoked? Where does the policy interest lie? For example, if siblings qualify, do step-brothers and step-sisters also qualify? Do engaged or same-sex couples in a long and loving relationship qualify? Does a close and lifelong friendship offer any prospect that a court might qualify the severely traumatised survivor where a lifelong friend and companion dies through the negligence of another? At the opposite extreme, should policy considerations, which must include some recognition of the burden on insurers called upon to meet the cost of multiple claims, exclude secondary victims altogether? Ultimately, of course, this burden falls on the policy holders and, by extension, the public. Should not the possibility of exaggeration, or even fraudulent claims, in this area not weigh heavily with judges whose sympathies may all too easily be won over by horrifying accounts of such accidents and their aftermath?
>
> The difficulty of resolving these issues is self-evident, even where the other elements of the proximity test are met and the considerations last

---

[14] ibid 108.

mentioned above would, it must be said, most commend themselves to this court. However, it seems to me that I must accept what has been decided in other cases and that in the instant case I therefore should apply a 'close proximate relationship' test which, by implication at least, seems to qualify the close family relationship between the plaintiff and his brother and sister. At least such an interpretation has the benefit of being consistent with the legislative policy evident in Part IV of the Civil Liability Act, 1961 when it identified those entitled to recover damages for mental distress in fatal accident cases as being 'any member of the family of the deceased'.[15]

The willingness of the court to restrict recovery for reasons of policy was again demonstrated in *Devlin v National Maternity Hospital*.[16] There it was accepted that the plaintiff had suffered a post-traumatic stress disorder as a result of the wrongful retention of her son's organs following a post mortem examination. Her claim was disallowed, however, by O'Donovan J and, on appeal, by the Supreme Court, on the grounds that the plaintiff had not established that her injury arose as a consequence of actual or apprehended physical injury to herself or another person. Accordingly, the plaintiff failed to satisfy the fourth condition in *Kelly*. In the course of her judgment Denham J stated:

> Thus there are limits in law to liability for nervous shock. The common law provides illustrations of successful cases where damages for nervous shock were awarded. However, those cases relate to persons perceiving an accident or its immediate aftermath ...
>
> This is a tragic case. In essence it arises because of the receipt of bad and sad news in a letter from the hospital. It is a hard case. The parents are entitled to deepest sympathy for their loss. However, the law as it stands does not entitle them to damages and I would not extend the law. Any such development would give rise to uncertainty in the law of liability generally and to potentially unforeseeable repercussions. Consequently, I would dismiss this aspect of the appeal also.[17]

One of the rare cases in which a plaintiff succeeded in obtaining an award of damages for nervous shock in a medical negligence case is that of the High Court in *Courtney v Our Lady's Hospital & ors*.[18] In that case the plaintiff's claim was, however, conceded and the case proceeded as an assessment of damages only. The plaintiff's daughter was two-and-a-half years of age when she became ill one night in February 2006. The plaintiff and her partner became concerned, as the infant was hallucinating, and they brought her to hospital. She was diagnosed as having a viral gastric bug, whereas she was in fact suffering from meningitis. She then developed purple spots and was

---

[15] ibid 113–114.
[16] *Devlin v National Maternity Hospital* [2008] 2 IR 222.
[17] ibid 239–240.
[18] *Courtney v Our Lady's Hospital & ors* [2011] IEHC 226.

transferred to the intensive care unit but died of a heart attack. The plaintiff had stayed with her daughter throughout the night.

O'Neill J found that the plaintiff had suffered a depressive illness 'which was caused by her exposure to and experiencing of the shockingly traumatic sequence of circumstances in the defendant's hospital, culminating in the death of Aisling',[19] and awarded the sum of €150,000 in respect of general damages. An important aspect of this case is the fact that it appears that O'Neill J considered that the requirement that a psychiatric injury be 'shock induced', as laid down by *Kelly*, does not mean that the shock must be a single act or event but can instead be a culmination of events.

The most recent medical negligence claim involving a claim for nervous shock is that of *Ruth Morrissey and Paul Morrissey v Health Service Executive, Quest Diagnostics Incorporated and MedLab Pathology Limited*.[20] Here the High Court had to consider quite a different scenario to the 'aftermath' situation which had arisen in previous nervous shock cases, i.e., nervous shock allegedly caused to a husband on learning of the return of his wife's cancer, following a negligently delayed diagnosis of her condition. In *Morrissey* the first plaintiff had undergone two cervical smear tests, in 2009 and 2012, both of which were reported as normal. In 2014, following complaints of postcoital bleeding, she was referred for investigations which ultimately revealed cervical cancer. The first plaintiff then underwent radical surgery, which appeared initially to be successful.

In the meantime, unknown to the plaintiffs, the second and third defendants, being the proprietors of the respective laboratories which had examined her smear tests in 2009 and 2012, undertook audits, both of which determined that the original results of the cervical smear tests were incorrect. In 2015 the results of these audits were communicated to the first defendant but it was not until June 2016 that this information was made available by it to the plaintiffs. Unfortunately, in October 2017, the first plaintiff experienced significant pain in her right leg, which led to further investigations and, ultimately, the diagnosis of a recurrence of her cancer. As a result, her husband, the second plaintiff, claimed that he had suffered an exacerbation of his physical condition of colitis and a psychiatric injury.

The second plaintiff claimed damages for nervous shock. Cross J accepted that he had suffered, *inter alia*, a recognised psychiatric injury when he was advised that his wife's cancer had returned. His claim for nervous shock was, however, rejected. Having referred to the five requirements set out by Hamilton J in *Kelly*, Cross J stated that it was the last of these which was open to debate. In the course of his judgment he stated:

---

[19] ibid 228.
[20] *Ruth Morrissey and Paul Morrissey v Health Service Executive, Quest Diagnostics Incorporated and MedLab Pathology Limited* [2019] IEHC 268.

believe that approaching this case on the basis of the duty of care issue is more satisfactory than an analysis as is sometimes engaged in courts in England as to distinctions between 'primary' and 'secondary' victims. The neighbour principle established by Lord Atkins in *Donoghue* is the principal basis for establishing a duty of care. However, since the decision of the Supreme Court in *Glencar Explorations Plc v Mayo County Council (No. 2)* a court must consider three or four (and whether it be, there are three or four, is not of any great significance) preliminary conditions in cases where the issue of whether a duty of care is owed arises, i.e. is there reasonable foreseeability, is there proximity of relationship, are there any countervailing public policy considerations and, finally, the justice and reasonableness of imposing a duty of care ...

Mr. Morrissey has a recognised physical and psychiatric injury. His injuries started when he was advised in Galway of the return of the cancer. Clearly, there is a close proximity of relationship between him and his wife, especially so given the nature of the disease being suffered by Mrs. Morrissey. In relation to issues of countervailing policy, insofar as Mr. Morrissey's claim is for physical injury caused by reason of his wife's misdiagnosis, issues of countervailing policy do arise in that every spouse or close family member of a victim of medical malpractice is not *per se* entitled to compensation for psychological or physical stress related injury. To so hold would be to broaden considerably and unacceptably the number of plaintiffs who could claim damages in respect of a legal wrong done to their family members. Accordingly, Mr. Morrissey's claim for damages for personal injuries arising from the misdiagnosis of cancer should fail on public policy alone. I make this point even assuming it was established that a duty of care exists ...

I do not believe that a reasonable person in 2009, 2012 or 2016 could reasonably have concluded that if they negligently misread the slides or failed to tell Mrs. Morrissey of the results of the audits that her husband would be so affected that he would suffer a recognisable physical and mental injury. Accordingly, I have come to the conclusion with some reluctance that Mr. Morrissey is not entitled to maintain a claim for his personal injuries apart from naturally the issues that are compensatable under the heading of general damages for loss of consortium.[21]

Thus it would appear that Cross J dismissed Mr Morrissey's claim on the basis that he failed to satisfy the fifth requirement set out by Hamilton CJ in *Kelly*, namely that the defendant owed him a duty of care not to cause him a reasonably foreseeable injury in the form of nervous shock. He also indicated, however, that he would have dismissed the case on the grounds of public policy alone, even if a duty of care had been established.[22]

---

[21] ibid 332–333.
[22] ibid 333.

A more recent case dealing with the issue of nervous shock in a non-medical context is the judgment in the Court of Appeal in *Harford v Electricity Supply Board*[23] where the plaintiff's claim failed on the basis that it did not satisfy the second and fourth requirements in *Kelly*. The Court of Appeal also referred to the policy considerations which arise when an extension to the existing law is sought. In that case the plaintiff, a network technician, was assigned the task of repairing a public streetlight. A hole in the road had been excavated on the previous day to expose the relevant electrical cables. The plaintiff attended at the locus in order to identify an appropriate live cable to which the faulty street light cable could be attached in order to restore its functionality. Although the facts of the case are fairly complex, it would appear that in the course of so doing, the plaintiff inadvertently handled cabling which was far in excess of that which he ought to have and indeed which could have led to him having been electrocuted. On realising that this had happened, the plaintiff immediately closed up the site and reported the incident to his superiors. It was common case that the plaintiff subsequently developed a recognised psychiatric illness, although there was disagreement between the experts as to whether this amounted to a post-traumatic stress disorder or a clinical depression.

The plaintiff issued proceedings claiming damages for nervous shock and was initially successful in the High Court. The defendant appealed the decision and the issue on appeal was whether or not damages could be recovered for nervous shock where there was no sudden calamitous event but rather an appreciation that physical injury had been narrowly avoided and where that appreciation led to psychiatric injury.

Noonan J carried out an extensive review of the authorities, including the decision of *Kelly v Hennessy* and concluded:

> In my judgment, the plaintiff cannot satisfy the requirements of the second and fourth principles identified by Hamilton CJ in *Kelly v Hennessy*. The injury was not 'shock-induced', as the second principle requires, in the sense that this expression is explained in the authorities to which I have referred. There was no sudden calamitous or horrifying event in the nature of an accident. There was thus no qualifying event and on one view, no event at all. There was instead a post hoc realisation that injury had been avoided by a decision not to proceed with what, with hindsight, was a dangerous course. The implications of that realisation unfolded over a period of hours for the Plaintiff.
>
> Hamilton CJ's fourth principle requires that the Plaintiff must sustain the nervous shock by reason of actual or apprehended physical injury to the Plaintiff or some other person. There was much debate during this appeal so as to the meaning of 'apprehended' but in my view, its

---

[23] *Harford v Electricity Supply Board* [2021] IECA 112.

meaning in this context is clear. The apprehension must be prospective or forward-looking to something yet to happen.[24]

Noonan J also touched upon the issue of policy in such cases, stating:

> Were liability to be imposed in this case, it would inevitably involve an extension of the existing law in this jurisdiction. Policy considerations of the kind discussed in *Fletcher* and *Devlin* will become relevant. A case such as the present, dependant on a purely internal realisation by the Plaintiff, unaccompanied in many instances by any verifiable event or incident, would give rise to considerable practical problems and real uncertainty in the law.
>
> The case, in my view, is governed by *Kelly v Hennessy* which, like *Fletcher* and *Devlin*, is binding on this court. There is, therefore, no basis for a consideration by this court of any extension of the law. That would ultimately be a matter for the Supreme Court in a future case where it arises. While I have considerable sympathy for the Plaintiff who undeniably suffered psychiatric injury, I am satisfied that the answer to the question posed in paragraph 1 above must be 'no'.[25]

There has also been a very helpful discussion of the law, both in this jurisdiction and in the United Kingdom, in the Circuit Court decision of Judge McMahon in *Curran v Cadbury Ireland Limited*[26] and the recent Court of Appeal decision in *Sheehan v Bus Éireann/Irish Bus and Vincent Dower*.[27]

As can be seen from the foregoing, *Kelly v Hennessy* remains the only Supreme Court authority in relation to claims for nervous shock in Ireland. Accordingly, it would appear that plaintiffs who wish to maintain a claim for nervous shock will have to satisfy all of the five conditions set out in the judgment of Hamilton CJ in that case. This may not prove insurmountable in medical negligence claims where the negligence exposes family members to the type of frightening scenes witnessed by the plaintiff in *Courtney*, assuming the remainder of the conditions are met. Far more problematical, however, are the situations where the plaintiff has not witnessed such scenes (referred to as the 'sudden perception of a frightening event or its immediate aftermath'[28] by Keane CJ in *Fletcher*). Difficulties may also arise in cases where the horrifying event suffered by family members is removed in time from the negligent act complained of. Both of these situations arose in *Morrissey*, but were not specifically adverted to by Cross J when discussing why the claim ought to be refused.

---

[24] ibid paras 78–79.
[25] ibid para 83–84.
[26] *Curran v Cadbury Ireland Limited* [2000] 2 ILRM 343.
[27] *Sheehan v Bus Éireann/Irish Bus and Vincent Dower* [2022] IECA 28.
[28] *Fletcher v Commissioners of Public Works* [2003] 1 IR 465, at p 481.

PRINCIPLES OF LAW RELATING TO NERVOUS SHOCK IN THE UNITED KINGDOM

The first leading decision in the United Kingdom is that of the House of Lords in *McLoughlin v O'Brian*.[29] In that case, the plaintiff's husband and their three children had been involved in a traffic accident caused by the defendant's negligence. One of the plaintiff's children died almost immediately and her husband and two other children were injured. The plaintiff was told of the accident by a motorist, who drove her to the hospital. There she came upon the surviving members of her family who were in a state of great distress and disarray. The plaintiff suffered severe shock, organic depression and a change of personality. In the course of his judgment, Wilberforce LJ emphasised the need for strict controls in relation to claims of this nature, stating:

> But, these discounts accepted, there remains, in my opinion, just because 'shock' in its nature is capable of affecting so wide a range of people, the real need for the law to place some limitation upon the extent of admissible claims. It is necessary to consider three elements inherent in any claim: the class of person whose claim should be recognised; the proximity of such persons to the accident; and the means by which the shock is caused.

Ultimately, the House of Lords held that the plaintiff was entitled to succeed in her claim but was divided as to the applicable test to be applied in this regard. Lord Scarman and Lord Bridge considered that the test of reasonable foreseeability was the sole test for determining whether there was a duty of care on the part of the defendant. Factors such as spatial, physical and temporal proximity, and the relationship of the plaintiff to the immediate victim of the accident were important as bearing on the degree of foreseeability of the plaintiff's psychiatric illness. Lord Wilberforce and Lord Edmund-Davies, on the other hand, thought that reasonable foreseeability was not the sole test in determining the existence of a duty of care and that in cases of psychiatric illness there should be overriding limitations on the principle of liability for reasonably foreseeable harm.

Whilst it is difficult to discern a clear *ratio* from the differing judgments in *McLoughlin*, the position has now been resolved by the decision of the House of Lords in *Alcock v Chief Constable of South Yorkshire Police*.[30] This case resulted from the tragedy at Hillsborough, where 95 spectators died and many hundreds were injured in a crush at a football stadium which had become overcrowded, due to negligent management on the part of the police. Sixteen claims were brought by persons who were relatives, or in one case the fiancé, of persons involved in the disaster. It was admitted that the deaths and injuries of the primary victims occurred as a result of negligence by the police and it

---

[29] *McLoughlin v O'Brian* [1983] AC 410.
[30] *Alcock v Chief Constable of South Yorkshire Police* [1992] 1 AC 310.

was assumed for the purposes of the case that each of the plaintiffs had proved the infliction of psychiatric illness.

Ten of the plaintiffs succeeded at trial but the Court of Appeal allowed the defendant's appeal in respect of nine of those successful plaintiffs and dismissed cross-appeals by the six unsuccessful plaintiffs. Ten of the fifteen plaintiffs unsuccessfully appealed to the House of Lords. Of these, Brian Harrison, who lost his brother and Robert Alcock, who lost his brother-in-law, were both present at the match. Brian Harrison had stayed up all night and was informed about the deaths the next morning and Robert Alcock searched until about midnight, when he identified the body of his brother-in-law in the temporary mortuary. The House of Lords held that in the case of these two plaintiffs, the necessary close tie of love and affection had not been proved and could not be presumed for brothers or brothers-in-law. In the cases of the eight other plaintiffs, who were not present at the match but had viewed the disaster on television or viewed the bodies in the mortuary, the court held that this could not be said to be equivalent to being within sight and hearing of the event or its immediate aftermath. (In this regard Ackner and Oliver LJJ indicated that there may be circumstances where the element of direct visual perception may be provided by witnessing the actual injury to the primary victim on simultaneous television.) Only one plaintiff succeeded, namely William Pemberton, in respect of whom the defendant did not appeal. He was a father who had travelled with his son to the match, stayed on the coach and watched the events as they happened on its television. He then searched for his son until he identified him in the temporary mortuary.

Importantly, in an oft-quoted phrase, Lord Ackner described the kind of shock which might give rise to a claim of nervous shock as follows:

> 'Shock', in the context of this cause of action, involves the sudden appreciation by sight or sound of a horrifying event, which violently agitates the mind. It has yet to include psychiatric illness caused by the accumulation over a period of time of more gradual assaults on the nervous system.

It was held by the House of Lords that a plaintiff who sustained nervous shock which caused psychiatric illness as a result of apprehending the infliction of physical injury or the risk thereof to another person could only recover damages in negligence against the wrongdoer if:

(i) His relationship to the primary victim was sufficiently close that it was reasonably foreseeable that he might sustain nervous shock if he apprehended that the primary victim had been or might be injured;
(ii) His proximity to the accident in which the primary victim was involved or its immediate aftermath was sufficiently close both in time and space and

(iii) He suffered nervous shock through seeing or hearing the accident or its immediate aftermath.[31]

It appears from the foregoing cases that in order to succeed as a secondary victim under UK law, claimants must establish, *inter alia*, proximity to the incident or its immediate aftermath. In clinical claims, however, the aftermath of a negligent event may be far removed from the event itself. It is important, therefore, to examine how this problematical issue has been dealt with in the United Kingdom.

In the case of *Taylor v Somerset Health Authority*,[32] the claimant's husband suffered a heart attack at work, caused by the defendant's negligent failure (many months before) to diagnose and treat his serious heart disease. He died shortly after being taken to hospital. The claimant went to the hospital, where she was told of the claimant's death and identified his body. Auld J in the High Court considered whether the claimant's attendance at the hospital an hour after her husband's death brought her within the immediate aftermath of the incident:

> All their Lordships in Alcock, in considering the application of the immediate aftermath test to the various claims before them, did so, understandably in the circumstances of the case, by reference to the accident, the disaster in the stadium. But regardless of the particular circumstances of that case, all their lordships clearly regarded some external, traumatic, event in addition to its primary consequence of injury or death as a necessary starting point when considering what Lord Oliver described, at p. 410, as 'the essential but elusive concept of "proximity" or "directness"'.

It was argued on behalf of the claimant that the event to which the proximity test applied was the consequence of the defendant's negligence, namely her husband's death from a heart attack. The defendant argued, firstly, that there was no event to which the proximity test could be applied and the deceased's death, long after the negligence which had caused it, was the culmination of a natural process of heart disease, and the death, however unexpected and shocking to Mrs Taylor when she learnt of it, was not in itself an event of the kind to which the immediate aftermath extension could be attached.

Secondly, it was contended that even if the deceased's death at work could be considered an event of the kind to which the immediate aftermath extension could be attached, the claimant's discovery of it at the hospital from the doctor

---

[31] See also *White v Chief Constable of South Yorkshire Police* [1999] 2 AC 455 which also arose from the Hillsborough disaster.
[32] *Taylor v Somerset Health Authority* [1993] 1 WLUK 683.

and subsequent identification of the body did not satisfy the third of the *Alcock* control mechanisms, that is that the claimant directly perceived the incident.

Auld J held that the claim failed for both of the reasons advanced by the defendant, stating:

> The immediate aftermath extension is one which has been introduced as an exception to the general principle established in accident cases that a plaintiff can only recover damages for psychiatric injury when the accident and the primary injury or death caused by that occurred within his sight or hearing. There are two notions implicit in this exception cautiously introduced and cautiously continued by the House of Lords they are of:
>
> (i) an external, traumatic, event caused by the defendant's breach of duty which immediately causes some person injury or death; and
> (ii) perception by the plaintiff of the event as it happens, normally by his presence at the scene, or exposure to the scene and/or to the primary victim so shortly afterwards that the shock of the event as well as of its consequences brought home to him.
>
> There was no such event here other than the final consequence of Mr Taylor's progressively deteriorating heart condition which the health authority, by its negligence many months before, had failed to arrest. In my judgment, his death at work and the subsequent transference of his body to the hospital where Mrs Taylor was informed of what had happened and where she saw the body do not constitute such an event.

Auld J then went on to say that, even if the fatal heart attack could be considered an event to which the 'immediate aftermath' extension applied, the doctor's communication to the claimant of that fact would not come within the extension.

In *Sion v Hampstead Health Authority*,[33] the claimant was a father of a young man injured in a motorcycle accident. The claimant did not see the accident but, for 14 days, stayed at his son's bedside, watching him deteriorate in health, fall into a coma and ultimately die. The claim was struck out. On appeal, Staughton LJ held that the appeal should be dismissed because the evidence did not disclose that the claimant had suffered any shock in the sense of a 'sudden appreciation by sight or sound of a horrifying event', but a continuing process of developing grief. Peter Gibson LJ agreed with Staughton LJ that the appeal should be dismissed on the ground that there needed to be a 'sudden appreciation by sight or sound of a horrifying event, which violently agitates the mind' (as per Lord Ackner in *Alcock*) rather than 'an accumulation of more gradual assaults on the nervous system over a period of time'.

---

[33] *Sion v Hampstead Health Authority* [1994] 5 Med LR 170.

It should be noted that it was argued on behalf of the defendant (based in part on the decision in *Taylor*) that 'the injuries to or the death of a primary victim in themselves or itself do not qualify as the horrifying event causing the shock needed for a valid claim', so that 'it was a precondition of a claim that the incident which resulted from a breach of duty should have characteristics of suddenness and violence additional to the injuries or death of the primary victim'. Peter Gibson LJ disagreed with this argument, stating:

> It is of course correct that in most of the decided cases there has been a sudden and violent incident resulting from a breach of duty, but it is the sudden awareness, violently agitating the mind, of what is occurring or has occurred that is the crucial ingredient of shock ... I see no reason in logic why a breach of duty causing an incident involving no violence or suddenness, such as where the wrong medicine is negligently given to a hospital patient, could not lead to a claim for damages for nervous shock, for example where the negligence has fatal results and a visiting close relative, wholly unprepared for what has occurred, finds the body and thereby sustains a sudden and unexpected shock to the nervous system.

Waite LJ agreed with both judgments, without distinguishing between them.

A successful outcome was achieved by the claimant in *North Glamorgan NHS Trust v Walters*.[34] In that case the claimant's baby was admitted to hospital on 17 June 1996 with signs of jaundice. The hospital negligently failed to diagnose that he was suffering from acute hepatitis. He needed a liver transplant and if he had received one he would probably have lived. Instead, he was given other treatment during the week and allowed home at weekends. On the weekend of 26 July 1996, the claimant brought him back to hospital. On 30 July 1996, the claimant, who was sleeping in the same room as the baby, was awoken at about 3.00 a.m. to see and hear him having a fit. She was then told, wrongly, that he had not suffered any serious damage as a result of the fit. He was later transferred to another hospital, where the claimant learnt that he had in fact suffered catastrophic brain damage. The baby died the following day. At first instance, the hospital was found liable for the claimant's psychiatric injury.

The Court of Appeal dismissed the defendant's appeal. The lead judgment was given by Ward LJ who stated that the issue was whether the claimant's psychiatric injury arose from the 'sudden appreciation by sight or sound of a horrifying event or its immediate aftermath'. He went on to analyse the case law, starting with Lord Wilberforce's speech in *McLoughlin*. He said that 'one looks to the totality of the circumstances which bring the claimant into proximity in both time and space to the accident'. It followed that, when Lord Wilberforce said that '"the shock must come through sight or hearing of the event or of its immediate aftermath", he was not intending to confine "the event" to a frozen moment of time'.

---

[34] *North Glamorgan NHS Trust v Walters* [2002] EWCA Civ 1792.

On the question as to whether the judge had erred in holding that the 36-hour period, beginning with the baby's epileptic fit and ending with his dying in his mother's arms, was one single 'horrifying event', Ward LJ stated:

> In my judgment the law as presently formulated does permit a realistic view being taken from case to case of what constitutes the necessary 'event'. Our task is not to construe the word as if it appeared in legislation but to gather the sense of the word in order to inform the principle to be drawn from the various authorities ... it is a useful metaphor or at least a convenient description for the 'fact and the consequence of the defendant's negligence', per Lord Wilberforce, or the series of events which make up the entire event beginning with the negligent infliction of damage through to the conclusion of the immediate aftermath whenever that may be. It is a matter of judgment from case to case depending on the facts and circumstances of each case. In my judgment on the facts of this case there was an inexorable progression from the moment when the fit occurred as a result of the failure of the hospital properly to diagnose and then to treat the baby, the fit causing the brain damage which shortly thereafter made termination of this child's life inevitable and the dreadful climax when the child died in her arms. It is a seamless tale with an obvious beginning and an equally obvious end. It was played out over a period of 36 hours, which for her both at the time and it subsequently recollected it was undoubtedly one drawn-out experience.

Again, in the non-clinical case of *Galli-Atkinson v Seghal*,[35] the claimant's daughter was fatally injured in a car accident, dying shortly thereafter. The claimant came upon the scene, witnessed a police cordon and was told of her death. She later saw the injuries at the mortuary and suffered psychiatric injury. It was held by the Court of Appeal that the aftermath could be seen to encompass more than one component. The test was as to proximity. Latham LJ explained that the claimant's visit to the mortuary could not be excluded from the events regarded as part of the aftermath of the accident. Those events stretched from the moment of the accident until the moment she left the mortuary. An event might be made up of a number of components, as could the aftermath, 'provided that the events alleged to constitute the aftermath retain sufficient proximity to the event'.[36]

There are limits to the cumulative approach demonstrated in the *Walters* and *Atkinson* cases, which are exemplified in the non-clinical negligence case of *White v Lidl UK*.[37] In that case the primary victim suffered an accident in a supermarket carpark when a crash barrier which had been poorly maintained

---

[35] *Galli-Atkinson v Seghal* [2003] EWCA Civ 697.
[36] See also the decision of the House of Lords in the non-clinical case of *W v Essex County Council* [2001] 2 AC 592.
[37] *White v Lidl UK* [2005] EWHC 871 (QB).

came through her windscreen. Her mental state deteriorated and, some months later, she committed suicide by hanging herself. The secondary victim was her husband, who found her hanging body and suffered psychiatric injury. In her judgment of the High Court, Hallett J considered what constituted the shocking event. She stated that if the shocking event was the original accident, the claim would fail as the secondary victim did not witness this. If the shocking event was, however, the suicide, the claim could succeed. Hallett J held that the claimant was bound to fail stating:

> Even with the benefit of hindsight his injury was not reasonably foreseeable. He cannot bring himself within the category of people who suffer shock as a result of seeing or hearing a tragic event or its immediate aftermath. This is because in my judgment the relevant event for the purposes of this case is the incident with the barrier.
>
> I agree with [counsel for the respondent] that one cannot simply ignore the incident in which injury was actually and negligently caused to the primary victim. Mrs White's cause of action based on the respondent's negligence arose at that time. Had Mr White come across the accident and his wife's car and suffered shock as a result, he would no doubt have had a claim. But he did not. It took a second event six months later for that to happen. This was not a combination of circumstances making up one event or even one series of events of a seamless nature. Nor was there an inexorable progression. The shocking event in this case was a completely distinct event, a second event separated in time and space from the accident ...
>
> It follows from what I have said that I do not accept that the decision in *Walters* extends the law in the way that [counsel for the claimant] might wish. In *Walters* it is clear from the judgment that the event with which the court was concerned was the fit suffered by the baby and its aftermath. The defendant's negligence caused the fit, which caused the brain damage, which in turn led to the death. Thus the event or series of events began with the fit, 'the negligent infliction of damage' and continued 'through to the conclusion of its immediate aftermath'. That is why there was, as the court found, an inexorable progression from fit to death, which occurred in the mother's sight and hearing. It was in that context that the court found the claimant succeeded in bringing herself within the class of people with a legitimate claim in law.
>
> As I have indicated, I am not persuaded that Mr White can do the same. He could not have sued for his own personal injury had his wife's health simply deteriorated after the accident. A distraught parent cannot sue for the progressive assaults upon him or her caused by the despair of looking after a brain-damaged child. Sadly, not all those who suffer can be compensated in damages. It is difficult to see therefore why the law should be extended to cover Mr White's reaction to his wife's death simply because six months after the accident it was for him an undoubtedly shocking event.

Similarly, in *Taylor v A Novo (UK) Ltd*,[38] the claimant's mother sustained an injury to her head and foot when a fellow employee caused a stack of racking boards to fall on her. She seemed to be making a good recovery but, three weeks later, she collapsed and died at home as a result of deep vein thrombosis leading to pulmonary embolism, caused by the accident. Her daughter did not witness the original accident but did witness her collapse and death at home and suffered post-traumatic stress disorder as a result. The claimant was successful at first instance in her claim for damages for psychiatric injury. The defendant's appeal, however, was successful. Lord Dyson MR, delivering the judgment in the Court of Appeal, stated that to allow the daughter's claim as a secondary victim would be to go too far, for two reasons. Firstly, the daughter would have been able to recover damages for psychiatric illness even if her mother's death had occurred months, and possibly years, after the accident, and the concept of proximity to a secondary victim cannot reasonably be stretched this far. Secondly, to allow liability would extend the scope of liability to secondary victims considerably further than had been done up to that time.

In the course of his judgment Lord Dyson stated:

> It follows that, in my view, the judge was wrong to hold that the death of Mrs Taylor was the relevant 'event' for the purposes of deciding the proximity question. A paradigm example of the kind of case in which a claimant can recover damages as a secondary victim is one involving an accident which (i) more or less immediately causes injury or death to a primary victim and (ii) is witnessed by the claimant. In such a case, the relevant event is the accident. It is not a later consequence of the accident. Auld J put the point well in *Taylor v Somerset Health Authority* [1993] PIQR P262: see para 11 above. Ms Taylor would have been able to recover damages as a secondary victim if she had suffered shock and psychiatric illness as a result of seeing her mother's accident. She cannot recover damages for the shock and illness that she suffered as a result of seeing her mother's death three weeks after the accident.

Lord Dyson distinguished the facts of the case from those in *Walters* in the following manner:

> The court was able on the facts of that case to hold that the event was a 'seamless tale with an obvious beginning and an equally obvious end ... played out over a period of 36 hours'. It was 'one drawn-out experience'. I do not see how this sheds any light on the question that arises in this case where the injuries and death suffered by Mrs Taylor were certainly not part of a single event or seamless tale. The judge held (correctly) that the sustaining of the injuries and the death were distinct events.

---

[38] *Taylor v A Novo (UK) Ltd* [2014] QB 150.

The question whether the death, being a separate event, was a relevant event for the purposes of a claim by a secondary victim did not arise in the *Walters* case.

It is interesting to note that Lord Dyson did not approve the comments made by Peter Gibson LJ in *Sion* above cited, when he stated:

> As I have explained at paragraph 13 above, the observations of Peter Gibson L.J. in *Sion* were *obiter dicta* and they are therefore not binding on this court.

The issue was revisited in the clinical context in the case of *Shorter v Surrey and Sussex Healthcare NHS Trust*.[39] In that case the hospital had failed to diagnose an aneurysm as a result of which the deceased suffered a subarachnoid haemorrhage about a week later. The deceased's sister was with her in hospital from the point when she was told about the haemorrhage to her death. The claim failed because there was no shocking event equivalent to the seizure in *Walters*. Of note were the comments made by Swift J about *Taylor v Somerset Health Authority* and *Walters*:

> Cases of clinical negligence present particularly difficult problems. The factual background of cases can be very different and often quite complex. The nature and timing of the 'event' to which the breach of duty gives rise will vary from case to case.
> In *Taylor v Somerset Health Authority*, the claimant's husband's heart attack and death occurred as a consequence of negligent treatment which had occurred many months before. The claimant did not observe the occurrence of the heart attack or death. She came onto the scene an hour later and viewed her husband's body at the mortuary. The trial judge found that there was no 'qualifying event', just the final consequence of her husband's progressively deteriorating heart condition which the defendant, by its negligence many months before, had failed properly to treat. It was not the kind of external, traumatic event which, when perceived by a secondary victim, would give rise to a successful claim for damages. He further found that, even if the heart attack and death were to be treated as a qualifying 'event', the claimant did not see her husband's body soon enough after his death to convey to her the shock of the heart attack as well as its consequence.
> In the case of *Walters*, it is not clear how long prior to the baby's seizure the negligence had taken place. It is, I suppose, arguable that the negligence continued from the point when the wrong diagnosis was made right up to the time of the seizure. However, in that case, the Court of Appeal made clear (paragraph 34 of Ward LJ's judgment) that the 'event' was a convenient description for 'the fact and consequence of the defendant's negligence' and that it had begun 'with the negligent

---

[39] *Shorter v Surrey and Sussex Healthcare NHS Trust* [2015] EWHC 614 (QB).

infliction of damage', i.e. at the time of the baby's convulsion. That was the time when the consequence of the negligence first became evident. There would of course have been ongoing consequences affecting the baby's biological processes for some time previously but it was only at the time of the convulsion that those consequences became evident and impacted on the claimant. The Court of Appeal found that the 'event' began at that time and continued for the 36 hours up to the baby's death.

Swift J continued:

> In the case of *Walters*, the trial judge and the Court of Appeal laid considerable emphasis on the start of the 'event', when the mother awoke to find her baby rigid and choking after a convulsion, with blood pouring out of his mouth. Ward LJ likened that to the 'assault upon her senses' the mother would have suffered if she had seen her child bleeding in a seat after a road traffic accident. That sort of 'assault upon the senses' is, it seems to me, of a very different order to the scene in the A & E Department at [the hospital] on 12 May. Indeed, even if Mrs Sharma had for a short time been in the state described by the Claimant, I do not consider that the sight would have come within the type of 'event' described in Walters and the other relevant authorities. Mrs Sharma's condition was fluctuating; she did not have obvious injuries; she was not – or at least did not appear at that stage to be – in any obvious or immediate danger.

Similarly, in the case of *Liverpool Women's Hospital NHS Foundation Trust v Ronayne*,[40] the claimant sustained a psychiatric injury from the shock of seeing his seriously ill wife in hospital, suffering from septicaemia and peritonitis, as a result of a negligently performed hysterectomy in which her colon had been stitched. The claim succeeded at first instance. The defendant's appeal to the Court of Appeal, however, was successful. Tomlinson LJ commented:

> In hospital one must expect to see patients connected to machines and drips, and as [counsel for the defendant] put it, expect to see things that one may not like to see. A visitor to a hospital is necessarily to a certain degree conditioned as to what to expect, and in the ordinary way it is also likely that due warning will be given by medical staff of an impending encounter likely to prove more than ordinarily distressing.

Again, in *Wild v Southend University Hospital NHS Foundation Trust*[41] the claimant was unsuccessful in his claim for psychiatric illness caused by the admitted negligence of the defendant. The claimant's wife had been admitted to hospital expecting to deliver a baby, but midwives were unable to find its heartbeat. When other medical professionals assessed the claimant's wife and

---

[40] *Liverpool Women's Hospital NHS Foundation Trust v Ronayne* [2015] EWCA Civ 588.
[41] *Wild v Southend University Hospital NHS Foundation Trust* [2014] EWHC 4053 (QB).

the foetus, it became apparent to the claimant that something was wrong. A fifth person arrived with a scanner, assessed the claimant's wife and said 'I concur', which deeply distressed the claimant, who thereby learnt that the foetus had died. The claimant and his wife were told that the baby would have to be delivered the following day. The trust admitted that its negligence had led to the stillbirth and that it was liable to the claimant's wife for nervous shock. It was not disputed that what the claimant had experienced had generated sufficient shock to have foreseeably caused psychiatric illness. The issue was whether the claimant could recover damages for nervous shock as a secondary victim. The claimant was ultimately unsuccessful in his claim as the court held that his experience did not equate to actually witnessing horrific events leading to a death or serious injury.

A different conclusion was reached, however, in the case of *Re (A Child) v Calderdale and Huddersfield NHS Foundation Trust*[42] where the mother and grandmother of a child who sustained injury arising from the circumstances of her birth, were both awarded damages for nervous shock. The child was also awarded damages for personal injury. The child had suffered a hypoxic injury due to a lack of oxygen to the brain immediately prior to and following her birth at a midwifery unit that had been under the defendant's control. Both the child's mother and grandmother, who had been present throughout the birth and witnessed the aftermath sustained post-traumatic stress. Causation was not in issue. Goff J was of the view that the child's mother was entitled to damages for nervous shock as her post-traumatic stress disorder had been triggered by the birth of a lifeless baby who required a sustained period of resuscitation, and who she thought was dead either as a primary or secondary victim. The grandmother was also awarded damages for post-traumatic stress disorder as a secondary victim as the event was sufficiently sudden, shocking and objectively horrifying to establish a claim for nervous shock.

In contrast, in the case of *Purchase v Ahmed*,[43] the defendant, a general practitioner, saw the claimant and her 20-year-old daughter at an out of hours consultation on a Thursday evening. The defendant prescribed medication for the claimant's daughter and they both returned home. The claimant's daughter remained at home for the next two days, while the claimant and her younger daughter travelled for a pre-arranged outing. In the early hours of Sunday morning, the claimant returned home to find her daughter unresponsive. A paramedic pronounced her daughter dead soon afterwards and the claimant also discovered a voicemail message from her daughter, left shortly prior to her death. The claimant alleged that she had suffered psychiatric injury, in the form of post-traumatic stress disorder, as a result of witnessing 'the shocking event' of the aftermath of her daughter's death as aforesaid. She argued that she was a secondary victim and entitled to damages in these circumstances.

---

[42] *Re (A Child) v Calderdale and Huddersfield NHS Foundation Trust* [2017] EWHC 824 (QB).
[43] *Purchase v Ahmed* (Birmingham County Court, 6 May 2020).

The defendant argued that as the claimant's witnessing of the event took place 54 hours after the consultation with the general practitioner, her claim should be struck out as she did not qualify as a secondary victim.

The trial judge dismissed the claimant's claim on the following bases:

- The law in relation to secondary victim claims in clinical negligence matters is not 'a developing jurisprudence that would in itself provide a sufficient reason to dismiss a strike out/summary judgment application'.
- Clinical negligence cases are not a 'special category of cases in their own right', such that the same principles for all personal injury psychiatric injury claims apply to them.
- The Court of Appeal's decision in *Taylor & Anor v A Novo (UK) Limited* was 'the authority of the law as it presently stands that means that Mrs. Purchase's claim is doomed to failure. The death of Evelyn and the aftermath of the discovery of her body cannot be the relevant event for the purposes of deciding the proximity question'.
- Considering *Walters v North Glamorgan NHS Trust* and *Liverpool Women's Hospital NHS Foundation Trust v Ronayne*, the 54-hour period between the consultation with the general practitioner on Thursday evening and the death on Sunday morning could not constitute 'a seamless tale which was one drawn out experience'.

Finally, it appeared that there might have been some softening of the UK approach in the recent decision of *Paul (A Child) v Royal Wolverhampton NHS Trust*.[44] In that case Chamberlain J, giving judgment in the High Court, held that the Master had been incorrect in striking out the claims for psychiatric injury on the basis that the claimants were sufficiently proximate to the 'relevant event' to be owed a duty of care. The claimants were the daughters of the deceased, who had been admitted to the New Cross Hospital on 9 November 2012 with chest and jaw pain. Following investigations, he was discharged on 12 November 2012. Just over 14 months later, on 26 January 2014, whilst out with the claimants (aged nine and twelve respectively) he collapsed and died from a heart attack.

It was the claimants' case that the treatment the deceased received in November 2012 was negligent and that had he been treated correctly he would not have suffered the fatal heart attack. In turn, the claimants would not have witnessed his death and suffered psychiatric injury. They pleaded the heart attack was 'the first manifestation of the Defendant's breach of duty' and they were therefore sufficiently proximate. They relied upon *Walters* and submitted that the 'relevant event' could be the event caused by the negligence (the heart attack and the deceased's death), as opposed to the act of negligence (the treatment received in November 2012).

---

[44] *Paul (A Child) v Royal Wolverhampton NHS Trust* [2020] EWHC 1415 (QB).

In response, the defendant argued that the claimants did not satisfy the proximity requirements laid down in *Alcock*. In particular, the claimants were not sufficiently proximate in time and space to the 'relevant event', being the alleged negligence in November 2012 to which there was no immediate aftermath. They submitted that the tort became actionable at that point and relied on *Taylor v Somerset* and *Taylor v A Novo (UK) Ltd*, which affirmed the position in *Alcock*, and that to allow the claim would open the floodgates to many more claims of this nature.

Chamberlain J concluded that the Master had been wrong in striking out the claim and held that the 'relevant event' and 'scene of the tort' was the deceased's collapse and death in January 2014. He allowed the appeal on the basis that they were sufficiently proximate to the relevant event to be owed a duty of care. They were entitled, therefore, to bring claims as secondary victims with psychiatric injuries they sustained witnessing the death of their father, Mr Paul.

The Defendant, however, successfully appealed the decision in *Paul (A Child) v Royal Wolverhampton NHS Trust* and *Purchase v Ahmed* to the Court of Appeal, with the judgment in those cases being delivered together with that of a third case, namely *Polmear v Royal Cornwall Hospital NHS Trust*. The Court of Appeal in that decision[45] noted that all three cases were clinical negligence claims, rather than accident cases, and that the true question to be decided was how the authorities were to be applied to clinical negligence cases where there is a delay between the negligent act or omission and a horrifying event caused to the primary victim by that negligent act or omission. In allowing the appeals, it would appear that the Court of Appeal felt constrained by the earlier decision of the court in *Taylor v A Novo (UK) Ltd*, but indicated that, subject to hearing further argument, the court might grant permission to the claimants to appeal its decision to the Supreme Court.

Having carried out an extensive examination of the authorities, Sir Geoffrey Vos MR stated:

> For a secondary victim to be sufficiently proximate to claim for psychiatric injury against the defendant whose clinical negligence caused the primary victim injury, the horrific event cannot be a separate event removed in time from the negligence. If the negligence and the horrific event are part of a continuum as seems to me the best possible explanation of *Walters*, there is sufficient proximity. It may be that the negligence was continuing in *Walters* at the time the 36-hour shocking event began. Either way, *Novo* is binding authority for the proposition that no claim can be brought in respect of psychiatric injury caused by a separate horrific event removed in time from the original negligence, accident or a first horrific event. I am, for the reasons I have given, unable

---

[45] *Polmear v Royal Cornwall Hospital NHS Trust* [2022] EWCA Civ 12.

to agree with Chamberlain J's conclusion at [75]. In my judgment, *Novo* does preclude liability in the circumstances of these cases, even where a horrific event is the first occasion on which any damage is caused to the primary victim ...

I have, as I have already said, reservations about whether *Novo* correctly interprets the limitations on liability to secondary victims contained in the five elements emerging from the House of Lords authorities. Subject to hearing further argument, therefore, I would be prepared to grant permission to the claimants to appeal to the Supreme Court, if sought, so that it can consider the important issues that arise in this case.

Similarly, having referred to the decisions in *McLoughlin*, *Alcock* and *White*, Underhill LJ stated:

They were concerned with cases where the death of the primary victim, which (or the immediate aftermath of which) was the shocking event witnessed by the secondary victim, was broadly contemporaneous with the breach of duty; and it was unnecessary to consider what the position would be if it had occurred some time later. However, I find it hard to see a principled reason why there should be the requisite proximity in the one kind of case but not the other. The arbitrariness of the distinction is illustrated by the example given by Peter Gibson LJ in *Sion*: why should the doctor who negligently prescribes a fatal medicine be liable to the secondary victim if the patient takes it and dies (in the requisite shocking circumstances) straight away, but not if they do so a few days or weeks later? As the Master of the Rolls demonstrates, Lord Oliver's references in Alcock to the need for 'physical and temporal propinquity' are not directed to the relationship between the breach of duty and the shocking event but rather to the need for the claimant to be close in space and time to the shocking event.

It follows that if the point were free from authority I would be minded to hold that on the pleaded facts the Claimants in all three cases should be entitled to recover. I do not think that recognising the necessary proximity in such cases would be contrary to the 'thus far and no further' approach taken in *White*. It would not involve going beyond the elements established in *Alcock*: rather, it would represent their application in a different factual situation.

The question thus is whether we are prevented from reaching that conclusion by any decision of this Court. For the reasons given by the Master of the Rolls, the decisions in *Sion*, *Walters* and *Ronayne* are not authoritative on the present issue. The difficulty, however, is *Taylor v A. Novo*.

Having formed the view that he was so prevented by the decision in *Novo*, Underhill LJ concluded:

On that basis none of the present claims can succeed. I would accordingly agree with the Master of the Rolls' proposed disposal of these appeals. My strong provisional view, like his, is that the issues raised by them merit consideration by the Supreme Court.

Lady Justice Davies agreed with the judgments of both the Master of the Rolls and Underhill LJ. It remains to be seen whether these cases are to be considered by the UK Supreme Court.

What can be gleaned from the foregoing is that the UK courts have generally imposed strict requirements for recovery by family members of a primary victim. Plaintiffs have succeeded in obtaining compensation in cases where they have perceived a horrifying event, or its immediate aftermath, caused by the defendant's contemporaneous negligence. The recent Court of Appeal decision, however, in the cases of *Paul (A Child), Polmear* and *Purchase* indicates that where the horrifying event is separate and removed in time from the negligent act, the claim for psychiatric injury by a secondary victim will not succeed. The decision may be further considered if it is appealed to the UK Supreme Court.

CONCLUSION

As can be seen from an examination of the relevant case law, both here and in the United Kingdom, the courts have been keen to place limits on the recoverability of damages for nervous shock. This has resulted in the control mechanisms laid down by the UK House of Lords in the case of *Alcock* and by the Irish Supreme Court in the case of *Kelly*.

The decision of the Irish Supreme Court in 1985 in *Kelly* remains the leading authority on the subject in this jurisdiction and is indeed the only Supreme Court decision directly on the point. Clearly, there is no reason in principle why the decision in *Kelly* ought not to apply to medical negligence actions. So, if a family member suffers nervous shock in circumstances which are equivalent to those which occurred in *Kelly*, they will be entitled to succeed in a claim for damages.

The difficulty which arises in the context of many medical negligence cases, however, is that nervous shock may be suffered by family members in situations which are not readily comparable to the accident/aftermath situation in *Kelly* such as:

- Nervous shock caused as a result of being informed of the significant injury/death of a family member, caused by medical negligence, but which does not involve the sudden perception of a frightening event or its immediate aftermath, and

- Nervous shock which does involve the sudden perception of a frightening event or its immediate aftermath, but where the medical negligence concerned occurred some time previously.

It is clear from the case law cited above that claims under either of these headings would fail in the United Kingdom, the first as a result of the control mechanisms introduced by *Alcock* and the second as a result of the recent Court of Appeal decision in *Paul (A Child)*, *Polmear* and *Purchase*. This issue may be further considered by the UK Supreme Court, if the matter is appealed.

Both situations arose in *Morrissey*, where Cross J indicated that the claim should fail on the basis of public policy alone, even if the plaintiff had succeeded in establishing a duty of care, which he had not.

It remains to be seen how the Supreme Court will deal with this issue. The cases of *Fletcher* and *Devlin* demonstrate a willingness on the court's part to limit recoverability for nervous shock where it is considered necessary for reasons of policy. It might be argued that extending the parameters of *Kelly* so as to incorporate the wider medical negligence claims referred to above might significantly open the floodgates in relation to future claims and give rise to grave uncertainty on the part of indemnifiers. If this argument were to be accepted, the Supreme Court may decline to extend the parameters of *Kelly* on the grounds of public policy. Alternatively, the Supreme Court might follow the line of argument which appeared to find favour in the Court of Appeal in *Paul (A Child)*, *Polmear* and *Purchase*, although the court felt constrained by the decision in *Novo* from allowing the claims. If this transpires to be the case, family members who suffer psychiatric injury as a result of perceiving a frightening event or its immediate aftermath, might succeed in a claim for damages, even if the negligent act complained of occurred some time previously.

Based on the totality of the case law, however, it seems likely that, in order to succeed in a claim for nervous shock, family members would at the very least have to perceive a frightening event or its immediate aftermath. Thus, the mere receipt of information relating to a loved one's significant injury/death would be unlikely to suffice.

Chapter IV

WHAT IS THE EXTENT OF THE CAUSES OF ACTION FOR WRONGFUL CONCEPTION AND WRONGFUL BIRTH IN THE REPUBLIC OF IRELAND?

Sophie Treacy and Timothy O'Leary SC[1]

Introduction

The rapid advancement of reproductive technology in recent years has given rise to many challenging medico-legal issues for the courts to grapple with. The rise of procedural sterilisation and prenatal testing of foetuses *in utero* has opened the door to a new species of tort claim. Claims for the wrongful conception or wrongful birth of a child, born as a result of a medical practitioner's negligence, have raised difficult ethical questions as to the extent to which a parent should be compensated for the arrival of their child. This chapter aims to investigate the potential for such claims to succeed in the Republic of Ireland.

Although some authors have used the phrases synonymously,[2] it is important to recognise from the outset that 'wrongful conception' and 'wrongful birth' claims represent two distinct scenarios.[3] This distinction may prove significant either to the viability of a claim or to the assessment of damages thereafter.[4] The term 'wrongful conception' denotes a situation in which a male plaintiff has undergone a vasectomy or a female plaintiff has undergone a tubal ligation in order to prevent a pregnancy. With these claims, due to the negligent actions

---

[1] Sophie Treacy prepared this chapter as a final year undergraduate student at the School of Law at Trinity College Dublin. Timothy O'Leary SC is a member of the Inner Bar of Ireland.
[2] See C Symmons, 'The Problem of 'Informed Consent' in the 'Wrongful Birth' Cases' (1987) Professional Negligence 3(2):56–62, where Symmons discusses instances of 'wrongful births' arising out of failed sterilisation procedures, which could more accurately be categorised as 'wrongful conception' cases.
[3] B Daly, 'Wrongful Birth, Wrongful Conception, and the Irish Constitution' (2005) European Journal of Health Law, 12 (1) 57.
[4] J McInerney 'To Be or not to Be' Born – Ireland's position on Wrongful Birth and Wrongful Life Actions' available at http://www.ablesolicitors.ie/to-be-or-not-to-be-born-irelands-position-on-wrongful-birth-and-wrongful-life-actions.

of a medical professional in either performing the procedure,[5] in running post-operative testing or in advising the plaintiff of risk of failure,[6] a child is conceived. Wrongful birth claims, however, relate to situations in which a child is born following either a failed abortion or a failure to detect a congenital abnormality at the antenatal screening stage,[7] thus preventing the parents from having an opportunity to choose whether or not to terminate the pregnancy.[8] Another claim of this nature that has arisen in some jurisdictions is known as a 'wrongful life' claim, whereby children who alleged that they ought not to have been born advance a claim themselves.[9] This chapter will focus, however, on the viability of claims advanced by the parents of wrongfully conceived and wrongfully born children in this jurisdiction in the context of both children who are born fully healthy or have a disability.

THE WRONGFUL CONCEPTION OF A HEALTHY CHILD

The extent to which the parents of an allegedly wrongfully conceived healthy child should be compensated, if at all, for the birth of their child is not only an important legal question but also a complex ethical and social one too.[10] Indeed, it is a question to which there is no uniform response across the common law world.[11] Approaches adopted by the courts in common law jurisdictions may be viewed as falling upon a spectrum, with the view that parents of wrongfully conceived children should be able to recover the full costs of birth and child-rearing falling at one end[12] and the view that the parents should be awarded no compensation whatsoever, as the arrival of a healthy child is assumed to be a blessing, falling on the other. Whilst the approach of the Australian High Court, for instance, falls definitively upon the former end of this spectrum,[13] the approach taken in the United Kingdom, which will inevitably be influential upon the approach taken by the Superior Courts in this jurisdiction, falls closer

---

[5] *Sherlock v Stillwater Clinic* 260 NW2d 169, wherein a physician erroneously advised the plaintiff that the result of a post-vasectomy semen test was negative.
[6] M Karosaitė, 'Whether the Parents Have a Right to Seek for Damages for aA Birth of an Unwanted Child Caused by Doctor's Negligence?' (2015) available at https://www.vdu.lt/cris/handle/20.500.12259/ 123056.
[7] See note 2 above.
[8] Mary Donnelly, 'The Injury of Parenthood: The Tort of Wrongful Conception' (1997) Northern Ireland Legal Quarterly, Vol 48, No 1 10.
[9] For discussion on 'wrongful life' claims, see A Ruda, "'I Didn't Ask to be Born': Wrongful Life From a Comparative Perspective' (2010) Journal of European Tort Law Vol 1 Issue 2.
[10] S Birgitta Elste, 'Analysis Of Common Law Judgments In Regards Of 'Wrongful Birth' Cases' (2006) The New Zealand Postgraduate Law e-Journal Issue 4.
[11] Briana Walley, 'Wrongful Birth or Wrongful Law: A Critical Analysis of the Availability of Child-Rearing Costs after Failed Sterilisation Operations in New Zealand' (2018) 24 Canterbury Law Review 1.
[12] See note 5 above.
[13] See *Cattnach v Melchior* [2003] HCA 38.

to the latter end thereof in the wake of the decision of the House of Lords in *McFarlane v Tayside Health Board*.[14]

Up until the ruling of the House of Lords in *McFarlane v Tayside Health Board*,[15] the law regarding compensation for the wrongful conception of healthy children in the United Kingdom seemed to have been settled.[16] The ruling in *Thake v Maurice*[17] led to the parents of a 'wrongfully conceived' healthy child recovering damages for the rearing of their child by reason of their medical practitioner's negligent omission to warn them of the risk that the vasectomy might fail. Kerr LJ noted that 'there is no such rule of public policy'[18] to prevent the court from awarding such compensation. The court focused on the economic strains that come with raising a child as 'every baby has a belly to be filled and a body to be clothed',[19] and awarded damages upon the application of conventional principles of tort law on the basis of the defendant being entirely liable.[20] The court ruled that the elements of negligence had been satisfied as the doctor was in breach of his duty of care, the conception of the child arose out of this breach and the damage incurred was sufficiently proximate.[21]

The subsequent decision in *Udale v Bloomsbury Area Health Authority*[22] seemed to undermine this reasoning somewhat, however, as the English High Court, in this instance, was not prepared to award maintenance for a wrongfully conceived child until the age of 16[23] on the basis of four public policy grounds enumerated by Jupp J. In his judgment, Jupp J pronounced that:

(i) it would be 'highly undesirable'[24] for a child to learn that a Court had declared his or her life a 'mistake';
(ii) the joy of having a child offsets the financial burden of raising this child;
(iii) awarding full compensation might put medical practitioners under a pressure to encourage abortions and
(iv) the birth of a healthy child is always a 'blessing'.

The case of *Emeh v Kensington and Chelsea and Westminster Area Health Authority*,[25] however, presented the English Court of Appeal with an

---

[14] *McFarlane v Tayside Health Board* [2000] 2 AC 59.
[15] ibid.
[16] See note 2 above.
[17] *Thake v Maurice* [1986] QB 644.
[18] ibid, per Kerr LJ.
[19] See note 16 above, per Pain J.
[20] J Manning, 'Health Care Law Part 1 Common Law Developments' (2004) 1 NZLR 181, 181–182.
[21] See note 10 above.
[22] *Udale v Bloomsbury Area Health Authority* [1983] 1 WLR 1098.
[23] See note 2 above.
[24] See note 21 above, per Jupp J.
[25] *Emeh v Kensington and Chelsea and Westminster Area Health Authority* [1985] QB 1012.

opportunity to settle this issue with the court choosing to endorse the line of reasoning set out in *Thake v Maurice*.[26] Accordingly, damages for raising wrongfully conceived healthy children were considered recoverable in the United Kingdom.

In the 15 years following the *Emeh*[27] decision, the ability of parents of 'wrongfully conceived' healthy children to recover damages for the costs of rearing a child was by no means met with universal approval.[28] Moreover, during this period the House of Lords began to reconsider the law of negligence as it applies to 'non-traditional claims',[29] such as nervous shock and pure economic loss,[30] and the view began to emerge that 'society simply cannot and should not require the tort system to provide monetary compensation for every harm resulting from carelessness, not even every physical harm'.[31]

Accordingly, in the case of *McFarlane v Tayside Health Board*[32] the tide finally turned against allowing the full recovery of the costs of rearing a child for wrongfully conceived healthy children. This case concerned a man who had undergone a vasectomy and subsequently impregnated his wife with their fifth child. Following a normal pregnancy, Mrs McFarlane gave birth to a healthy child. She proceeded to claim for the physical discomfort arising from her pregnancy, confinement and delivery. Both parents also claimed for the cost of rearing the child. When the case ultimately reached the House of Lords, the court had no difficulty in awarding damages for the former claim as the judgment of Lord Slynn stated that there is 'no doubt that there should be compensation for the physical effects of the pregnancy and birth, including of course solatium for consequential suffering by the mother immediately following the birth'.[33]

In respect of the claim for child-rearing costs, however, the court noted that this was a 'difficult'[34] legal issue that was 'still developing [with] no universal and clear approach'.[35] In a departure from the reasoning in *Emeh*,[36] the House of Lords refused to award damages for the raising of the child as the jurisprudential seeds which had been sown in the judgment of *Udale v Bloomsbury Area*

---

[26] See note 16 above.
[27] See note 24 above.
[28] In *Allen v Bloomsbury Health Authority* [1993] 1 All ER 615, Brooke J drew a distinction between loss for personal injury and pure economic loss.
[29] Jane Stapleton, 'Legal Cause: Cause-in-Fact and the Scope of Liability for Consequences' (2001) 54, Vanderbilt Law Review 941.
[30] The Rt Hon Lady Justice Hale, 'The Value of Life and the Cost of Living – Damages for Wrongful Birth' (2001) British Actuarial Journal Vol 7, No. 5 747.
[31] See note 28 above.
[32] See note 13 above.
[33] ibid, per Lord Slynn.
[34] ibid.
[35] ibid 73.
[36] See note 24 above.

Health Authority[37] finally came to fruition. All five judges of the House of Lords took five different routes, however, in arriving at this conclusion resulting in a ruling that fails to deliver a clear and sound precedent on this issue.[38] Lord Slynn considered it not to be 'fair, just or reasonable to impose on the doctor or his employer liability for the consequential responsibilities, imposed on or accepted by the parents to bring up a child'.[39] Lord Steyn observed that 'instinctively, the traveller on the Underground would consider that the law of tort has no business to provide legal remedies consequent upon the birth of a healthy child, which all of us regard as a valuable and good thing'[40] and refused to award child-rearing costs on the basis of a rationale grounded in distributive justice. Lord Hope ruled that the costs of rearing the child could not be recovered on the basis that the benefits of raising the child, which would offset the financial burden, were immeasurable.[41] Lord Clyde echoed the distributive justice reasoning of Lord Steyn, while Lord Millet held that it would be 'subversive of the mores of society'[42] if parents were able to benefit from having a child without shouldering the financial responsibility that comes with it. The resounding outcome of the *McFarlane*[43] decision was that parents could no longer successfully claim for the costs of raising their 'wrongfully conceived' and healthy child. The rationale underpinning this decision, however, is far less coherent.

With the *Emeh*[44] judgment representing one side of the argument and the dismissal of the claim of Mrs McFarlane by the House of Lords representing the other, it is clear that the issue of whether child-rearing costs should be recoverable in these instances turns on many complicated sub-issues, including issues of public policy, distributive justice and proximity, to name but a few. Arguments against the recoverability of child-rearing damages for 'wrongfully conceived' and healthy children are often based upon a merging of compatible perspectives which include that it is unduly harsh on the medical profession if parents should be allowed the benefits from raising a child without any of the expense that it usually entails,[45] the arrival of a healthy child is a blessing, the benefits of raising the child outweigh the expense and that it would be damaging should a child learn that his or her birth was a 'mistake'.

The argument based upon distributive justice for the non-recoverability of child-rearing damages has also been influential. It is grounded upon the rationale that burdens and losses must be justly distributed amongst all members of society and it would not be a socially just distribution of resources

---

[37] See note 21 above.
[38] See note 9 above.
[39] See note 13 above.
[40] ibid, per Lord Steyn.
[41] See note 10 above.
[42] See note 13 per Lord Millet.
[43] ibid.
[44] See note 24 above.
[45] See note 7 above.

to award full child-rearing expenses to parents of a healthy child, albeit one born against the wishes of the parents. Other reasons for denying compensation for child-rearing in cases such as these include issues in relation to causation, the difficulty with assessment and quantification of damages[46] and concerns centred upon the encouragement of abortion.[47]

By contrast, arguments supporting the recovery of child-rearing costs tend to view the situation through an economic lens. Strasser observes that parents are 'suing for money to help raise the child rather than to rid themselves of an unwanted burden'.[48] Proponents for full recovery view the damage of child-rearing costs as an economic harm incurred by the birth, as opposed to the birth itself constituting the harm.[49] It would be contrary to the dignity of the child[50] if his or her life was deemed to amount to 'damage'[51] and thus, those in favour of recovery distinguish the purported damage of the birth child from the alleged financial damage which arises from raising the child. In this context, it is also often argued that parents have a right to determine the size of their family[52] and the deprival of this right necessitates appropriate compensation. Furthermore, it has been argued that courts categorising the birth of a child as 'always a blessing' is an intrusive value judgment which fails to respect the couples' reproductive choices and autonomy.[53]

In respect of these competing positions on whether child-rearing costs for healthy and 'wrongfully conceived' children should be recoverable, this jurisdiction appears to have followed the United Kingdom in ruling that they are not. In *Byrne v Ryan*[54] a negligently executed tubal ligation led to the birth of two healthy children. The defendant successfully challenged the ability of the plaintiff to recover child-rearing costs as the Irish High Court approved the ruling of the House of Lords in *McFarlane*[55] in this jurisdiction. Kelly J cited Lord Gill, with approval, from the judgment of first instance in *McFarlane*[56] that 'the privilege of being a parent is immeasurable in money terms' and pointed to 'a certain incongruity' in the plaintiff seeking child-rearing costs while having acknowledged 'the joy and satisfaction that [her] two children

---

[46] See note 10 above.
[47] ibid.
[48] Mark Strasser, 'Misconceptions and Wrongful Births: A Call for a Principled Jurisprudence' (1999) 31 Arizona State LJ 161 at 195.
[49] M Hogg, 'Damages for Pecuniary Loss in Cases of Wrongful Birth' (2010) 1 JETL 156.
[50] WP Keeton, D Dobbs, R Keeton, D Owen, *Prosser and Keeton on Torts* (5th edn 1984) 372.
[51] Ewa Baginska, 'Wrongful Birth and Non-Pecuniary Loss: Theories of Compensation' (2010) 1 JETL 171.
[52] Yasmin Moinfar, 'Pregnancy Following Failed Sterilisation Under the Accident Compensation Scheme' (2009) 40 VUWLR 805.
[53] Shaun Elijah Tan, 'The Right Approach to Wrongful Conception' (2015) OULJ Vol 4 28.
[54] *Byrne v Ryan* [2009] 4 IR 542.
[55] See note 13 above.
[56] ibid.

... brought to her'. Kelly J also rejected the Australian judgment in *Cattanach v Melchior*,[57] which permitted recovery of damages for a claim of this nature and instead favoured the position opted for in the 'vast majority of state courts in the United States, the courts of England and Wales, Scotland and a number of civil law courts'.[58]

In disallowing child-rearing costs, the High Court was persuaded by a number of the arguments advanced in the United Kingdom in this context. Kelly J also cited the Irish Supreme Court decision of *Fletcher v The Commissioners for Public Works*[59] which invoked legal policy based upon distributive justice in establishing that, in certain circumstances, it is proper for the court to refuse to award damages on grounds of public policy. The court also endorsed what can be termed the 'benefits off-set' rationale proffered by Lord Gill and Lord Millet in *McFarlane*[60] in ruling that it 'would not be fair or reasonable'[61] to award child-rearing damages in this instance. Kelly J further advanced an argument unique to the Irish context in ruling that the value placed upon the family and the dignity of human life in the Irish constitutional order would be better served by disallowing child-rearing costs for 'wrongfully conceived' and healthy children. Thus, as the law currently stands in this jurisdiction, the costs of rearing a healthy child, who is alleged to have been born against the wishes of the parents, are not recoverable by them.

It was conceded from the outset in defence of the claim in *Byrne v Ryan*[62] that the plaintiff was entitled to personal injury compensation arising from her pregnancy. Kelly J queried this concession but, in light of it having been made, proceeded to award the plaintiff €90,000 for the two respective periods of an unplanned pregnancy and childbirth and €10,000 for the recourse by her to a second sterilisation procedure. This concession in the defence of this claim is of significance because the making of it, coupled with the award of damages to the plaintiff in this case, suggested that a pregnancy could constitute a 'personal injury' in this jurisdiction. The medical status of pregnancy does not seem to sit comfortably with the traditional concepts of personal injury and illness at common law.[63] Section 2 of the Civil Liability Act 1961, however, defines a personal injury as including 'any disease and any impairment of a person's physical or mental condition'. According to Rogers,[64] pregnancy amounts to such an impairment as it 'involves an element of danger, certain discomfort and possibly severe disruption of a woman's employment and pattern of life'.

---

[57] *Cattanach v Melchior* (2003) 199 ALR 131.
[58] *Byrne v Ryan* [2007] IEHC 206, per Kelly J.
[59] *Fletcher v The Commissioners for Public Works* [2003] 1 IR 465.
[60] See note 13 above.
[61] See note 58 above.
[62] *Byrne v Ryan* [2009] 4 IR 542.
[63] Mullis, 'Wrongful Conception Unravelled' (1993) Med Law Rev 320, at 324.
[64] Rogers, 'Legal Implications of Ineffective Sterilisation' (1985) 5 Legal Studies 296 at 310.

Accordingly, the decision of Kelly J in *Byrne v Ryan*[65] paved the way for the establishment of damages for pregnancy as a result of wrongful conception in this jurisdiction.[66]

In March of 2021, the Judicial Council of Ireland issued the document *Personal Injuries Guidelines*, which affirm the position taken by Kelly J in the judgment of *Byrne v Ryan*.[67] Pursuant to these guidelines, a 'failed sterilisation leading to unwanted pregnancy where there is no serious psychological impact or depression' should give rise to an award of damages between €17,500 and €30,000.[68] In light of this specific guideline, it is clear that before the Irish courts, general damages for a wrongful conception leading to the birth of a healthy child, will be granted. Where there is no psychiatric sequalae claimed, however, the award for general damages falls within the lower end of the jurisdiction of the Circuit Court.

THE WRONGFUL CONCEPTION OF A DISABLED CHILD

If the decisions of *McFarlane v Tayside Health Board*[69] and *Byrne v Ryan*[70] establish clear precedents that damages cannot be recovered for having to rear a healthy child arising from an alleged wrongful conception, they raised the question as to whether the position is the same when the child conceived is subsequently born with a disability. In the United Kingdom, the courts have distinguished cases involving allegedly wrongfully conceived disabled children from the strict position in *McFarlane*.[71] In the case of *Parkinson v St James & Seacroft University Hospital NHS Trust*,[72] being the seminal ruling on this issue, a negligently performed laparoscopic sterilisation procedure led to Mrs Parkinson becoming pregnant with a child. She was warned that her child may be born with a disability but chose not to terminate her pregnancy. When her son was born with a severe lifelong disability, she sought damages under certain headings, including for the cost of raising him. The English Court of Appeal acknowledged that, as in *Emeh*,[73] Mrs Parkinson's decision not to terminate her pregnancy was immaterial to the recoverability of child-rearing damages as she could not be coerced into having an abortion on the grounds of another's negligent act.[74]

---

[65] *Byrne v Ryan* [2009] 4 IR 542.
[66] This is also the position in the United Kingdom: see *Walkin v South Manchester Health Authority* [1995] 1 WLR 1543.
[67] *Byrne v Ryan* [2009] 4 IR 542.
[68] The Judicial Council, *Personal Injuries Guidelines* 6 March 2021, Section 6(E)(d), at p 31.
[69] See note 13 above.
[70] *Byrne v Ryan* [2009] 4 IR 542.
[71] See note 13 above.
[72] *Parkinson v St James & Seacroft University Hospital NHS Trust* [2001] EWCA Civ 530.
[73] See note 24 above.
[74] J K Mason, 'Wrongful Pregnancy, Wrongful Birth and Wrongful Terminology' (2002) 6 Edinburgh L Rev 46.

It would seem that if the English Court of Appeal strictly applied *McFarlane*[75] in this instance, irrespective of the child's disability, no costs for the raising of the child would be recoverable. This was not, however, the decision which this court arrived at. Rather, the court embraced the opportunity to limit the scope of the sort of recovery that was precluded by *McFarlane*[76] in ruling that Mrs Parkinson was entitled to recover the financial costs for child-rearing that flowed from the child's disability. Although it has been suggested that this decision could represent a possible row back on *McFarlane*,[77] the judgment of Brooke LJ in *Parkinson*[78] may equally be viewed as an affirmation of it. Indeed, Brooke LJ focused on the distributive justice line of argument which had prevented the recovery of child-rearing damages in *McFarlane*.[79] He applied them to the situation at hand in finding that it would be a fair, just and reasonable allocation of resources to award extra general damages for the raising of the disabled child.

In so doing, Brooke LJ made reference to Lord Steyn's concession in *McFarlane*[80] that the balance of distributive justice may fall differently in the event of the child, allegedly being wrongfully conceived, then being born with a serious disability because distributive justice is a 'moral theory'[81] which ultimately comes down to what an ordinary person would deem fair, just and reasonable in the particular circumstances. Brooke LJ also cited Lord Woolf MR in *Heil v Rankin*[82] in relying upon his assertion that 'compensation must remain fair, reasonable and just' and be 'what society as a whole would perceive as being reasonable'. Thus, in implementing this analysis of what a 'fair, just and reasonable' degree of compensation would constitute, Brooke LJ cited with approval the Supreme Court of Florida's decision in *Fassoulas v Ramey*[83] which awarded damages for the cost of rearing a child, arising from that child's disability, on the basis of the 'financial and emotional drain' that comes from raising such a child. Accordingly, on the grounds of distributive justice and what an ordinary person would consider fair, just and reasonable, being a rubric adopted from the decision of the House of Lords in *McFarlane*,[84] Brooke LJ found that the extra child-rearing expenses associated with the child's disability were recoverable.

In the other judgment given in *Parkinson*,[85] Lady Hale concurred with Brooke LJ in respect of the extra child-rearing costs incurred by bringing up a disabled

---

[75] See note 13 above.
[76] ibid.
[77] ibid.
[78] See note 69 above.
[79] See note 13 above.
[80] ibid.
[81] ibid, per Lord Steyn.
[82] *Heil v Rankin* [2000] 2 WLR 1173.
[83] *Fassoulas v Ramey* 450 So 2d 822 (Fla 1984).
[84] See note 14 above.
[85] See note 69 above.

child being recoverable. Rather than approaching the issue through the lens of distributive justice, however, she emphasised the profound psychological and physical impact of pregnancy which, if visited upon a woman against her will, amounts to an invasion of her bodily integrity. Lady Hale acknowledged the 'additional stresses and strains'[86] and 'extra care and extra expenditure'[87] that may come with raising a disabled child, even if they 'bring as much pleasure and as many advantages as does a normal healthy child'.[88] In applying a version of the 'benefits offset' test which had been utilised in *McFarlane*,[89] Lady Hale ruled that child-rearing costs related to the child's disability were recoverable. She observed that this approach still afforded the disabled child the same dignity and status as a healthy child while simply acknowledging that the costs of raising this child are more.[90]

The *Parkinson*[91] decision, therefore, adds a layer of nuance to the *McFarlane*[92] authority when the question of whether damages for the rearing of a child, who is born disabled, having been conceived against the wishes of the parents, falls to be determined. It affirms, both through a 'benefits offset' test and a distributive justice analysis, that the ordinary costs for raising a healthy child are not recoverable. While affirming that healthy and disabled children are equal in their dignity and status, the court has considered it fair, just and reasonable that the extra costs of associated with raising a disabled child are provided for in an award of damages.

The English Court of Appeal in *Parkinson*[93] managed to distinguish between cases involving healthy and disabled children, conceived against the wishes of their parents, in a sensitive manner which recognises the full human dignity and equality of disabled children. Indeed, in the past, this distinction between healthy and disabled children has not always been well expressed in such a manner.[94] Many commentators have cautioned that the granting of greater awards to parents of wrongfully conceived disabled children risks implying that disabled children are valued less than healthy children.[95] Bradfield has argued that if a healthy child is considered a blessing and thus no damages for the rearing of this child are recoverable, allowing such compensation for the birth of a disabled child implies that they are not a blessing, which is 'not only unequal and unfair, but offensive'.[96] This is a view which has been very

---

[86] See note 69, per Lady Hale.
[87] ibid.
[88] ibid.
[89] See note 13 above.
[90] See note 69, per Lady Hale.
[91] ibid.
[92] See note 13 above.
[93] See note 69 above.
[94] See note 49 above.
[95] Anthony Jackson, 'Wrongful Life and Wrongful Birth' (1996) 17 The Journal of Legal Medicine 349–381.
[96] Owen M Bradfield, 'Healthy Law Makes for Healthy Children: *Cattanach v Melchior*' (2005) 12 JLM 305 at 312.

influential in the Australian courts, with McMurdo P in *Cattanch v Melchior*[97] commenting that it would be 'offensive' if it was suggested that disabled children could not enrich their families and wider community to the same degree as a healthy child. It is submitted that the line of reasoning in *Parkinson*[98] which led to an award of extra general damages for raising a disabled child recognises that disabled children are just as much a benefit and blessing to their families as healthy children. It is only because raising a disabled child incurs greater financial expense that the balance of what is fair, just and reasonable is tipped in favour of some degree of compensation for the rearing of a disabled child. This does not suggest that disabled children in and of themselves are of any less worth than healthy children. It merely suggests that a reasonable person would think it fair that a family with extra financial needs on account of their child's disability receives additional financial compensation.

In the Irish context, a factual scenario similar to that which arose in *Parkinson*[99] gave rise to the case of *Hurley Ahern and anor v Moore & Southern Health Board*.[100] In this case, a failed laparoscopic sterilisation resulted in the birth of a child with severe congenital abnormalities, who then died six months later. The High Court followed the judgment of *Byrne v Ryan*[101] in holding that irrespective of the child's disability, the mother was entitled to compensation for the pain and suffering arising from her pregnancy. Ryan J awarded a further €100,000 in general damages on the basis of the events that led up to the child's death. The court did not take the opportunity, however, to clarify whether the *Parkinson*[102] ruling applies in this jurisdiction in respect of whether or not child-rearing damages that flow from the disability of a child conceived against the wishes of the parents are recoverable. Accordingly, the question still remains as to whether the Irish courts would follow the *Parkinson*[103] line of authority should such a scenario arise. The willingness of Ryan J to award general damages on account of raising this disabled child, for the six months of this child's life, may indicate that the Irish courts would be inclined to follow the United Kingdom approach of *Parkinson*.[104] The explicit incorporation of *Parkinson*[105] into this jurisdiction, however, is yet to occur.

---

[97] See note 57 above. This observation was made by McMurdo P when these proceedings were before the Queensland Court of Appeal. Special leave was later granted thereafter for the defendants to appeal to the High Court of Australia exclusively on the issue of the award of damages for the cost of raising and maintaining a healthy child.
[98] See note 69 above.
[99] ibid.
[100] *Hurley Ahern and anor v Moore & Southern Health Board* [2013] IEHC 72.
[101] *Byrne v Ryan* [2009] 4 IR 542.
[102] See note 69 above.
[103] See note 69 above.
[104] ibid.
[105] ibid.

THE WRONGFUL BIRTH OF A DISABLED CHILD

Developments in modern medicine have given rise to extensive testing procedures that allow foetal conditions to be detected in the early stages of pregnancy.[106] If these tests are negligently preformed, or if a medical practitioner fails to inform expectant parents of such prenatal tests and a child is born with a disability, parents may advance a claim on the grounds that they were deprived of the opportunity to seek an abortion.[107] In contrast to the scenario of wrongful conception, claims for the wrongful birth of a disabled child arise when the conception of the child was originally planned, but had the parent been informed of the probability that their child would be born with a disability, they would have terminated the pregnancy.[108] Such claims usually constitute pure economic loss, mainly the costs of raising the disabled child, in conjunction with a claim for damages for emotional distress.[109] It is interesting to examine the development of this issue in this jurisdiction given that the repeal of the Eighth Amendment of the Constitution of Ireland, which prohibited abortion, occurred relatively recently in 2018.

There appear to be two jurisprudential avenues through which a claim for wrongful birth may be advanced. The first analysis upon which a wrongful birth action may be based is that of factual causation. In other words, but for the medical practitioner's negligence in screening for foetal abnormalities, the disabled child would not have been born as the parents would have opted to terminate the pregnancy. Thus, on the basis of the ordinary principles of tort law, the parents should be compensated for raising their disabled child. An alternative argument which may be advanced in this scenario is that the mother had a right to choose whether or not to continue her pregnancy and as she was deprived of the opportunity to make an informed choice by reason of the misinformation given to her about the health of the foetus in her womb, she should be financially compensated.

In light of the repeal of the ban on abortion under the Eighth Amendment of the Irish Constitution, an approach based on the infringement of the mother's right to choose whether or not to continue with her pregnancy has surely been strengthened. Before the repeal of the Eighth Amendment, an argument maintaining an infringement of the plaintiff's 'right' to travel outside of the jurisdiction for an abortion would have been tenuous at best. As Geoghegan J pointed out in the case of *A & B v Eastern Health Board*,[110] the Thirteenth and Fourteenth Amendments of the Irish Constitution, popularly known as

---

[106] See note 5 above.
[107] ibid.
[108] *C S v Nielson* 767 P 2d 504 (Utah 1988), where a physician failed to inform plaintiff that tubal ligation procedure was not 'absolute in nature' and that alternative sterilisation procedures existed with different success rates.
[109] Mariam Gaiparashvili, 'Wrongful Birth and Wrongful Life Cases from a Human Rights Perspective' (2020) Herald of Law 11.
[110] *Byrne v Ryan* [1998] IR 464.

the Travel and Information Amendments, respectively, did not confer a right to abortion outside of this jurisdiction, but merely prevented injunctive relief being granted against travelling for that purpose. This was later affirmed by the Supreme Court in the *IRM v Minister for Justice, Equality, Ireland and the Attorney General*.[111] The repeal of the Eighth Amendment of the Irish Constitution, however, must entail that mothers will have stronger grounds in the future for advancing the argument that their right to avail of an abortion was infringed as a result of being negligently misinformed of the health of the foetus *in utero*, and hence, that they should be financially compensated for the raising and maintenance of the child subsequently born. Nonetheless, the simpler and more direct approach is to proceed on the basis of factual causation when maintaining a wrongful birth claim. Indeed, in 2018, a settlement of €1.8 million was granted in a case involving the wrongful birth of a disabled child which occurred prior to the repeal of the Eighth Amendment.

Conclusion

As Lord Macmillan observed in the foundational case of the concept of a duty of care at common law, *Donoghue v Stevenson*,[112] '[t]he categories of negligence are never closed' and the law must 'adapt itself to the changing circumstances of life'. Wrongful conception and wrongful birth claims seem to embody this characterisation as they have pushed the law of tort 'into wholly uncharted waters'.[113] The question of whether parents of wrongfully conceived and wrongfully born children should be compensated for raising and maintaining their children, together with the additional question as to whether it is appropriate to make greater awards in these respects when the child born is disabled, provide challenging moral and legal dilemmas for the courts. The answers to these questions in this jurisdiction are far from settled because the case law concerning them is at an early stage of development. Given the scientific and medical advances in prenatal screening, together with the increasingly widespread reliance upon medical practitioners to provide contraceptive and sterilisation procedures, these issues are likely to be at the forefront of medical negligence litigation practice in this jurisdiction in the years ahead.

---

[111] *IRM v Minister for Justice, Equality, Ireland and the Attorney General* [2017] IESC 61.
[112] *Donoghue v Stevenson* [1932] UKHL 100.
[113] Charles Foster, 'It Should Be, Therefore It Is' (2004) 154 New Law Journal 1644.

PART C
CAUSATION

CHAPTER V

HAS CAUSATION IN MEDICAL NEGLIGENCE LITIGATION NOW MOVED FROM THE 'BUT FOR' TEST TO ONE OF 'MATERIAL CONTRIBUTION'?

Anne Spillane and Eoin McCullough SC[1]

INTRODUCTION

Causation is a crucial battleground in medical negligence litigation. The prerequisite proof without which the turnstile is locked against liability and damages has been widely acknowledged as the most difficult hurdle for the plaintiff to overcome.[2]

Legally, causation is comprised of two tiers: the *cause in fact* and the *cause in law*.[3] At its simplest, 'factual causation' is concerned with the physical connection between the act of the defendant and the damage complained of. Traditionally, the *sine qua non* test, otherwise known as the 'but for' test, has served as the dominant threshold question of liability when determining factual causation.[4] Controversies have erupted, however, across the common law world. The perceived unfairness of the classic litmus test has forced courts to re-examine the appropriateness of the doctrine in clinical negligence actions.[5] Various modifications, such as the 'material contribution' test, have gained currency in many jurisdictions. Thus, a crucial question arises: has the 'but for' test been cast aside in favour of a more pragmatic approach to the issue of causation?

The following chapter critically reviews whether causation in medical negligence litigation has now moved from the 'but for' test to one of 'material

---

[1] Anne Spillane prepared this chapter as a final year undergraduate student at the School of Law at Trinity College Dublin. Eoin McCullough SC is a member of the Inner Bar of Ireland.
[2] Eilin O'Dea BL, 'Causation and the 'Loss of Chance' Doctrine in Medical Negligence Cases' The Bar Review, June 2007, Vol 12 Issue 3.
[3] Simon Mills and Andrea Mulligan, *Medical Law in Ireland* (3rd edn, Bloomsbury 2017) 235.
[4] John D Rue, 'Returning to the Roots of the Bramble Bush' Fordham Law Review 71 (2002–2003) 2680.
[5] John Healy, *Medical Malpractice* (1st edn, Round Hall 2009) 687.

contribution'. It begins by outlining the 'but for' test and the inherent subtleties of its application in difficult cases of evidential uncertainty and multiple contribution that leave a plaintiff with virtually insuperable difficulties of proof. It then moves on to evaluate the alternative approach to factual causation, the 'material contribution' test. It establishes how the rule emerged in case law, examines its relevance in medical negligence claims and determines the position adopted by the Irish courts. The next section then offers an alternative solution to address proof of causation, the 'loss of chance' doctrine, and analyses the possible incorporation of elements of this doctrine into common law rules on civil liability. Finally, the chapter proposes future developments of the 'but for' test and its modifications in Irish medical negligence litigation.

Ultimately, this review leads to the conclusion that the *sine qua non* test remains the touchstone of causation in clinical negligence cases. In exceptional circumstances, however, justice and logic may require the conventional test to be modified. The precise extent of that modification remains to be determined in future cases.

CONVENTIONAL CAUSATION: THE 'BUT FOR' TEST

The 'but for' test is the traditional indicator of causation. Quite simply, it asks whether the plaintiff would have been unscathed, 'but for' the tortious act of the defendant.[6] A straightforward application of this principle in Ireland may be found in *Purdy v Lenihan*.[7] This case turned on the issue of whether the cerebral palsy from which the plaintiff suffered was caused by bleeds prior to the critical period or, alternatively, by obstetric breach of duty in the final 20 minutes of delivery. Ultimately, the 'but for' test was applied by the Supreme Court to find that there was credible evidence to support the conclusion that the later breach of duty had not, in fact, caused the injury.

The *sine qua non* test works in the vast majority of cases concerning factual causation. No test of causation, however, can provide 'infallible threshold guidance'.[8] As Mills points out, 'there are some subtleties involved in the "but for" test'.[9] Though the test does not necessarily require evidence that the defendant's negligence was the sole source of the injury complained of,[10] logically, it requires evidence that it was the proximate cause of injury. This feature does not cause difficulty in most cases where the fact patterns lend themselves well to the 'but for' test, resulting in outcomes that accord with common sense. Where the medical evidence satisfactorily isolates the possible

---

[6] William L Prosser, *Torts* (4th edn, West Publishing 1971) 41.
[7] *Purdy v Lenihan* [2003] IESC 7.
[8] *Kuwait Airways Corporation v Iraqi Airways Company* [2002] 3 All ER 209.
[9] Mills and Mulligan, at note 3 above, p 237.
[10] *Athey v Leonati* [1996] 3 SCR 458.

causalities and where the net question is whether the plaintiff's injury was avoidable in the hypothetical event that the defendant had exercised reasonable care, as in *Purdy*, the 'but for' test is generally accepted to function well within the framework of negligence litigation.

Medical negligence actions, however, necessarily give rise to cases where the damage is multi-factorial in origin and there may be no easily identifiable proximate cause of injury.[11] The 'but for' test can become a 'blunt instrument and a lever to injustice'[12] in circumstances where the causative contribution of the defendant's negligence was only partial or was one of a number of other causes that coalesced in the ultimate injury. Thus, the plaintiff may ultimately fail on the basis that they cannot establish the defendant's negligence as being the proximate cause of injury. Where the courts use the classic litmus test in these situations, the plaintiff cannot possibly succeed.

As such, a question arises: is it fair and just to place on the plaintiff a burden of proof which, as a consequence of circumstances outside of their control, they simply cannot overcome?[13] Often, the difficulty in establishing any one factor as being the proximate cause of injury arises due to the limitations of science. It may be that the causes are concurrent and/or cumulative, or alternatively sequential and/or successive, so that there is no one specific causative factor. In other circumstances it is the failure of the doctor to conduct an appropriate examination that gives rise to the inherent medical uncertainties. For this reason, a number of modifications to the 'but for' test have emerged in an attempt to address the glaring deficiencies of the contingent cause rule.[14] Whether such modifications have, however, resulted in the courts' abandonment of the classic litmus test as the supreme indicator of factual causation is considered below.

'MATERIAL CONTRIBUTION': A NEW ERA FOR PROOF OF CAUSATION

In order to discern whether the test for causation has moved from the 'but for' test to one of 'material contribution', it is necessary to establish the emergence of the modified rule in case law, critically evaluate its application in claims of clinical negligence and then establish the perspective of the Irish courts on this contentious point of law.

An overview

The orthodox question of factual causation has been a source of judicial dissatisfaction. Throughout the latter half of the last century, various

---

[11] O'Dea, at note 2 above.
[12] Healy, at note 6 above, p 691.
[13] O'Dea, at note 2 above.
[14] Sandy Steel and David Ibbetson, 'More Grief on Uncertain Causation in Tort' (2011) Cambridge Law Journal Vol 70 No 2 451.

jurisdictions, in exceptional cases, have applied a more flexible approach to causation in response to cases in which it is not possible to establish the precise cause of an injury.[15] In some instances, courts have relieved the plaintiff from the rigours of the 'but for' rule by reference to the test of whether the defendant's negligence *materially contributed* to his injury.[16]

Developments in English law have been at the forefront of this debate in the common law world. The first significant judicial attempt to alleviate the strictures of the 'but for' test arose in *Bonnington Castings Ltd v Wardlaw*.[17] The House of Lords held that the plaintiff does not have to establish that the defendant's breach of duty was the main cause of the damage provided that it materially contributed to the damage. Applying this test, Lord Reid concluded that the 'guilty' dust was a material contributory cause to the damage, holding the employer liable for the full extent of the loss. The potential scale of this altered approach was evident from Lord Reid's concept of *materiality* which he said might include any contribution which does not fall within the exception *de minimis non curat lex*.[18]

A similar departure from the 'but for' test was subsequently attempted in *McGhee v National Coal Board*,[19] another case vexed by evidential difficulties in the endeavour to segregate the multiple sources of the plaintiff's injury. The decision consolidated the approach in *Bonnington* but also augmented it by premising it upon broader policies and principles. The plaintiff contracted dermatitis as a result of exposure to coal dust. Due to the current state of medical knowledge, however, the plaintiff could not establish, as a matter of probability, that his employer's negligence had caused or contributed to his illness. In a further relaxation of causation principles, the House of Lords held the defendant liable on the basis that it was sufficient to show that the defendant's breach of duty made the *risk* more probable even though it was uncertain whether it was the actual cause. A majority of the House of Lords treated a 'material increase in the risk' as equivalent to a 'material contribution to the damage'.[20] Lord Wilberforce recognised that this process involves overcoming an 'evidential gap' by drawing an inference of fact, an inference that is rooted in policy reasons:

> The answer as a matter of policy or justice should be that it is the creator of the risk who, *ex hypothesi*, must be taken to have foreseen the possibility of damage, who should bear its consequences.[21]

---

[15] Mills and Mulligan, at note 3 above, p 241.
[16] *McGhee v National Coal Board* [1973] 1 WLR 1.
[17] *Bonnington Castings Ltd v Wardlaw* [1956] AC 613.
[18] ibid.
[19] *McGhee v National Coal Board* [1973] 1 WLR 1.
[20] ibid [8].
[21] ibid [6].

In *McGhee*, therefore, the defendant's breach of duty resulted in an increase of an existing risk.

In *Wilsher v Essex Area Health Authority*,[22] a medical negligence case, the question was whether that modification could be applied to a case where there were up to five discrete possible causes of the plaintiff's injury and where the defendant's negligence had been causative only of one of the multiple risk factors. The House of Lords sought to rein in the *McGhee* formulation, endorsing a narrower interpretation of its scope. The court in *Wilsher* interpreted *McGhee* as based on an ordinary evidential inference that arose from facts established in the case. It was held, therefore, not to establish a new principle of law capable of more general application and did not have the effect of reversing the burden of proof.

This narrow, revisionist interpretation of the *McGhee* modification, however, was not accepted by the same court in *Fairchild v Glenhaven Funeral Services Ltd*.[23] The problem in demonstrating causation in this case was that the employees had been negligently exposed to asbestos fibres by a number of employers. With the current level of scientific knowledge, the plaintiffs could not identify which employer was responsible. Faced with a clear 'evidential gap', the House of Lords restored the approach in *McGhee* to the status of a special rule of law that modified the nature of proof required to discharge causation, reducing it in exceptional circumstances to proof of increase in the risk of injury. The court accepted that jurisdictions across the common law worlds had resolved difficulties of proof in the plaintiff's favour where scientific knowledge was not sufficiently advanced to prove the existence or extent of the defendant's causative bearing on damage.[24]

Essentially, the House of Lords provided that in the special circumstances of this type of case, justice demands the relaxation of the rigid requirements of the 'but for' test and favours the modified causal avenue of 'material contribution'. The special circumstances in *Fairchild* were that an employee had been exposed by different defendants, during different periods of employment, to inhalation of asbestos dust, in breach of each defendant's duty to protect him from the risk of contracting mesothelioma and/or that risk had been realised but, in current medical knowledge, the onset of the disease could not be attributed to any particular or cumulative wrongful exposure.[25]

---

[22] *Wilsher v Essex Area Health Authority* [1988] AC 1074.
[23] *Fairchild v Glenhaven Funeral Services Ltd* [2002] UKHL 22, [2003] 1 AC 32.
[24] *Fairchild v Glenhaven Funeral Services Ltd* [2003] 1 AC 32 at [66].
[25] Subsequently, the House of Lords made it clear in *Sienkiewicz v Greif (UK) Ltd* [2011] 2 AC 229 that the exception established in *Fairchild* applies also in cases involving a single defendant. In cases of both single and multiple defendants, the plaintiff will succeed if they prove, on the balance of probability, that the defendant's breach of duty had materially increased the risk that they would develop the disease.

It is important, however, to note that the court in *Fairchild* did not overrule *Wilsher*. Rather it deemed that the case was correctly decided on its facts. It is one thing, according to Lord Bingham in *Fairchild*, to treat an increase of risk as equivalent to the making of a material contribution where a single noxious agent was involved, but another thing where any one of a number of noxious agents may equally probably have caused the damage.[26]

It is submitted that the distinction drawn between *Wilsher* and *Fairchild* is problematic. The unfairness to the plaintiffs of requiring proof of the impossible in circumstances where the defendant is in breach of duty is what usually leads the courts to relax the causal requirements of the 'but for' test. In recognition of this justification, Lord Hoffmann acknowledged that the distinction between a case involving a single agent and number of different agents was not a principled distinction.[27] Nonetheless, *Wilsher* is still accepted to retain currency in cases with a similar causal matrix.[28]

Having established the departure of the orthodox test in exceptional circumstances of multiple causality, Lord Bingham declined in *Fairchild* to address the further question of whether in cases where liability is deemed to flow from a partial cause, damages should be reduced to reflect the approximate degree to which the negligence is causatively contributed to the injury.

Should the courts abandon the 'all or nothing' rule of common law that conventionally entitles the plaintiff to full compensation for their personal injury irrespective of the partially causative nature of the defendant's contribution?[29] It was subsequently decided by the House of Lords in *Barker v Corus UK Ltd*[30] that where causation is established on the part of multiple tortfeasors because of their material contributions to the injury or their material increase of the risk of injury, under the modified rules in *McGhee* and *Fairchild*, a court should then proceed to divide liability between the defendants severally, not jointly, according to the extent of their causative contribution to injury. Due to the possibility that plaintiffs would receive reduced damages if any one of the multiple tortfeasors was judgment proof, the legislature immediately reversed the *Barker* ruling in the specific context of mesothelioma damage caused by exposure at work to asbestos,[31] ensuring joint liability, subject to each defendant's right to seek contribution from other contributory wrongdoers.

The 'material contribution' test in medical cases

While the *Fairchild* ruling clearly established a judicial willingness to modify the 'but for' rule of causation to one of 'material contribution' in special

---

[26] ibid 66.
[27] ibid 77.
[28] Healy, at note 6 above, p 700.
[29] ibid 707.
[30] *Barker v Corus UK Ltd* [2006] 2 AC 572.
[31] Compensation Act 2006 (England), s 3.

circumstances where the justice of the case requires it, a cloud of uncertainty was simultaneously cast over the application of this exception to medical negligence litigation. Lord Hoffmann's reference in *Fairchild* to the 'massive increase in the liability of the National Health Service' in his justification for approving the *Wilsher* decision suggests that there may be policy considerations that will push the courts to adopt a stricter approach to exceptional matters of causation in clinical negligence cases.[32] Indeed, in *Wootton v J Docter Ltd*[33] it was left as an open question whether *Fairchild* could apply in the medical context. Such uncertainty was finally dispelled, however, in *Bailey v Ministry of Defence*[34] by Waller LJ who remarked that 'one cannot draw a distinction between medical negligence cases and others'.[35]

In *Bailey v Ministry of Defence*,[36] partly as a result of pancreatitis but also partly as a result of the hospital's negligence, the defendant was in a weakened state, which meant that when she subsequently vomited, while in hospital, she could not expel the vomit and this caused her serious harm. The Court of Appeal approved the extension of the causation exception to medical actions and summarised the position in relation to cumulative causes cases. Waller LJ concluded that:

> In a case where medical science cannot establish the probability that 'but for' an act of negligence the injury would not have happened but can establish that the contribution of the negligent cause was more than negligible, the 'but for' test is modified, and the claimant will succeed.[37]

It is respectfully suggested that this analysis is correct. Once it had been found that the plaintiff's damage was caused by her 'weakened state' and that her weakened state was 'contributed to' by both negligent and non-negligent acts, the conclusion that the former had 'materially contributed to the damage' was unavoidable.

The approach in *Bailey* was applied in *Canning-Kishver v Sandwell and West Birmingham Hospitals*[38] in which the claim succeeded after the contributing act of negligence was found to be a material cause. Furthermore, in the recent decision of *John v Central Manchester Children's University Hospitals NHS Foundation Trust*,[39] *Bailey* was applied in this case where there were three casual factors involved in the claimant's brain damage. The defendants argued that *Bailey* applied only to 'single agency' cases, not multiple casual factors.

---

[32] ibid para 69.
[33] *Wootton v J Docter Ltd* [2008] EWCA Civ 1361.
[34] *Bailey v Ministry of Defence* [2008] EWCA Civ 883.
[35] ibid [46].
[36] ibid.
[37] ibid.
[38] *Canning-Kishver v Sandwell and West Birmingham Hospitals* [2008] EWHC 2384.
[39] *John v Central Manchester Children's University Hospitals NHS Foundation Trust* [2016] 4 WLR 54.

Picken J held that the approach of 'material contribution' to the damage can apply just as much to multiple casual factor cases as it does to 'single agency' cases. Whether it can be applied in any given case will depend on whether the evidence points to the agency or factor for which the defendant was responsible as a probable contributing factor in causing the plaintiff's damage.

The Irish perspective

While the 'material contribution' test has emerged as an exceptional modification to the orthodox rule of causation in medical negligence litigation across the common law world, the 'but for' test remains the primary threshold question of liability in Ireland. As outlined above, the English courts have, in special cases, been willing to apply a more flexible approach to causation in response to cases in which it is not possible to establish the proximate cause of an injury, particularly in circumstances inhibited by the limitations of science. No Irish court has yet accepted material contribution as an element in clinical medical negligence cases. Despite the anticipation expressed by O'Flaherty J in *Best v Wellcome Foundation Ltd*,[40] where he believed that *McGhee* was likely 'to find a frequent resonance in our courts', the Irish judiciary has applied the 'but for' test as the dominant means of establishing factual causation.

The case of *Quinn v Mid Western Health Board and anor*[41] displays the unwillingness of the courts in this jurisdiction to modify the conventional rule. In this case, the defendants admitted breach of duty in the management of the plaintiff's mother's pregnancy. They argued, however, that the plaintiff's brain damage was caused by an acute episode during her gestation and that she would have suffered this injury regardless of how the later stage of the pregnancy was managed. In *Quinn*, therefore, the plaintiff sought to rely on the *Fairchild* ruling to alter the question of causation from the 'but for' test to one of material contribution.

The Supreme Court was not persuaded. In the judgment of Kearns J, he took the view that the *Fairchild* decision was exceptional and turned on its own unique facts:

> I would be firmly of the view that [the *Fairchild* decision] turns on its own unique facts and it was expressly confined by the House of Lords to a particular set of circumstances where it would be patently unjust not to allow the appeal ... the fact that the House of Lords took an exceptional course in *Fairchild* was expressly acknowledged to have been the case by Lord Hoffmann in the course of his judgment in the recent case of *Gregg v Scott* [2005] UKHL 2.

---

[40] *Best v Wellcome Foundation Ltd* [1993] 3 IR 421.
[41] *Quinn v Mid Western Health Board and anor* [2005] 4 IR 1.

Kearns J found that the 'but for' approach to causation should be followed by the Supreme Court. Flagging the decision in *Wilsher*, he stated that any approach which had the effect of reversing the onus of proof or transferring the onus of proof to the defendant would be one of such importance that it could only be done by a full court of the Supreme Court or even by legislation. The judgment in *Quinn* therefore exposes the potential injustice of applying the 'but for' test to cases of medical negligence where there is no clearly identifiable 'proximate cause of injury'.[42] The binary nature of the 'but for' test, which requires a yes or no answer, has garnered criticism in cases such as *Quinn* where it is not possible to achieve a certain determination of causation due to the state of science.[43] Notwithstanding this, it is important to note, however, that Kearns J also made the following observation in his judgment:

> Nor do special circumstances arise or exist in this case to bring it within the more relaxed requirements for establishing causation which are found to exist in *McGhee v National Coal Board* and *Fairchild v Glenhaven Funeral Services Ltd*.[44]

This comment suggests that circumstances may arise in which the orthodox causation requirement could be relaxed, as long as this does not involve the significant step of transferring the onus of proof. In view of the more recent English decisions in which the 'material cause' approach has been more thoroughly explored in the medical context, it is foreseeable that this is a matter that may be brought before an Irish court for further consideration.[45]

'Loss of chance': an alternative approach

As discussed above, the English courts have determined that 'material contribution' is an appropriate modification to the conventional test in circumstances where it cannot be shown, with the requisite certainty, that the act caused the harm complained of but where it was a contributing factor. There is another line of authority, however, being the 'loss of chance' doctrine, which addresses the deficiencies of the 'but for' test in a different way. This section seeks to consider this alternative avenue of causal inquiry in medical negligence litigation 'which has divided courts and commentators throughout the common law world'.[46]

'Loss of chance' arises most often where a plaintiff has been deprived of the opportunity of making a full or proper recovery from an illness or injury for which they first sought treatment. Applying traditional 'but for' analysis, if,

---

[42] O'Dea, at note 2 above.
[43] Bob Siegerink, 'Causal Inference in Law: An Epidemiological Perspective' (2016) European Journal of Risk Regulation Vol 7 Issue 1 175.
[44] *Quinn v Mid Western Health Board and anor* [2005] 4 IR 1.
[45] Mills and Mulligan, at note 3 above, p 242.
[46] *Gregg v Scott* [2005] 2 AC 176.

on the balance of probabilities, competent treatment would have prevented the deterioration which has occurred, or produced an improvement, the negligence is causally linked to the damage and the defendant is liable. Where the patient's prospects of a successful outcome to the treatment were estimated to be less than 50%, however, the patient cannot satisfy the 'but for' test.

The English courts have considered loss of chance on a number of occasions.[47] In the leading case of *Gregg v Scott*,[48] the House of Lords maintained a stringent approach to the 'loss of chance' type of approach and upheld the application of the strictures of the 'but for' requirements to such a claim. In *Gregg*, the plaintiff, who suffered a delayed diagnosis of cancer, was found to have originally had only a 42% chance of making a full recovery, which had been reduced to a 25% chance by reason of the defendant's negligent misdiagnosis. The court found that the plaintiff was not entitled to damages, on the basis that even if there had been no misdiagnosis it was more likely than not that the plaintiff would not recover. Therefore, by reference to traditional 'but for' principles, the negligent action had not caused the injury.

The appellant's invocation of the *Fairchild* exception in *Gregg* was rejected by the majority. Baroness Hale alluded to *Fairchild* as an example of the common law's flexible approach to causation in difficult cases but regarded it as of no application in a case such as *Gregg*.[49] While Lord Philips accepted that this might be seen as unfair, he said that using this robust test, which produced rough justice, was justifiable on policy grounds. Similar policy considerations were voiced by Lord Hoffmann who emphasised the undesirable ripple effects of permitting recovery in this case:

> To allow people to claim for the loss of chance would be a radical change in tort law and should be made by legislation, not judicial decision. The impact of such a change of the law on the NHS and insurers would be enormous. It would be improper for the House of Lords to make such a potentially significant change.[50]

Given that the House of Lords had regarded itself as enjoying the power to relax conventional causation rules in *Fairchild*, it is not immediately obvious why the majority in *Gregg* was not equally comfortable with taking such an approach in that case. After all, just weeks prior to the decision in *Gregg*, the House of Lords had decided that the claim in *Chester v Afshar*[51] could be upheld notwithstanding apparent difficulties of causation in that case. In *Chester*, the doctor failed to warn the plaintiff of the 1–2% risk of significant nerve damage

---

[47] *Hoston v East Berkshire Area Health Authority* [1987] AC 750.
[48] *Gregg v Scott* [2005] UKHL 2, [2005] 2 AC 176.
[49] ibid.
[50] ibid [3].
[51] *Chester v Afshar* [2005] 1 AC 134 and subsequently cited in Irish case law in *Winston v O'Leary* [2006] IEHC 440 and *Healy v Buckley* [2016] IESCDET18. The case was distinguished in *O'Leary (A Minor) v Health Service Executive, Ireland* [2016] IECA 25, on the basis that the plaintiff in *Chester v Afshar* [2005] AC 134 would have deferred the operation if she had been informed of the risks and the decision.

associated with the surgery. Ms Chester agreed to the operation and the risk of nerve damage materialised leaving her partially paralysed. While the majority accepted that, on conventional causation principles, the decision could not be supported, the House of Lords nevertheless found in favour of Ms Chester.

Crucially, for present purposes, some of the majority had regard to *Fairchild* flexibility as a justification for their approach. In light of this, it is surprising that four out of five judges ignored *Chester* in their opinions in *Gregg*. Baroness Hale did briefly refer to *Chester* as a good example of a case where 'well settled principles may be developed or modified to meet new situations and new problems'.[52] She distinguished *Gregg* on the basis that it was dealing with a particular problem which could be remedied without altering the principles applicable to the great majority of personal injury cases which give rise to 'no real injustice or practical problems'.[53] It is difficult to argue with the suggestion that *Chester* was 'unconvincingly distinguished'[54] in *Gregg*.

Notably, the House of Lords placed great emphasis on the proposition that the law of torts is concerned with outcomes, not with chance of outcomes. There are passages in Baroness Hales's speech in *Gregg* which apparently leave the door open for recovery for loss of chance in a case where death has occurred.[55] Overall, there appears to be some flexibility in very exceptional cases, but on the whole a strict application of the 'but for' test to 'loss of chance' claims pertains in English law.

The Irish perspective

In Ireland, arguments relating to the 'loss of chance' doctrine in medical negligence actions may be advanced in future with greater frequency.[56] Of particular interest to Irish practitioners are two, seemingly contradictory, Supreme Court decisions.

In *Philp v Ryan*[57] the Supreme Court approaches the problem from the perspective of compensable damage, rather than causation. The plaintiff had been told that he had prostatitis when in fact he had prostate cancer. In the Supreme Court, Fennelly J framed the question of whether the plaintiff could be compensated for this negligent action largely as a question of damage rather

---

[52] ibid [192].
[53] ibid.
[54] Morgan, 'A Chance Missed to Recognise Loss-of-a-Chance in Negligence' [2005] LMCLQ 281.
[55] ibid [226].
[56] Ryan and Ryan, 'Recent Judicial Approaches to 'Loss of Chance' in Medical Negligence Cases' in Craven and Binchy (eds), *Medical Negligence Litigation: Emerging Issues* (First Law 2005).
[57] *Philp v Ryan* [2004] 4 IR 241 and subsequently cited in *Quinn v Mid Western Health Board* [2005] 4 IR 1, *Law Society of Ireland v Walker* [2007] 3 IR 581, *IBB Internet Services Ltd and others v Motorola Ltd* [2013] IESC 53, *Hegarty v Mercy University Hospital Cork Ltd* [2016] IECA 24, *Dineen v Depuy International Ltd* [2019] 2 IR 238, *Brandley v Deane* [2018] 2 IR 741; followed in *Daly v Mulhern* [2008] 2 IR 1 and *Lett & Company Ltd v Wexford Borough Council & others* [2012] 2 IR 198.

than one of causation. He drew a distinction between past events, where the normal rule of proof on the balance of probability applies and future uncertain events. He commented that it would be:

> contrary to instinct and logic that a plaintiff should not be entitled to be compensated for the fact that, due to the negligent diagnosis of his medical condition, he has been deprived of appropriate medical advice and the consequent opportunity to avail of treatment which might improve his condition.[58]

Fennelly J concluded that the plaintiff was entitled to damages for the loss of the opportunity to be advised correctly and treated accordingly. In framing the question in this way, it seemed that the Irish courts rather neatly sidestepped the thorny issues of causation that vex the question in English law.

As highlighted above, however, the Supreme Court in *Quinn v Mid Western Health Board and anor*[59] maintained that the 'but for' approach must be followed. No claim for damages for loss of a chance was made in *Quinn* and the central issue instead was the proper test for causation. Kearns J nevertheless appeared to throw some doubt on the doctrine of 'loss of chance' applying in this jurisdiction when he referred to *Gregg v Scott* and said:

> It may be noted *en passant* that this decision of the House of Lords is also the most recent authority in support of the proposition that actionable claims for loss of a chance do not lie. ... Given that the decision of Peart J. in *Philp v Ryan* was referred to in the judgment of Lord Hoffmann, it is perhaps appropriate to comment that that judgment, containing as it does an excellent analysis of the facts on which that particular case turns, does not purport to address the underlying legal principles.[60]

Thus, the state of the law is not wholly certain in Ireland. *Quinn* raises a degree of doubt about how a court would approach the question of loss of chance if that were to be the central issue in a clinical negligence case. The position appears to be that a patient may recover for the loss of chance, but what remains unknown is whether, in Irish law, the plaintiff must satisfy the *Gregg* standard and show that their chance of a successful outcome would have been more than 50% but for the negligence.[61]

---

[58] ibid [24].
[59] *Quinn v Mid Western Health Board and anor* [2005] 4 IR 1.
[60] ibid.
[61] McQuillan, 'Judicial Belief in Statistics as Fact: Loss of Chance in Ireland and England' (2014) 30(1) Professional Negligence 9.

Development of the 'but for' test in Irish medical negligence litigation

Given the deficiencies of the 'but for' test, the courts need to adopt a model whereby that test is enshrined as the dominant test for causation but can still be abandoned when it becomes unworkable to allow an alternative test to be applied. There is much to recommend in the approach taken in Canada. In *Athey v Leonati*,[62] the Supreme Court of Canada describes the 'but for' test as 'of general, but not conclusive' application. Pursuant to the judgment in *Athey*, the 'but for' test still remains the default test to determine factual causation. The 'material contribution' test is to be employed only when the default test results in some 'logical impossibility'[63] or a result that is 'obviously unjust'.[64]

In order to apply the 'material contribution' test, the facts of the case must satisfy a two-limb test. Firstly, the 'but for' test must be unworkable and the reason for this must be outside of the plaintiff's control, for example, the limitations of science. Secondly, there must be a breach in the duty of care by the defendant, exposing the plaintiff to an unreasonable risk of injury with the plaintiff ultimately sustaining that injury. With this approach, the dominance of the 'but for' test is maintained, as the test is only usurped under exceptional circumstances.

Conclusion

The 'but for' test is undoubtedly the dominant question to which the Irish courts will turn when considering factual causation in medical negligence litigation. Causation has not moved from the 'but for' test to one of 'material contribution' in this jurisdiction. Although the possibility has not been excluded, no Irish court has yet applied 'material contribution' as an element in a clinical negligence case.

The appropriateness of such a stringent approach, however, to questions of causation must be questioned. It is submitted that the Irish courts should adjust this approach and allow the adjustment of the 'but for' test in cases of multiple causality where the limitations of science would cause the test to produce an unfair or illogical result. In such situations, the 'material contribution' test should serve as a modified alternative that does not jeopardise the general dominance of the 'but for' test. The Canadian example offers a way forward. Furthermore, the approach to the 'loss of chance' doctrine requires clarification. Ultimately, while no test of causation can provide 'infallible threshold guidance',[65] the 'but for' test continues to work in the vast majority of cases.

---

[62] *Athey v Leonati* [1996] 3 SCR 458.
[63] Erik Knutsen, 'Clarifying Causation in Tort' DLJ Vol 33 No 1 153.
[64] ibid.
[65] *Kuwait Airways Corporation v Iraqi Airways Corporation* [2002] 3 All ER 209.

PART D
TIME LIMITS

CHAPTER VI

ARE THE TIME LIMITS FOR MEDICAL NEGLIGENCE LITIGATION ESSENTIALLY DIFFERENT TO THOSE WHICH APPLY IN PERSONAL INJURIES LITIGATION?

Hugh Kelly and Rónán Dolan SC[1]

INTRODUCTION

There is no discrete statutory time limit for bringing medical negligence actions but while they are not expressly characterised as any different from other personal injuries claims, this chapter is concerned with whether, as a matter of practical reality, such actions typically have greater potential to avail of the statutory extension of the limitation period of two years within which a claim for damages for personal injury must be commenced.

Identifying any practical distinction between medical negligence and other personal injuries claims requires an examination of the legislation in the context of the practical challenges more likely to face the injured plaintiff in a medical negligence claim and whether such discrete circumstances are more likely to trigger the statutory extension than is the case in other personal injuries actions.

The Statute of Limitations (Amendment) Act 1991 defines personal injuries as 'any disease and any impairment of a person's physical or mental condition'. The limitation periods for claims for damages for sustaining such injuries are contained in s 11(2)(b) of the Statute of Limitations 1957, as amended by the Statute of Limitations (Amendment) Act 1991 and the Civil Liability and Courts Act 2004.

THE LIMITATION PERIOD

Section 11(2)(b) of the Statute of Limitations 1957 originally established a limitation period of three years for personal injuries actions, arising from

---

[1] Hugh Kelly prepared this chapter as a final year undergraduate student at the School of Law at Trinity College Dublin. Rónán Dolan SC is a member of the Inner Bar of Ireland.

the date of the accrual of the cause of action. This limitation period applied until the advent of legislative reform in 1991. In the Statute of Limitations (Amendment) Act 1991 a statutory basis for the extension of this limitation period was introduced in cases claiming damages for personal injuries. Section 3 of this Act provides as follows:

> 3. (1) An action, other than one to which section 6 of this Act applies, claiming damages in respect of personal injuries to a person caused by negligence, nuisance or breach of duty (whether the duty exists by virtue of a contract or of a provision made by or under a statute or independently of any contract or any such provision) shall not be brought after the expiration of three years from the date on which the cause of action accrued or the date of knowledge (if later) of the person injured.

The key concept in determining whether this extension should apply is the plaintiff's 'date of knowledge'. A legislative definition of the 'date of knowledge' is provided in s 2(1) of the same Act as follows:

> 2. (1) For the purposes of any provision of this Act whereby the time within which an action in respect of an injury may be brought depends on a person's date of knowledge (whether he is the person injured or a personal representative or dependant of the person injured) references to that person's date of knowledge are references to the date on which he first had knowledge of the following facts:
>
> a. that the person alleged to have been injured had been injured,
> b. that the injury in question was significant,
> c. that the injury was attributable in whole or in part to the act or omission which is alleged to constitute negligence, nuisance or breach of duty,
> d. the identity of the defendant, and
> e. if it is alleged that the act or omission was that of a person other than the defendant, the identity of that person and the additional facts supporting the bringing of an action against the defendant;
>
> and knowledge that any acts or omissions did or did not, as a matter of law, involve negligence, nuisance or breach of duty is irrelevant.

Subsections (a) to (e) of s 2(1) of the 1991 Act list, therefore, a defined set of factual variables for determining the 'date of knowledge'. On a literal interpretation, without one or more of these five facts, a plaintiff cannot be said to have the requisite knowledge so as to allow the limitation period to commence. One disregards any knowledge that the acts or omissions of the defendant alleged to have caused the harm could be actionable. No extension of time arises because the plaintiff may not have realised that the acts or omissions of the potential defendant were tortious as a matter of law.

Section 2(2) of the 1991 Act tempers s 2(1) by further providing as follows:

> 2. (2) For the purposes of this section, a person's knowledge includes knowledge which he might reasonably have been expected to acquire –
>
> (a) from facts observable or ascertainable by him, or
> (b) from facts ascertainable by him with the help of medical or other appropriate expert advice which it is reasonable for him to seek.

Accordingly, s 2(2)(b) of the 1991 Act explicitly requires a plaintiff to seek out expert advice where it is reasonable to do so but it is important to note that the requirement is only to seek advice. The fact that it is (a) *or* (b) in s 2(2) must not be forgotten. A court may fix a plaintiff with knowledge from facts observable or attainable by him alone, depending on the circumstances, so no generalised assumption may be made.

Section 2(3) of the 1991 Act explicitly prevents the court from imposing expert knowledge on a plaintiff, however, by providing:

> 2. (3) Notwithstanding subsection (2) of this section –
>
> (a) a person shall not be fixed under this section with knowledge of a fact ascertainable only with the help of expert advice so long as he has taken all reasonable steps to obtain (and, where appropriate, to act on) that advice; and
> (b) a person injured shall not be fixed under this section with knowledge of a fact relevant to the injury which he has failed to acquire as a result of that injury.

The provisions may be considered to implicitly contemplate circumstances where a plaintiff is misdirected, misinformed or for some other reason may be incapable of obtaining advice – this chapter will look at cases where such circumstances were considered.

It is also important to note that the three-year limitation period, which survived legislative reform in 1991, has since been amended by s 7 of the Civil Liability and Courts Act 2004, reducing the limitation period for claims for damages for personal injuries from three years to two.

THE APPLICATION OF THE 'DATE OF KNOWLEDGE' IN RELATION TO CLAIMS OF MEDICAL NEGLIGENCE

The cases of *O'Sullivan v Ireland, The Attorney General & ors*[2] and *Green v Hardiman*[3] comprise the leading statement of the law in this jurisdiction

---

[2] *O'Sullivan v Ireland, The Attorney General & ors* [2019] IESC 33.
[3] *Green v Hardiman* [2019] IESC 51.

in relation to the application of ss 2 and 3 of the 1991 Act addressing claims arising from allegations of medical negligence. Both of these cases came before the Supreme Court at the same time and the court decided to hear the respective appeals together.

In *O'Sullivan v Ireland, The Attorney General & ors* a hospital lost its appeal to the Supreme Court against the finding that the two-year limitation period for issuing personal injury proceedings began when the plaintiff received a doctor's medical report based on hospital records and not when he was informed in the weeks after his surgery that he had contacted MRSA. In the leading judgment of the Supreme Court, Charleton J agreed with the High Court and the majority judgment of the Court of Appeal that the claim was not statute barred because the date of knowledge, as defined by s 2 of the 1991 Act, was when a medical report was furnished almost a year and a half after the operation and the limitation period only commenced at this point in time. The hospital had argued that the starting point was the contraction by the plaintiff of MRSA. He had thereafter watched a programme on television about MRSA and contacted the man featured in the show. Thereafter, he contacted a solicitor and made a freedom of information request to the hospital for medical records.

Charleton J held that the plaintiff was not in a fit state following his surgery to appreciate that he had caught MRSA and that this was the cause of his condition. In short, the plaintiff was held not to have been physically or mentally able to receive or process this information. Charleton J further held that the receipt of hospital records making reference to a positive swab result for MRSA was not enough to commence the limitation period and that this only occurred when a report from a general practitioner was received thereafter. Accordingly, he held that the date of knowledge started once the plaintiff knew both of the injury and that it was attributable to the defendant in broad terms. It was not necessary for the plaintiff to have knowledge that this attribution constituted negligence or breach of duty.

It is of note that O'Donnell J (as he then was) gave a dissenting judgment in this case. He held that when the plaintiff was informed that he had become infected with MRSA during his initial operation, either on its own or in conjunction with the television programme, if not providing the plaintiff with the relevant knowledge under s 2(1)(c) of the Statute of Limitations (Amendment) Act 1991, this at least put him on enquiry. O'Donnell J further held that advice directed towards s 2(1)(c) of the 1991 Act could have been readily and speedily given and that the limitation period began from that point onwards.

The decision of the Supreme Court in the case of *Green v Hardiman* (which also comprised O'Donnell J) was, however, unanimous. Once again, Charleton J gave a leading judgment in this case. He considered that in circumstances where expert advice is required to establish undiscovered injuries caused by negligence, incorrect expert advice about the injury could have the effect of preventing time from running for the purpose of calculating the limitation period for commencing the claim.

Charleton J referred to his judgment in *O'Sullivan v Ireland, The Attorney General & ors* and identified that the core issue in this case was the stage a plaintiff might have broad knowledge from the facts known to him, or might reasonably be expected to acquire such facts, from either facts knowable to him or on the basis of consulting an expert. Charleton J was of the view that the plaintiff had not failed to make reasonable inquiries in relation to the cause of his injury but was instead sent in the wrong direction by reason of the medical advice which he had received. It was only after inquiries made by the solicitor whom he instructed, in conjunction with expert opinion which this solicitor obtained, that the plaintiff could be fixed with having knowledge of his claim as defined by s 2 of the 1991 Act.

In the concurring judgment of O'Donnell J, he commented that there is a broad spectrum for knowledge in cases of medical negligence which can dictate whether a particular case is further or closer to this dividing line. The essential reason why the plaintiff in this case fell on the right side of this line was because he had sought medical advice in January 2009 and had been specifically informed that his ongoing complaints were not connected to the bowel surgery which he had undergone in December 2007. Accordingly, in both of the judgments of Charleton and O'Donnell JJ, the critical factor was that the plaintiff had been given a wrong steer in the medical advice which he had received and this prevented him being fixed with the requisite knowledge, as defined by s 2(1) of the 1991 Act for the limitation period to commence. Both of these judgments concluded that it was reasonable for the plaintiff not to immediately question the medical advice which he had received and to take time before consulting with a solicitor in relation to his claim.

THE TEST WHEN DETERMINING THE 'DATE OF KNOWLEDGE'

In her judgment in *O'Sullivan v Ireland, The Attorney General & ors*, when concurring with the judgment given by Charleton J, Finlay Geoghegan J helpfully elaborated on the test that should be availed of when applying the provisions of s 2 of the Statute of Limitations (Amendment) Act 1991 and, more particularly, when determining the time at which a plaintiff can be held to have the requisite knowledge for the limitation period to commence. At paragraph 33 of her judgment, she set out a three-step test as follows:

> First, when did the plaintiff have actual knowledge? Second, is the defendant seeking to have the plaintiff imputed to have constructive knowledge of all of the relevant facts at an earlier date? If so, thirdly can the court impute this knowledge and on what date?

Accordingly, a distinction was made between actual and constructive knowledge with constructive knowledge held to be knowledge imputed by the court to a plaintiff pursuant to s 2(2) of the 1991 Act. Finlay Geoghegan J further clarified the use of the term actual knowledge by stating:

> I wish to make clear that in referring to 'actual knowledge', I am not seeking to indicate a level of knowledge different to that which has been set out in the earlier judgments of this Court including *Gough v Neary* in the majority judgments and the English cases referred to therein.[4]

Finlay Geoghegan J went on to state that:

> The advantage, in practical terms, of the two or three step approach I am suggesting in determining a plaintiff's date of knowledge for the purposes of s. 2 of the 1991 Act and distinguishing between actual knowledge and constructive knowledge, if necessary, is that the Court in the first step, in relation to the date of actual knowledge, is not required to consider issues such as whether or not a plaintiff was put on inquiry of certain facts or whether the plaintiff acted reasonably in ascertaining facts or seeking expert advice.[5]

In the judgment given by Charleton J in this case, he provides a helpful commentary in relation to this test as provided by Finlay Geoghegan J. He said that if it is alleged, on her analysis, by a defendant that knowledge has to be attributed to a date earlier than the date of actual knowledge due to a plaintiff failing to take all reasonable steps to obtain and act on expert advice, that earlier date should be identified by the defendant; if necessary the second step. Charleton J went on to comment that on the basis of the analysis of Finlay Geoghegan J, the third step is the ascertainment of when the plaintiff was aware that injury is attributable, in whole or in part, to such facts as are 'alleged to constitute negligence'. He said:

> As she later analyses the decided cases, a patient a month after leaving hospital following a procedure or operation may know that he or she is seriously ill. That is not knowledge of itself according to the statutory definition. Knowing that the illness is due to infection may not be enough either since some hospital infections, according to counsel in this case, may be transmitted to a patient while in hospital through no fault in procedures for clinical cleaning and sterilization. The difficulty arises in the last test, that is knowledge that the serious injury is due to attribution to some act or omission that may, as a matter of later legal analysis, which for the purpose of ascertaining knowledge, turn out to

---

[4] ibid para 34.
[5] *O'Sullivan v Ireland, The Attorney General & ors* [2019] IESC 33, para 32.

be an actionable wrong but which the plaintiff is aware of as an act or omission.[6]

At the core of this test, when determining whether a plaintiff has actual and constructive knowledge, are the factual criteria prescribed in s 2(1)(a) to (e) of the 1991 Act. Finlay Geoghegan J confirmed in her judgment that these five criteria apply to the definitions of both actual and constructive knowledge and she further describes them as cumulative.[7] In addressing these cumulative facts, however, Finlay Geoghegan J identified one of these facts as being of primary importance and concern:

> The most difficult is that specified in para. (c), the fact 'that the injury was attributable in whole or in part to the act or omission which is alleged to constitute negligence, nuisance or breach of duty'.[8]

APPLYING S 2(1)(C) OF THE STATUTE OF LIMITATIONS (AMENDMENT) ACT 1991

In considering s 2(1)(c) of the 1991 Act, Finlay Geoghegan J identified three related areas which require consideration, namely:

(1) the identification of the facts of which a plaintiff must have knowledge;
(2) what level of certainty is required; and
(3) what level of detail is required to have 'knowledge' of those facts for the purposes of the section.[9]

It is the answers to these three questions which identify the facts a plaintiff must be in possession of, or could be held to have been in possession of, in determining his or her date of knowledge for the purpose of s 2 of the 1991 Act. A consideration of these three questions is pivotal to determining whether medical negligence claims, by reason of how they arise, are more likely to enjoy the benefit of extensions of the statutory limitation in accordance with ss 2 and 3 of the 1991 Act.

The term which is central to the identification of the relevant facts is 'attributable'. Finlay Geoghegan J was also explicitly clear in her judgment in following the precedent of the Supreme Court in *Gough v Neary* that 'the phrase 'the injury was attributable to' must be interpreted as meaning 'capable of being attributed to' or 'potentially attributable to'.[10] An important distinction is made in the judgment of Charleton J in *O'Sullivan*, which is that it is not

---

[6] ibid para 6.
[7] ibid para 24.
[8] ibid para 33.
[9] ibid para 53.
[10] ibid para 52.

enough for the injury to be capable of attribution to the defendant but that it must be capable of attribution to the specific act or omission alleged to have caused the injury.[11] This is similar to the approach in the United Kingdom.[12] It is clear the plaintiff must have knowledge that the injury complained of is possibly related to a specified and identifiable act or omission of the defendant but the question then to be determined is what degree of detail is required.

The level of detail necessary to constitute knowledge under s 2(1)(c) of the 1991 Act is one of broad knowledge. In *O'Sullivan*, Charleton J considered the reasoning of Brooke LJ in *Spargo v North Essex District Health Authority*[13] as follows:

> Taking a similar approach, Brooke LJ in *Spargo* considered that time began to run where a potential plaintiff had 'a broad knowledge of the essence of the causally relevant act or omission to which the injury is attributable' by which is meant 'capable of being attributed to' as 'a real possibility'. In a sensible way, that judge refers to the limitation period as starting where a plaintiff has 'such knowledge' to go to a solicitor to seek advice on the basis of a broad knowledge that an injury or condition 'is capable of being attributed to an act or omission' which, in broad terms, a plaintiff 'can identify'.[14]

Similarly, in her judgment in *O'Sullivan*, Finlay Geoghegan J confirmed that a plaintiff must have broad knowledge of the causally relevant acts or omissions which are alleged to constitute negligence and to which the injury is potentially attributable.[15] A broad knowledge of the causally relevant acts or omissions alleged to constitute negligence is now, therefore, firmly established as the level of knowledge which is required by s 2(1)(c) of the 1991 Act.

The level of certainty necessary for a plaintiff to be said to have knowledge is a complex question as it interacts frequently with an area of knowledge explicitly precluded from consideration – legal knowledge. The general statement of the certainty required is explicitly not one of legal certainty. It needs only to be at a level sufficient to make it reasonable for a plaintiff to commence the claim. The leading test in this area was set out by Donaldson MR in *Halford v Brookes* as follows:

> In this context 'knowledge' clearly does not mean 'know for certain and beyond possibility of contradiction'. It does, however, mean 'know with sufficient confidence to justify embarking on the preliminaries to the

---

[11] See the comments of Charleton J in *O'Sullivan* at para 34 and those of Hoffmann LJ in *Hallam-Eames v Merrett Syndicates Ltd (No 1)* [1996] 7 Med LR 122, at p 177.
[12] See the comments of Lord Mance in *Haward v Fawcetts* [2006] UKHL 9, [2006] 1 WLR 682, at para 133.
[13] *Spargo v North Essex District Health Authority* (1997) 37 BMLR 99.
[14] ibid para 27.
[15] ibid para 60.

issue of a writ, such as submitting a claim to the proposed defendant, taking legal and other advice, and collecting evidence,' and suspicion, particularly if it is vague and unsupported, will indeed not be enough, but reasonable belief will normally suffice.[16]

THE RELATIONSHIP BETWEEN SS 2 AND 3 OF THE 1991 ACT AND MEDICAL NEGLIGENCE CLAIMS

It is evident from the case law that medical negligence claims are the most frequent type of litigation seeking to invoke ss 2 and 3 of the Statute of Limitations (Amendment) Act 1991. Charleton J, in the course of his judgment in *O'Sullivan* stated:

> It is striking that the law has moved from miners and coal dust and builders suffering from the later manifestation of the effects of asbestos. Instead, the case law centres on the particular facts of occurrences in hospitals.[17]

Charleton J proceeds to offer several possible reasons for this development, the most striking of which are the entrusting of personal care to clinicians whose work can only be understood by other clinicians and these potential plaintiffs being incapacitated by their injuries or otherwise.

The typically, though not invariably, more complex nature of medical negligence cases renders them more likely to involve an engagement with the specific provisions of s 2(1) of the 1991 Act. Among the complicating factors faced by plaintiffs in medical negligence actions are the realities of obtaining medical records and experts' reports thereafter. Difficulties often arise in cases requiring multiple experts' reports addressing interrelated issues concerning liability and causation. These reports may not be consistent or reconcilable with each other and may fail to establish a discernible cause of action in terms of both liability and causation.

Similarly, a plaintiff will often require the opinion of a medical expert not just to offer an independent opinion upon the medical treatment and care which has been provided but also to interpret and communicate the contents of often highly technical records and reports. This essential process can easily impede a plaintiff from obtaining the necessary level of knowledge as defined in s 2(1) of the 1991 Act.

Given the inherent complexity of these claims, a plaintiff may also not know what is the cause of the injury complained of until the nature of the negligence and clinical breach of duty firstly has been established. This has long been

---

[16] *Halford v Brookes* [1991] 1 WLR 428, Donaldson MR, 443.
[17] ibid para 30.

recognised as a particular feature of this litigation and was identified by Smith LJ in *Forbes v Wandsworth Health Authority* in this manner:

> In many medical negligence cases the plaintiff will not know that his injury is attributable to the omission of the defendant alleged to constitute negligence, in the sense that it is capable of being attributable to that omission, until he is also told that the defendant has been negligent.[18]

This statement was fully endorsed by Geoghegan J in *Gough v Neary*[19] with which he expressed his complete agreement. Similarly, in her judgment in *O'Sullivan*, Finlay Geoghegan J recognised the frequency with which factual knowledge is unobtainable until the same time at which knowledge of unlawful behaviour has been found. She said:

> Whilst the authorities clearly distinguish between relevant factual knowledge of the causally relevant acts or omissions alleged to constitute negligence and irrelevant legal consequences that such acts or omissions may constitute negligence, they also recognise, correctly in my view, that in practice, and perhaps quite often in medical negligence claims, a plaintiff may not obtain the requisite factual knowledge (even in the broad terms next referred to) of the causally relevant acts or omissions of the defendant alleged to constitute negligence, until such time as the plaintiff has also received advice in relation to the probable or potential negligence of the defendant.[20]

Medical negligence claims represent the largest cohort of cases facing pleas by the defendants of being statute barred and of reliance being placed upon ss 2 and 3 of the 1991 Act. Both of the plaintiffs in *O'Sullivan* and *Green* were successful in having their claims heard after a strict application of the relevant limitation had long since expired. The plaintiff in *Gough* enjoyed a similar success. Many medical negligence claims have previously been unsuccessful in this regard, however, such as in *Dobbie*,[21] *Broadley*,[22] *Forbes*[23] and *Cunningham*.[24]

In his dissenting judgment in *O'Sullivan*, O'Donnell J noted that while the courts' methods of ascertaining the date of knowledge and determining the knowledge of the plaintiff have been inconsistent, to say the least, the courts' interpretation of s 2 of the 1991 Act has perhaps been more consistent than is obvious. He said that to that extent, the application of the section in practice

---

[18] Stuart Smith LJ in *Forbes v Wandsworth Health Authority* [1996] EWCA Civ 1318, at p 411.
[19] *Gough v Neary and Cronin* [2003] IESC 39, at p 127.
[20] ibid 58.
[21] *Dobbie v Medway HA* [1994] 1 WLR 1234.
[22] *Broadley v Guy Clapham & Co* [1994] 4 All ER 439.
[23] ibid.
[24] *Cunningham v Neary* [2004] 2 ILRM 498.

has not been perhaps unduly problematic. He also recognised, however, that the interpretation of the provision, particularly in borderline cases, is undoubtedly difficult.

The most likely reason for this is perhaps found in the judgment of Charleton J in *O'Sullivan*. Following a consideration of the principles of statutory interpretation, Charleton J explored the purpose of this legislation and how the courts should apply it. In doing so, he employed the concept of the 'ordinary and aware plaintiff'.[25] This plaintiff is anyone from the injured factory worker, to the pedestrian victim of a traffic collision, to a public transport patron who slips on waste and falls down the stairs of a bus. In the case of the factory worker injured by a machine at her place of work, Charleton J remarked that a court considers:

> What does that potential plaintiff know? She only knows that something has happened which should not have happened: that she has been seriously injured and that as she sees it something which should not have happened in accordance with standard training has occurred.[26]

Similarly, he noted that in relation to the pedestrian who brings such a claim:

> All that such a plaintiff will know is that, as a pedestrian, he should have seen the car and he perhaps also thinks that the motorist in the car ought to have noticed him. The outcome is uncertain. Nonetheless, time runs from the accident.[27]

Finally, the patron of the bus, who slips and falls down the stairs – what does he or she know? They know they have been injured and that there was waste present on the stairs but:

> The question of who put the ice cream there would be answered by the probability that it was another customer, but the question of liability of the bus company as to whether the method of inspection, including by internal cameras or by periodic checks by the driver, was adequate, can only be answered by an examination of the records and video recordings.[28]

Charleton J uses these three examples of the 'ordinary and aware' plaintiff as a baseline to which courts must endeavour to consider the claims of plaintiffs where their cases contain hidden elements. He said:

> It is beyond argument that the purpose of section 2(1) of the 1991 Act was to establish a reasonable degree of uniformity as between the ordinary

---

[25] ibid para 22.
[26] ibid.
[27] ibid.
[28] ibid.

case, such as the three examples mentioned in the preceding paragraph, and the case where there was a hidden element.[29]

Nonetheless, there remain numerous issues with the practical application of the detailed judgments of Charleton and Finlay Geoghegan JJ in *O'Sullivan*, such as the potential for variance in application where there are delays in receiving medical records and expert reports and where there are requests for further and better particulars. One key issue highlighted by O'Donnell J in his dissenting judgment in that case is where there are such delays and multiple requests for further and better particulars, there is the potential for establishing multiple time periods, each running from the date of receipt of the various particulars.[30] Having said that, these judgments of Charleton and Finlay Geoghegan JJ offer considerable assistance to potential plaintiffs and their legal representatives as to when the time limits may be extended in medical negligence cases.

CONCLUSION

One can conclude by asking whether, in both explicitly recognising the prominence of medical negligence cases in the interpretation and application of s 2 of the 1991 Act and in drawing the distinction between a plaintiff in a medical negligence action and the 'ordinary and aware plaintiff', Charleton J has implicitly answered our question. Is this a confirmation of different time limits for plaintiffs who are intent upon commencing proceedings claiming medical negligence? It would certainly seem to acknowledge that discrete practical difficulties are more likely to arise in cases such as these.

The answer to these questions is best given, however, by Charleton J himself when he reflects further upon the distinctions between these cases by saying as follows:

> the amendment as to the delay in time is not to be construed as putting the unaware plaintiff in a better position than the ordinary and aware plaintiff ... It is beyond argument that the purpose of section 2(1) of the 1991 Act was to establish a reasonable degree of uniformity as between the ordinary case, such as the three examples mentioned in the preceding paragraph, and the case where there was a hidden element. Where plaintiffs were handicapped by the slow emergence of a personal injury, a potential injustice due to an inflexible limitation period is ameliorated in their favour and for that purpose. Where such plaintiffs, however, have that degree of awareness that would have enabled a plaintiff injured in the ordinary way to commence a personal injuries action, their cases are not to be treated more favourably than cases where the injury is immediately, or soon, apparent and where there is a sense of wrong

---

[29] ibid.
[30] See the judgment of O'Donnell J in *O'Sullivan*, at para 12.

sufficient to enable a reasonable person to consult a solicitor with a view to commencing litigation. In both kinds of cases, if you only know a fact that may establish negligence when an expert has been consulted, then time begins to run only at that point.[31]

It should also be emphasised that Charleton J expressed a distinct willingness to examine each case on its own merits and refuses to establish any prescriptive precedent in that regard. We must return then to the nature of medical negligence cases. There is a recognised frequency of reliance upon s 2 of the 1991 Act in these cases, primarily due to a frequent and understandable delay with the plaintiffs in these cases acquiring the requisite knowledge in order to commence their claims. Nonetheless, no generalised assumptions may be made and each case must be considered on its own facts as the application of this section is entirely fact specific.

In order to do so correctly, it is perhaps prudent to conclude with a final section from this critical judgment of Charleton J in *O'Sullivan* in which he sets out how one can best proceed in this manner:

> Where a plaintiff claims that he or she did not commence a case due to knowledge of their injury, and of the broad facts alleged to constitute an actionable negligence, coming to them at a date later than the occurrence of the wrong in question, a number of factors must be considered.
>
> The first step in determining whether time begins to run at that later date, or on the earlier date of the occurrence of the alleged wrong, requires judges to examine the way the plaintiff puts his or her case and to distil what he or she is complaining about. That inquiry is into the truth of any such assertion, to determine the point at which such a plaintiff had, in broad terms, knowledge of the facts on which that complaint is based. Such knowledge is sufficient to start the time running if it justifies the plaintiff in both consulting a solicitor and also in being able to give an outline of the broad factual parameters of his or her case; that is what happened to the plaintiff as a result of a wrong by someone else. In this context, the limitation period may be delayed because a potential plaintiff did not have such broad knowledge of one or more of the following: knowledge that they had been injured by what they complain of; or knowledge that the proposed defendant had done something wrong; or knowledge that the injury was significant; or knowledge as to the identity of the proposed defendant or defendants. It is knowledge that the proposed defendant had done something wrong which is the key factor in most cases; that is, broad knowledge of the act or omission in consequence of which that plaintiff says that he or she was subject to an act or omission that should not have occurred. Any later legal analysis as to whether, as a matter of law, such act or omission is negligence is not

---

[31] ibid para 23.

relevant. What caused the accident is relevant, whether or not that act or omission amounted in law to negligence.

The core issue is always at what stage such a plaintiff had such broad knowledge from facts which he or she either had, or might reasonably have been expected to acquire, from observable or ascertainable facts, or only on the basis of consulting an expert to ascertain such fact or facts. Having been consulted in such a timely fashion as a reasonable person would pursue that step, it is then the task of the expert to identify any act or omission that is alleged to constitute a wrong. Failure to take timely steps to pursue broad knowledge of facts by consulting an expert, or inertia in acting on such knowledge when received, does not stop time running.[32]

---

[32] ibid paras 33 to 35.

Chapter VII

ISSUING PROCEEDINGS BUT NOT SERVING THEM – IS THERE A WIDER TOLERANCE AND JUSTIFICATION FOR THIS PRACTICE IN MEDICAL NEGLIGENCE LITIGATION?

Trinity Geddis and Richard Kean SC[1]

There can be no dispute that the institution and service of legal proceedings require time limits which demand that litigants proceed with reasonable expedition in the prosecution of their claims. As far back as 1825, Best CJ described this necessity with some colour in his judgment in the case of *A'Court v Cross*[2] when he stated that: 'Long dormant claims have often more of cruelty than of justice in them'.[3] Naturally, with the passage of time memories become blurred, witnesses die or become untraceable or unable to give evidence, whilst evidence can be lost, damaged or destroyed. By prescribing certain time limits for the commencement and service of legal proceedings, the Statutes of Limitations and Order 8 of the Superior Courts Rules apply in unison to provide the necessary certainty and finality to litigation.

The time limits which apply to the commencement and service of proceedings in medical negligence litigation are, however, unique. The flexibility of the time limits applicable to this branch of civil litigation reflects the complexities inherent in it. The particular features of medical negligence litigation have allowed a distinctive approach to emerge from the Superior Courts in relation to how the time limits for the commencement and service of such proceedings are to be applied. In such cases, it is common to issue a protective writ within the requisite limitation period, while awaiting an expert medical report to establish that a cause of action can be established in evidence in terms of liability and/or causation. By examining the recent judgment of the Court of Appeal in *Murphy v Health Service Executive*,[4] this approach of the Superior

---

[1] Trinity Geddis prepared this chapter as a final year undergraduate student at the School of Law at Trinity College Dublin. Richard N Kean SC is a member of the Inner Bar of Ireland.
[2] *A'Court v Cross* (1825) 130 ER 540.
[3] ibid 541.
[4] *Murphy v Health Service Executive* [2021] IECA 3.

Courts, which has emerged in the specific context of medical negligence litigation, is considered below.

MEDICAL NEGLIGENCE LITIGATION: TWO TEMPORAL HURDLES

Statutes of Limitations

The justifications underpinning the Statutes of Limitations are twofold: they safeguard defendants against stale claims and they deter plaintiffs from unduly delaying the institution of legal proceedings. The Statute of Limitations 1957 (the 1957 Act) is the primary source of limitation provisions in the Republic of Ireland.[5] Whilst a uniform limitation period does not exist in Irish law, the general principle enshrined within the 1957 Act is that the time period to commence proceedings 'runs from the date of accrual of the cause of action until the date that an action is brought'.[6] Failure to commence proceedings during the prescribed limitation period will result in the relevant claim becoming statute barred.

Pursuant to s 3(1) of the Statute of Limitations (Amendment) Act 1991 (the 1991 Act), as amended by s 7(a) of the Civil Liability and Courts Act 2004, the special time limit for actions in respect of personal injuries cases is two years. Unlike other limitation periods, s 3 (1) of the 1991 Act also provides that the limitation period for personal injuries proceedings will commence on the 'date on which the cause of action accrued' or the 'date of knowledge' if later, of the person injured.

Section 2 of the 1991 Act defines the 'date of knowledge' as occurring when the plaintiff first had knowledge of the facts that the person alleged to have been injured had been injured, that the injury in question was significant, that the injury was attributable in whole or in part to the act or omission which is alleged to constitute negligence, nuisance or breach of duty and the identity of the defendant. If it is alleged that the act or omission was that of a person other than the defendant, the 'date of knowledge' is further dependent upon the plaintiff first having knowledge of the identity of that person and the additional facts supporting the bringing of an action against the defendant. This critical section further provides that knowledge that any acts or omissions did or did not, as a matter of law, involve negligence, nuisance or breach of duty is irrelevant.

The application of this statutory 'date of knowledge' test in the context of medical negligence litigation is particularly challenging. Central to its

---

[5] In the context of medical negligence litigation, the Statute of Limitations 1957 has been amended by the Statute of Limitations (Amendment) Act 1991, the Statute of Limitations (Amendment) Act 2000, the Personal Injuries Assessment Board Acts 2003 to 2019 and the Civil Liability and Courts Act 2004.
[6] Martin Canny, *Limitation of Actions* (2nd edn, Round Hall 2016) [2-02].

complication is that the plaintiff may be proceeding on the basis of an alleged cause of action against a former treating physician who is further alleged to have failed to disclose to that plaintiff the relevant information which would have allowed for knowledge of the claim to have been given. The complex issues that arise in this regard are addressed elsewhere in this publication and need not be rehearsed further here.[7] For the purpose of this chapter, however, it is necessary to briefly review two recent decisions of the Irish Supreme Court which specifically considered the application of the 'date of knowledge' test in the context of medical negligence litigation. For in determining when proceedings need to be issued and served, one must first ascertain the date when the plaintiff first had the requisite knowledge that a cause of action against the intended defendant had arisen.

In *O'Sullivan v Ireland, The Attorney General & ors*,[8] the Supreme Court, by a majority, found that the time for the commencement of the plaintiff's cause of action, which arose from him contracting 'MRSA' at the defendant hospital, did not commence when he was informed that he had contracted it, as this did not encompass knowledge of any causally relevant act or omission of the hospital to which the plaintiff's injury was attributable. In his judgment, Charleton J stated that the 'date of knowledge' of the plaintiff commenced when he knew both of the injury and that it was attributable to the defendant in broad terms.[9] It was not until the plaintiff was furnished with the general practitioner's medical records, detailing an outbreak of MRSA in the hospital from which the plaintiff should have been protected, that there was 'congruence of all the requisite elements under the statute to start the clock ticking'.[10]

A similar approach is reflected in the decision of the Supreme Court in *Green v Hardiman*[11] which was heard by the Supreme Court immediately after the case of *O'Sullivan v Ireland, The Attorney General & ors*. In that case, the Supreme Court unanimously held that where expert advice is required to establish that an injury has arisen from clinical negligence, professional medical advice can halt the expiry of the statutory limitation period if a plaintiff has been wrongly advised that his injury is not attributable to a negligent act.

In his judgment, Charleton J referred to his judgment in *O'Sullivan* and reiterated that the date of knowledge only commences when a plaintiff knows both of the injury and that it was attributable to the defendant in broad terms. In this case, the limitation period was delayed due to the exceptional circumstances of the plaintiff being given a misleading set of facts on the basis of a professional assessment. In these exceptional circumstances, the Supreme

---

[7] As set out by Hugh Kelly and Rónán Dolan SC in the preceding chapter in this publication entitled 'Are the time limits for medical negligence litigation essentially different to those which apply in personal injuries litigation?' at page 107.
[8] *O'Sullivan v Ireland, The Attorney General & ors* [2019] IESC 33.
[9] ibid.
[10] *O'Sullivan v Ireland, The Attorney General & ors* [2018] IECA 8 at [10].
[11] *Green v Hardiman* [2019] IESC 51.

Court concluded that the plaintiff only acquired a sufficient level of knowledge when an expert opinion was obtained which first disclosed the correlation between the nature of the injury suffered by the plaintiff and the negligence and breach of duty which gave rise to it. As a practical consequence, the two-year limitation period did not begin to run until four and a half years after the alleged negligent treatment.

These two leading decisions of the Supreme Court underline the influence which expert medical advice has in determining the application of the statutory limitation period. They confirm that there is no all-encompassing test which applies to determining the accrual of a cause of action for clinical negligence. Rather, the commencement of the limitation period in these cases must be determined in a fact specific manner. Accordingly, the courts enjoy a unique degree of flexibility when applying time limits in cases based upon an allegation of clinical negligence and breach of duty.

This has a corresponding and highly important significance for practitioners in determining whether a personal injuries summons is to be issued and when it is to be served. The specific facts of each case determine whether it is necessary to issue a summons within the basic two-year limitation period even when an expert report has not yet been procured establishing that a cause of action arises in relation to both liability and causation. By reason of the nature of clinical negligence claims, where a potential plaintiff has often to ascertain whether a cause of action arises with the assistance of expert medical advice, the prudent course of action is to issue a personal injuries summons within the statutory limitation period but not serve it while the report of a medical expert is awaited, disclosing whether a cause of action in terms of liability and causation actually arises. If the summons is served upon a potential defendant and the medical expert subsequently advises that a cause of action does not arise, a plaintiff will then be liable for the costs of that prospective defendant when a notice of discontinuance of the proceedings is served. It is, therefore, of critical importance in clinical negligence claims as to when a personal injuries summons, which has been issued, has to be served without needing to be renewed by order of the High Court or, if needing to be so renewed, what the criteria are for such an application to be successful.

ORDER 8 OF THE RULES OF THE SUPERIOR COURTS 1986, AS AMENDED

Order 1A of the Rules of the Superior Courts 1986, as amended (RSC), was introduced to give effect to s 10 of the Civil Liability and Courts Act 2004, which provides that clinical negligence claims, being personal injuries actions, are to be initiated by way of personal injuries summons. Order 8 of the RSC stipulates that a personal injuries summons, once issued from the High Court Central Office, must be served on a defendant within 12 calendar months from the day that it is issued.[12] Failure to serve the summons during

---

[12] RSC Ord 8, r 1 provides that 'no original summons shall be in force for more than twelve months from the day of the date thereof, including the day of such date'.

Issue and Service of Proceedings 125

the requisite 12-month period will result in the expiry of the summons. This means that service cannot be validly effected unless the summons is renewed in accordance with the provisions of Order 8 Rule 1 of the RSC.[13]

The original formulation of Order 8 Rule 1, in the RSC, allowed a summons to be renewed for six months where the High Court or the Master of the High Court, whichever the case may be, was satisfied that 'reasonable efforts' had been made to serve the defendant, or there was 'other good reason' for renewal. Order 8 Rule 1 has since been amended by the Rules of the Superior Courts (Renewal of Summons) 2018.[14] The amended Order 8 came into effect on 11 January 2019 and introduced significant changes to the conditions which must be satisfied for a summons to be renewed. Different rules now apply depending on whether the application to renew the summons is made before or after the 12-month period from when the summons was issued.

Similar to its previous iteration, Order 8 Rule 1(1) of the RSC now provides that applications for leave to renew a summons, before it expires, may be made to the Master of the High Court. Under Order 8 rule 1(2), however, the Master is only now authorised to grant leave to renew for a reduced period of three months 'if satisfied that reasonable efforts have been made to serve' or 'for other good reason'. Furthermore, Order 8 Rule 1(3) states that applications for leave to renew a summons, after it has expired, can only be made to the High Court. Finally, and perhaps most significantly, Order 8 Rule 1(4) provides that the High Court may grant leave to renew for a three-month period 'if satisfied that there are special circumstances which justify an extension'.

When considering the provisions of this Order, it should be stated from the outset that the requirement of solicitors to act expeditiously, not just in the service of the summons but also in its renewal within the prescribed time period, cannot be over emphasised. The inherent risk of non-renewal of a summons by the courts remains a real threat, being entirely dependent upon a court's view as to what constitutes 'special circumstances' or 'other good reason'. Legal practitioners will be at the mercy of the court where they fail to renew a summons within the prescribed time frame as to whether the court is satisfied that the 'special circumstances' requirements have been met. Whilst a summons can be renewed twice, once with the Master and once in the High Court, where a solicitor decides to hold off serving proceedings (albeit for the legitimate reason that an expert report is awaited) the plaintiff must not be in any way dilatory in obtaining this report and it is hard to see the disadvantage of furnishing the defendants with a copy of the summons within the required time frame to dilute any subsequent argument they may attempt to make. An application to the Master of the High Court for renewal of the summons, prior to the expiry of the initial 12-month period, requires demonstration of good reason to justify a renewal and is a lower threshold than the 'special circumstances' which will be required for an extension of time for leave to

---

[13] Hilary Delany and Declan McGrath, *Civil Procedure in the Superior Courts* (4th edn, Round Hall 2018) [2-29].
[14] SI 2018/482.

renew a summons before the court. While each case will depend on its own facts, the issues of when to issue, when to notify, when to serve and when to renew require the most careful of consideration in the context of medical negligence litigation.

INTERPRETING ORDER 8 RULE 1(4) OF THE RSC: A TWO-PART TEST?

Since the commencement of this new formulation of Order 8 of the RSC, this test has received extensive consideration from the High Court before this new provision was the subject of a comprehensive judgment of the Court of Appeal in *Murphy v Health Service Executive*.[15] As a plaintiff in a clinical negligence claim may not have received a report from a medical expert, grounding a cause of action in terms of liability and causation within a period of 12 months from the date of the issue of the personal injuries summons, the critical question arises as to what constitutes such 'special circumstances' in such litigation.

Prior to the judgment of the Court of Appeal in *Murphy v Health Service Executive*, the test for renewing a summons, pursuant to the new formulation of Order 8 of the RSC, where a plaintiff had failed to serve it upon a defendant within the 12-month period while it was alive, was the subject of conflicting judicial interpretation in the High Court. Far from providing clarity, the newly substituted rule sparked uncertainty amongst litigants as a series of High Court decisions revealed diverging views as to how the test was to be applied. In *Murphy and Cullen v ARF Management Limited*,[16] *Ellahi v The Governor of Midlands Prison and others*[17] and *Downes v TLC Nursing Home*,[18] the High Court appeared to confirm that the applicable test for renewing an expired summons under Order 8 Rule 1(4) of the RSC was that two conditions must be met, that is:

(i) the court must be satisfied that there are 'special circumstances' to justify an extension of time to apply for leave to renew the summons and
(ii) the court must be satisfied that there is 'other good reason' for renewing the summons.

Other members of the judiciary of the High Court have been critical of this two-tiered approach. Most notably, in *Brereton v The Governors of the National Maternity Hospital*,[19] Hyland J noted that 'it seems somewhat unlikely that the drafters of Order 8, Rule 1(4) would have imposed a two-tiered test for renewing a summons'.[20] Furthermore, when *Murphy v Health Service Executive* was

---
[15] *Murphy v Health Service Executive* [2021] IECA 3.
[16] *Murphy and Cullen v ARF Management Limited* [2019] IEHC 802.
[17] *Ellahi v The Governor of Midlands Prison and others* [2019] IEHC 923.
[18] *Downes v TLC Nursing Home* [2020] IEHC 465.
[19] *Brereton v The Governors of the National Maternity Hospital* [2020] IEHC 172.
[20] ibid [9].

Issue and Service of Proceedings 127

originally heard in the High Court before Cross J, he stated that 'it would not be my reading of O.8. that a Court would first be obliged to consider "special circumstances" and then decide on "good reasons"'.

The interpretation of Order 8 has now, however, been settled by two judgments of the Court of Appeal in the cases of *Murphy v Health Service Executive* and *Nolan v The Board of Management of St Mary's Diocesan School*. The Court of Appeal gave judgment in the former case on 15 January 2021 and in the latter case on 11 January 2022. It is of note that Noonan J gave the judgment on behalf of the Court of Appeal in *Nolan* and he was also a member of the Court of Appeal in *Murphy* in which the judgment was given by Haughton J. Accordingly, both of these key judgments of the Court of Appeal should be read as one. While the judgment in *Nolan* is the more recent of these two judgments, we will consider it first as the case did not arise in the context of a clinical negligence claim. The judgment of the Court of Appeal in *Murphy* does, however, provide very helpful guidance in relation to the application of Order 8 to the specific nature of clinical negligence claims. With these claims, the process of establishing expert evidence to determine that a cause of action arises both in terms of liability and also in terms of causation, can be arduous and time consuming and create particular time pressures in terms of the service of a personal injuries summons within the prescribed period.

SATISFYING THE 'SPECIAL CIRCUMSTANCES' TEST

In this more recent decision of the Court of Appeal, entitled *Irene Nolan v The Board of Management of St Mary's Diocesan School*,[21] Noonan J delivered an *ex tempore* judgment on 11 January 2022, further examining the criteria and principles to be applied in respect of summons renewal applications. The case itself is a bullying and harassment claim alleged to have occurred by teachers at a school on various dates between 30 April 2008 and 24 October 2017. A diagnosis of depression of the plaintiff was made in October 2017 and a medical report furnished to the then solicitor. An application to the Personal Injuries Assessment Board was made and the plaintiff instructed a new firm of solicitors in May 2018.

On 7 November 2019 the plaintiff lodged an *ex parte* docket with the High Court seeking to renew the summons and this was heard before Murphy J on 18 November, who ordered that the summons be renewed for a period of three months. As required by the Rules, the Order also stated the reason for the renewal as being circumstances where a delay occurred by reason of the change of solicitors. The summons was subsequently served on the defendant who then successfully applied to the court to set aside the renewal.

---
[21] *Irene Nolan v The Board of Management of St Mary's Diocesan School* [2022] IECA 10.

Issues had arisen in relation to the plaintiff's entitlement to early retirement due to ill health. In the application, it was suggested that this had been a very stressful procedure for the plaintiff and a decision was taken not to serve the personal injuries summons to avoid 'adding to the stress the Plaintiff was under in having to deal with two separate matters'.

The notice of motion was grounded in the normal way on affidavit and the solicitor averred that the decision not to serve the summons appears to have been a decision of the solicitor himself. It was unclear whether he had obtained instructions from the plaintiff in that regard. The Court concluded, having considered the affidavit, that the decision by the solicitor was taken without instruction. The Court found this surprising as there was no suggestion that the plaintiff was at any relevant time incapable of giving instruction.

After a detailed analysis of the facts and law, Barr J, after hearing the defendant's application to set aside the renewal of the summons in the High Court, was not satisfied that the reasons advanced by the plaintiff's solicitor for not serving the summons constituted special circumstances. He considered that in the absence of medical evidence there was no factual basis for the decision not to serve. He also went on to consider the issue of prejudice and held, in any event, that there was in fact prejudice to the defendant. Having considered the relevant provisions of the RSC and in particular Order 8, he stated that: 'I think it is fair to say that the new rule was introduced to tighten up and limit the circumstances in which a renewal would henceforth be given'.

When the matter then came before the Court of Appeal, Noonan J carried out an analysis of the tension that exists being the clear policy behind limitation periods to protect parties against stale claims and bring finality to litigation, on the one hand, and the courts' jurisdiction to, in effect, extend the limitation period by renewing a summons that has expired, on the other. Again, Noonan J pointed out that at one time in the past the bar was relatively low in terms of renewal applications which were frequently granted more or less for the asking. He then referred to the significant change in this 'endless indulgence'.[22] He was influenced also by the court's obligation under Article 6 of the European Convention on Human Rights to ensure that, in the determination of civil rights, everyone is entitled to a fair and public hearing within a reasonable time.

Noonan J pointed out that the question of prejudice has, in general, no relevance to limitation periods and its application to the renewal of summonses must be carefully scrutinised. He reiterated that the court must be satisfied that there are 'special circumstances which justify an extension'. The Court concluded that 'the pre-requisite is that there is a special circumstance which once established requires a court to consider whether the circumstances justify renewal'. The court obviously must also consider whether it is in the interests of justice

---

[22] See *Gilroy v Flynn* [2004] IESC 98.

to renew the summons and this entails considering any general or specific prejudice or hardship alleged by a defendant and balancing that against the prejudice or hardship that might result for a plaintiff if renewal is refused.

Noonan J was of the opinion that Haughton J, when giving judgment on behalf of the Court of Appeal in *Murphy v Health Service Executive*, recognised that special circumstances alone are not enough and placed emphasis on the requirement for these circumstances to justify extension. At paragraph 74 of his judgment in *Murphy*, Haughton J stated that, in considering whether 'special circumstances … justify an extension':

> The court should consider whether it is in the interests of justice to renew the summons, and this entails considering any general or specific prejudice or hardship that may result for a plaintiff if renewal is refused.

Furthermore, at paragraph 76 of his judgment in *Murphy*, Haughton J further stated:

> In my view this is not a second tier or limb to the test. The need for the court to consider under sub-rule (4) the interests of justice, prejudice and the balancing of hardship is in my view encompassed by the phrase 'special circumstances [which] justify extension'. Thus there may be special circumstances which might normally justify a renewal, but there may be countervailing circumstances, such as material prejudice in defending proceedings, that when weighed in the balance would lead a court to decide not to renew. The High Court should consider and weigh in the balance all such matters in coming to a just decision.

Noonan J was of the view that the reference by Haughton J in *Murphy* to there not being a second-tier limb to the test refers to the view of the Court of Appeal that special circumstances and the justification for renewal are not two separate and distinct matters. Rather, they fall to be considered together in the analysis of whether it is in the interest of justice to renew the summons. Prejudice is a component of that analysis. Accordingly, it seems clear that Noonan J, in giving judgment for the Court of Appeal in *Nolan*, has endorsed that these criteria are equally relevant and not mutually exclusive.

The approach set out by Noonan J is that the first plinth is to consider whether or not there are special circumstances and then to consider the question of prejudice. In the case at hand, Noonan J was of the view that the solicitor had in substance raised three reasons why at various stages he elected not to serve the summons. He was unimpressed by what he described as a lack of clarity in the affidavits on the issue and reminded the parties that the plaintiff carries the onus of establishing the special circumstances justifying renewal and that the court should not be left to speculate about matters of evidence.

Noonan J considered each of the factors in turn:

1. The stress to the plaintiff, and stress from litigation is nothing new and is an inevitable and unavoidable incident of litigation. He was not, therefore, impressed that the stress of litigation is ever, except in the rarest of cases, sufficient to amount to a special circumstance within the meaning of Order 8.
2. The Court was not convinced that there was anything particularly unusual about multifaceted litigation particularly in the context of bullying and harassment in the workplace.
3. The Court found it 'difficult therefore to understand that anyone who willingly embarks on such litigation can be heard to say that they should not be required to pursue it on such time as they feel emotionally equipped to do so'. The fact that the plaintiff may have been diagnosed by her general practitioner as suffering from depression as a result allegedly of the matters of which she complains 'hardly changes matters'.
4. The Court was unimpressed by the fact that there was no medical evidence but just a bare assertion that the solicitor was worried about subjecting his client to stress. The Court pointed out that the solicitor was not a doctor and the Court paid particular attention to the fact that there had never been any suggestion that the plaintiff was unable to give instructions but, on the contrary, she appeared to have been able to transact other legal business of significance to her during the period concerned.
5. Ultimately, the Court was quite satisfied that no matter how well motivated the solicitor was in wishing to protect his client from stress, this could not be viewed as a special circumstance for the purpose of Order 8 Rule 1(4).
6. The overlapping ground advanced by the solicitor that the personal injury action should not proceed until a retirement claim was disposed of received no sympathy from Noonan J. Referring to Lord Goddard in *Battersby v American Oil Company Limited*[23] where he said: 'It is a duty of a plaintiff who issues a writ to serve it promptly … ordinarily it is not a good reason that the plaintiff desires to hold up the proceedings whilst some other case is tried or await some future development'. His view in that regard was supported by *Darjohn Developments Limited (in liquidation) v IBRC Limited*,[24] where the Court stated 'in general it is not permissible to issue proceedings and then "park" them without service in the hope or anticipation for example that a change in the law may render them viable or an impecunious defendant may become a mark'.

---

[23] *Battersby v American Oil Company Limited* [1945] 1 KB 23, at p 23.
[24] *Darjohn Developments Limited (in liquidation) v IBRC Limited* [2016] IEHC 535.

7. Noonan J also dismissed the suggestion which had been advanced on behalf of the plaintiff that there was any difficulty in relation to the renewal of summons during the period of the Long Vacation.

Ultimately, the Court concluded that there was no special circumstance that had been demonstrated by the plaintiff in the appeal as would qualify within the terms of Order 8. There was also no need to consider the issue of prejudice as that only would arise for consideration where special circumstance had been demonstrated and none was shown on this case. The appeal was dismissed. This decision is a timely reminder to practitioners about the difficulties which must now be faced in relation to applications to renew summonses.

BETWEEN A ROCK AND A HARD PLACE – ISSUING PROCEEDINGS BUT NOT SERVING THEM

The shortening of the limitation period for personal injuries actions, from three years to two years, pursuant to the Civil Liability and Courts Act 2004, has placed plaintiffs in clinical negligence claims in a precarious position.[25] As such claims are excluded from the ambit of the Personal Injuries Assessment Board, this two-year limitation period cannot be extended by the assessment process which otherwise operates for the benefit of the plaintiff in personal injuries litigation. This is particularly anomalous when one considers the typically time-consuming and complicated task of investigating and substantiating where a cause of action arises in terms of both liability and causation in a potential clinical negligence action.

The onerous task of complying with these time constraints is exacerbated by the strict professional obligations imposed upon practising barristers. Rule 5.9 of the Code of Conduct for the Bar of Ireland, provides that barristers 'ought not to settle a pleading claiming professional negligence unless they have satisfied themselves that expert evidence is or will be available to support such claim'. Significantly, this rule permits barristers to settle pleadings claiming professional negligence on the part of a medical practitioner, without expert evidence, in certain circumstances, 'such as when the time for issuing proceedings is in danger of expiring'. As a statutory limitation period is approaching its expiration date, a legal practitioner retained to consider the commencement of a clinical negligence action, should, therefore, invariably choose to issue a protective summons pending receipt of an expert medical report to support the cause of action in terms of liability and causation. While the Code of Conduct for the Bar of Ireland duly authorises the issuing of a protective writ in the absence of expert evidence, it expressly directs barristers to advise instructing solicitors that the protective summons 'should issue without being served until the required expert evidence is available'.

---

[25] Michael Boylan, 'Time Waits for No Man' (2005) 99(8) Law Society Gazette (Oct) 8.

Given the new formulation of Order 8 of the RSC, prudence dictates that legal practitioners acting for plaintiffs in potential clinical negligence actions will try to secure the necessary report from a medical expert in relation to liability and causation, before the one-year period to serve the summons expires. Otherwise, a plaintiff is then subjected to the test prescribed by Order 8 of the RSC when applying to the High Court for a renewal of the summons for a further period of three months so that it can be validly served within this extended period. The recent decision of the Court of Appeal in *Murphy v Health Service Executive* suggests, however, that Order 8 of the RSC allows for a greater latitude for the renewal of a personal injuries summons in clinical negligence litigation where the difficulty of obtaining expert medical evidence in relation to liability and causation inhibits a personal injuries summons from being served within one year from it being issued.

MURPHY V HEALTH SERVICE EXECUTIVE

Facts

On 31 August 2018 the plaintiff issued proceedings against the Health Service Executive (HSE), claiming negligence and breach of duty in the treatment she received at University Hospital Mayo in March 2016. The proceedings were commenced by way of a protective summons, issued on a precautionary basis, so as to minimise the plaintiff's risk of her claim being held to be statute barred. The protective summons stated that as of the date of it being issued, the plaintiff was unable to plead the key elements of her claim in terms of alleged negligence and breach of duty, together with causation arising therefrom, but that the particulars thereof would be adduced upon receipt of medical reports from expert medical practitioners in the relevant field.

The plaintiff was alleging that when she presented to this hospital, she should have undergone a CT scan in order to assess whether she was suffering from internal cranial haemorrhaging. If not, she would then have commenced taking aspirin so as to reduce the likelihood of her suffering from a stroke. She did not undergo this scan, nor was she prescribed aspirin on the day of her admission to this hospital, nor was she referred to the specialist stroke unit therein at this time. She alleged that her condition significantly deteriorated on the day of her admission and that she suffered a progressive stroke on this day which would otherwise have been avoided had she been initially assessed correctly and treated appropriately thereafter.

In order to establish a cause of action, the plaintiff had, therefore, to adduce expert medical evidence in relation to liability and causation respectively as follows:

    (i) she had to procure an opinion from a consultant in accident and emergency medicine that she was neither initially assessed nor treated correctly on the first day of her admission to this hospital (i.e., a liability report) and

(ii) she had to also obtain an opinion from a consultant in stroke medicine that the failure to prescribe aspirin to her in a timely manner led to her suffering from a progressive and otherwise avoidable stroke during this day (i.e., a causation report).

Before the requisite report was received from a consultant in accident and emergency medicine, the one-year time frame to serve the proceedings pursuant to Order 8 of the RSC had elapsed and the personal injuries summons, therefore, expired on 1 September 2019 without being served upon the defendant. On 16 September 2019, a report was received by the plaintiff's solicitors from a consultant in this discipline which conclusively stated that there was negligence and breach of duty in the treatment afforded to the plaintiff on the date of her admission to this hospital. This report also advised that a separate opinion be obtained from a consultant in stroke medicine so that the question of causation, arising from the negligence and breach of duty, as alleged, would be addressed.

On the same day that he received this report, the plaintiff's solicitor contacted a consultant in stroke medicine and sought a report from him. The report from this expert was received on 14 January 2020. As expert evidence was now obtained by the plaintiff's solicitors to establish the claim in terms of both liability and causation, the plaintiff then made an *ex parte* application, pursuant to Order 8 Rule 1(4) of the RSC, to renew the personal injuries summons to the High Court. This application was successfully made to Murphy J on the 3 February 2020 and the summons was renewed for a period of three months. It was duly served upon the defendant 16 days later.

On 6 May 2020 the defendant issued a motion seeking to have this order renewing the personal injuries summons set aside. The defendant submitted that the five-month delay between the expiry of the summons and the renewal application was inordinate and that any order permitting the renewal of the summons would 'unquestionably and irreversibly prejudice the defendant'.[26] The defendant also argued that the suggestion that a delay in obtaining expert medical reports constituted a special circumstance was entirely 'unstateable'.[27]

After the application of the defendant to the High Court was heard before Cross J, he refused to grant it. In his judgment he noted that 'the prohibition on serving professional negligence proceedings until the receipt of verifying reports creates a conflict with the obligations to serve the proceedings within the time specified in the Rules'.[28] He found that the delay in obtaining the required medical reports was both 'justified and reasonable' and the defendant

---

[26] High Court, Outline Written Legal Submissions on behalf of the Defendant, at para 59.
[27] ibid para 36.
[28] *Murphy v Health Service Executive* [2020] IEHC 483 at [34].

had not been subject to any 'specific prejudice' as a result.[29] Consequently, it was concluded that this delay was a sufficient 'special circumstance' to justify the renewal of the summons. The defendant then appealed the High Court decision on the basis that Cross J applied an incorrect interpretation of the test as now prescribed by the amended Order 8 of the RSC. Specifically, the defendant contended on appeal that Cross J failed to apply the two-tier test which had previously been endorsed by the other judges of the High Court in the cases of *Murphy and Cullen*, *Ellahi* and *Downes*.

THE JUDGMENT OF THE COURT OF APPEAL

The Court of Appeal was, therefore, tasked with identifying the circumstances in which the High Court may renew a summons pursuant to the revised provisions of Order 8 of the RSC. In particular, the court had to address the correct interpretation of Order 8 Rule 1(4), that is as to what may constitute 'special circumstances which justify an extension' for the renewal of a summons for three months from the date of such renewal in the context of experts' reports being awaited to determine if a cause of action arose, in terms of both liability and causation, in clinical negligence proceedings.

In respect of the test to be applied for the renewal of an expired summons, as noted earlier, Haughton J, in giving judgment on behalf of the Court of Appeal, emphatically rejected the notion of a two-tier test and thus found the decisions in *Murphy and Cullen*, *Ellahi* and *Downes* to be incorrect statements of law. Following an in-depth examination of the wording of Order 8 Rule 1(4) of the RSC, Haughton J stated that had there been an intention to impose a two-tier test for renewing a summons, the revision of Order 8 'would have done so explicitly'.[30] He also stated that by adopting a two-step interpretation of the rule, the court would effectively be introducing 'words that simply are not there'.[31] As such, the Court of Appeal concluded that the only question that the High Court is required to consider, when faced with an application for the renewal of a summons, is whether there are 'special circumstances' which justify the renewal.

One of the general observations which the Court of Appeal made in relation to the 'special circumstances' test was that it would be 'unwise to lay down any hard and fast rules', as the question of whether special circumstances have arisen will turn on the individual facts of each case.[32] The Court of Appeal did direct, however, that when applying this test, the court should consider whether the renewal of summons is in the interests of justice.[33] This entails

---

[29] ibid [39].
[30] *Murphy v Health Service Executive* [2021] IECA 3, per Haughton J at [59].
[31] ibid.
[32] ibid [70].
[33] ibid [78].

considering any hardship alleged by a defendant and balancing this against the hardship that may be borne by the plaintiff if the renewal of the summons is refused.

Upon applying this test to the facts in *Murphy*, Haughton J chose to adopt a similar approach to that of Cross J in the High Court. In giving judgment, at first instance, Cross J found that the Code of Conduct for the Bar of Ireland expressly prohibited a barrister from settling a personal injuries summons, alleging negligence against a medical practitioner, without sufficient expert evidence to support such a plea. Ultimately, this led Cross J to conclude that the absence of the necessary expert opinion(s) to ground a medical negligence action is a special circumstance justifying, in the absence of any culpable delay, the renewal and extension of time.

In the course of the appeal hearing, the defendant contended that Cross J had erred in making this finding. In particular, the defendant contested his finding that obtaining 'necessary reports' was required prior to service of the summons. In making this argument, the defendant relied upon the judgment of McKechnie J in the decision of the Supreme Court in *Mangan v Dockery & ors*.[34] In that judgment, McKechnie J stated that 'a report is not an essential precondition' to the issuing of proceedings in a medical negligence action and that only 'a reasonable basis must exist' before medical negligence proceedings are issued.[35] This submission was rejected by Haughton J by reference to the professional obligation on legal advisors to obtain appropriate expert opinion before serving proceedings alleging professional negligence. He noted the courts' particular concern that practitioners comply with this duty when engaging in medical negligence litigation, stating that they:

> have consistently decried the issue and service of medical negligence proceedings, which put the competence or reputational integrity of doctors or institutions in issue, unless there is an appropriate/reasonable basis for doing so.[36]

It is unsurprising, therefore, that the Court of Appeal subsequently classified the present claim as being one of the 'vast majority of medical cases' which required the plaintiff's legal advisors to obtain expert reports before bringing an application to renew the summons.[37] Essentially, in upholding the substantive determination of the High Court, the Court of Appeal held that provided a plaintiff's legal representatives 'move with expedition', a delay in receiving the necessary expert medical reports, which are reasonably required to advise upon,

---

[34] [2020] IESC 67.
[35] ibid [97].
[36] *Murphy v Health Service Executive* [2021] IECA 3, per Haughton J at [83].
[37] ibid [86].

and prosecute, a claim, would constitute 'special circumstances' justifying the renewal of the summons under the amended Order 8 of the RSC.[38]

THE UNIQUE POSITION OF CLINICAL NEGLIGENCE LITIGATION

By reason of this judgment of the Court of Appeal, one can reasonably conclude that the failure to serve proceedings in the High Court, within the prescribed one-year time frame, is a practice which enjoys a wider tolerance and justification in the context of clinical negligence litigation, where considerable delays in obtaining expert opinion are commonplace. Legal practitioners acting for plaintiffs in such litigation have to navigate between their professional responsibility to comply with time limits imposed by the Statutes of Limitations and Order 8 of the RSC, on the one hand, and their obligation to only issue and serve proceedings alleging negligence on the part of a medical practitioner when supported by expert evidence, on the other. The facts of *Murphy v Health Service Executive* vividly illustrate the challenges posed by this balancing act. Indeed, the Court of Appeal recognised that the tension between these two duties is 'particularly acute' in medical negligence claims, as they often require the consideration of extensive medical records and the obtaining of professional opinions from numerous experts.[39]

In addition, Haughton J noted that even the task of identifying an appropriate expert, in clinical negligence litigation, who is willing to provide a medical report, can be challenging.[40] In making this statement, Haughton J cited a statement of O'Donnell J made by him in his dissenting judgment in *O'Sullivan v Ireland, The Attorney General & ors* that:

> It is plain that medical negligence cases pose particular difficulties. The two-year limitation period for the commencement of actions is short, given the necessity to obtain expert advice on liability, normally from witnesses with sufficient expertise to provide an authoritative opinion, and who are often based outside the jurisdiction.[41]

Indeed, even the distinction between medical negligence litigation and professional negligence claims generally, was highlighted by Haughton J when he stated that:

> In medical negligence cases in particular it is notoriously difficult to establish liability, and many cases risk foundering on the issue of causation.[42]

---

[38] ibid [93].
[39] ibid [88].
[40] ibid [90].
[41] *O'Sullivan v Ireland, The Attorney General & ors* [2019] IESC 33, per O'Donnell J, [24].
[42] *Murphy v Health Service Executive* [2021] IECA 3, per Haughton J, [87].

On balance, therefore, legal practitioners acting on behalf of claimants in medical negligence proceedings must take the time required to fully substantiate a claim of clinical negligence and breach of duty before serving unwarranted proceedings which could jeopardise the reputation of a medical practitioner and unnecessarily involve that practitioner's professional indemnifiers. It is of note that Haughton J also emphasised in his judgment that there is no means by which a solicitor can ensure that expert medical reports are received from medical professionals, retained to prepare such reports, in a timely manner.[43]

Considering all of these factors in unison, one can confidently infer from this judgment that the Superior Courts will demonstrate a greater willingness to renew an expired personal injuries summons, pursuant to Order 8 Rule 1(4) of the RSC, when the delay in the service of the summons has arisen because an expert medical report was being awaited to establish the claim in terms of liability or causation and when that report was being sought reasonably expeditiously. Having said that, allowing a summons to lapse is an added complication in the prosecution of a medical negligence action, which is, of itself, invariably complex by reason of its very nature. Notwithstanding the assuring nature of this judgment of the Court of Appeal, therefore, the lapse of a personal injuries summons in a medical negligence action is a further complication which any reasonable legal practitioner and that practitioner's indemnifiers will want to see avoided whenever possible.

---

[43] ibid [90].

PART E
PRACTICE AND PROCEDURE

Chapter VIII

FORWARD TO THE PAST: ARE THE CONCEPTS OF HINDSIGHT BIAS, BLIND REVIEWS AND INTER-OBSERVER VARIABILITY NOW ESTABLISHED IN MEDICAL NEGLIGENCE LITIGATION PRACTICE?

Ashling Gallagher and Conor Halpin SC[1]

Introduction

The recent litigation arising from the CervicalCheck screening controversy has shone a light upon the concepts of hindsight bias, blind reviews and inter-observer variability in the evaluation of cytology screening. This chapter examines those concepts and how the courts, both of first instance and appeal, have so far resolved the issues relating to these concepts arising from repeated case management applications and fraught debate amongst plaintiff and defendant legal teams in the course of protracted trials. The issues which have given rise to this controversy have firstly centred upon whether markings on cervical slides, which were placed upon them when they were originally screened by cytoscreeners, should or should not be removed prior to their review by experts engaged by the parties.

Furthermore, the ongoing and central issue is the effect upon the independence of experts' evidence, in reviewing the original screening of these slides, when they have been informed, prior thereto, of the patient to whom the slide relates having been diagnosed with cervical cancer and the results of the subsequent review or auditing of the screening slide after this diagnosis was made. In other words, does an expert have what is termed as 'hindsight bias' when reviewing the original screening of a slide knowing that the patient to whom it relates was subsequently diagnosed with cervical cancer? Alternatively, can an expert be truly independent in reviewing such a slide when he or she knows that after this patient was diagnosed with cancer, the screening of the slide was reviewed, that is the subject of an auditing process, which determined that the

---

[1] Ashling Gallagher prepared this chapter as a final year undergraduate student at the School of Law at Trinity College Dublin. Conor Halpin SC is a member of the Inner Bar of Ireland.

slide should have originally been reported as disclosing an abnormality, when it had originally been reported as showing no such abnormality.

The latter issue was central to the litigation in the case of *Morrissey and anor v Health Service Executive & ors*[2] (High Court) and *Morrissey and anor v Health Service Executive and ors*[3] (Supreme Court) and the former issue has recently been the subject of a decision from the Court of Appeal in *Vivienne Wallace v Health Service Executive and Sonic Healthcare (Ireland) Ltd and MedLab Pathology Ltd and Clinical Pathology Laboratories Incorporated*.[4] We analyse these decisions where relevant to this chapter with a view to determining whether they are likely to continue to arise in cytology litigation and whether either a judicial or a non-judicial roadmap can be established to avoid the constant revisiting of these issues as these cases continue to come before the courts.

The law in this jurisdiction regarding the duty of care in proceedings arising from clinical negligence and, in particular, cancer screening, has recently been clarified by the Supreme Court in the case of *Morrissey and anor v Health Service Executive & ors*.[5] In a single judgment of the Supreme Court, Clarke CJ encapsulates the legal standard of care in a clinical negligence claim as requiring:

> The court to assess whether or not a reasonable professional of the type concerned could have carried out their task in the manner which occurred in the case in question. That overall test requires a court to determine what standard a reasonable professional would apply.[6]

Additionally, Clarke CJ observed that the standard of care in medical negligence cases remains the test in *Dunne (An Infant) v National Maternity Hospital & another* per Finlay CJ.[7] The seminal decision in *Morrissey and anor v Health Service Executive and ors*[8] is an unsurprising reiteration of that standard in cases of alleged professional negligence. It resolves and sets out a clear pathway on multiple issues arising in *CervicalCheck* and cancer screening litigation. Notwithstanding that judgment, however, the contentious issues surrounding blind review, hindsight bias and inter-observer variability unfortunately remain unresolved. It is clear that the Supreme Court was of

---

[2] *Morrissey and Morrissey v Health Service Executive, Quest Diagnostics Incorporated and MedLab Pathology Limited* [2019] IEHC 268.
[3] *Morrissey and Morrissey v Health Service Executive, Quest Diagnostics Incorporated and MedLab Pathology Limited* [2020] IESC 6.
[4] *Vivienne Wallace v Health Service Executive and Sonic Healthcare (Ireland) Ltd and MedLab Pathology Ltd and Clinical Pathology Laboratories Incorporated* [2021] IECA 141.
[5] *Morrissey and Morrissey v Health Service Executive, Quest Diagnostics Incorporated and MedLab Pathology Limited* [2020] IESC 6.
[6] *Morrissey and Morrissey v Health Service Executive, Quest Diagnostics Incorporated and MedLab Pathology Limited* [2020] IESC 6, per Clarke CJ at [16.2].
[7] *Dunne (an Infant) v National Maternity Hospital and Jackson* [1989] IR 90, per Finlay CJ at [109].
[8] *Morrissey and Morrissey v Health Service Executive, Quest Diagnostics Incorporated and MedLab Pathology Limited* [2020] IESC 6.

the view that a judicial pronouncement was not required in its consideration of the appeal issues. Indeed, the recent Court of Appeal decision in *Wallace*[9] supports the judicial view that it is a matter for the court of first instance to consider and decide upon those issues on the basis of the facts and evidential merits of each case.

These issues are of particular importance and relevance when experts are firstly, reviewing prior screening with original cytology screening markings present on the slide and secondly, with the knowledge that the patient concerned has been diagnosed with cancer thereafter. Whether they consider that their subsequent expert opinions, provided for the purpose of litigation, are influenced by these factors, would appear to largely depend on whether an expert is instructed on behalf of a plaintiff or a defendant. In summary and in general terms, it seems to be the case that plaintiffs reject the contention that an expert is influenced by original slide markings and knowledge of a cancer diagnosis, while defendants argue the opposite. Where markings are present, the first of these issues has resulted in pre-trial applications, advanced by defendants, to have the markings removed prior to expert review, with these applications being resisted by plaintiffs. These pre-trial applications by necessity also introduce the additional elements of hindsight bias and inter-observer variability. The issue of whether it is appropriate for the High Court to make pre-trial orders in the absence of hearing evidence, which would presumably be expert evidence on the issue, is also examined in this chapter with reference to the recent Court of Appeal decision in *Wallace*.[10]

It is our view that these concepts have already become well established in cytology screening litigation even though such litigation is in its relative infancy. The recent development of such principles will be explored in the first section by defining the key concepts and particularly those which are controversial. The second part of this chapter will examine their application in recent case law.

Defining controversial concepts

As noted by Craven and Binchy,[11] medical negligence litigation, formerly a rarity, has become a daily feature of life in the Irish courts.[12] The exponential

---

[9] *Vivienne Wallace v Health Service Executive and Sonic Healthcare (Ireland) Ltd and MedLab Pathology Ltd and Clinical Pathology Laboratories Incorporated* [2021] IECA 141.
[10] *Vivienne Wallace v Health Service Executive and Sonic Healthcare (Ireland) Ltd and MedLab Pathology Ltd and Clinical Pathology Laboratories Incorporated* [2021] IECA 141.
[11] Ciarán Craven and William Binchy, *Medical Negligence Litigation: Emerging Issues* (1st edn, First Law 2008).
[12] Ciarán Craven and William Binchy, *Medical Negligence Litigation: Emerging Issues* (1st edn, First Law 2008) at p 1.

growth of litigation has been mirrored by ever-evolving technology and review mechanisms in a similar trajectory, the presentation of which is assisted by expert witnesses who are now routine participants in professional negligence actions, with their function woven into the adversarial fabric of the courtroom.[13] Objectivity and impartiality are of paramount importance when providing an expert opinion and giving sworn evidence before the court. The importance of their role has been further highlighted in the cervical cancer litigation when dealing with the complex issues of a blind review as a response to alleged hindsight bias and the issue of inter-observer variability within the context of the cervical screening programme.

CervicalCheck – The National Cervical Cancer Screening Programme

The National Screening Service, which is now part of the Health Service Executive, encompasses four national population-based programmes being:

- BreastCheck – The National Breast Screening Programme.
- CervicalCheck – The National Cervical Screening Programme.
- BowelScreen – The National Bowel Screening Programme.
- Diabetic RetinaScreen – The National Diabetic Retinal Screening Programme.

The national cervical cancer screening programme is, therefore, known as CervicalCheck. The purpose of CervicalCheck is to carry out an ongoing national cervical screening service for the early diagnosis and primary treatment of cervical cancer in women. The objective is to be achieved by the detection of changes in the cells of the cervix before they become cancerous.[14]

On examination of the cervical cancer screening procedure, one understands better why grey areas exist in cervical cancer testing. Samples are taken usually by a patient's general practitioner. Formerly, a sample was taken by scraping cells from the lining of the cervix, being what was termed as a 'smear' test. The current method is what is termed as 'liquid based cytology' (LBC) testing. This involves material being taken from the cervix by means of a brush which, in turn, is placed in a container holding a liquid solution. The container is then sent, by way of the CervicalCheck programme, to be examined in a laboratory which has been contracted to do so. The laboratories generate a slide based on the liquid from this container and the slide will have a pattern of cells upon it. There must be a sufficient density of cells upon the slide for it to be adequate for testing. Each slide is then screened using scientific methods which are comprised within the practice of cervical cytology, that is the interpretation of whether cells taken from the cervix can be seen to be regular or distorted in their appearance. This involves microscopic examination by a cytology screener of the slide in question.

---

[13] See generally Ormrod, 'Scientific Evidence in Court' [1968] Crim LR 241.
[14] *Morrissey and Morrissey v Health Service Executive, Quest Diagnostics Incorporated and MedLab Pathology Limited* [2019] IEHC 268 at [11].

Screening services, such as cervical cytology testing, are not designed to diagnose cancer. In *Freeney v HSE*,[15] which was a case concerning breast cancer screening and mammography, in the course of her evidence, Dr Given Wilson, consultant radiologist, distinguished between diagnostic processes and screening processes. The former focuses on people who are symptomatic whereas the latter is a safety net used to look for evidence of cancer.[16] A screening test is designed for populations of individuals who do not have any symptoms of disease. It aims to identify those with a risk marker for a disease and ensure early treatment. A screening test is not, therefore, a diagnostic test, the latter being designed for individuals with symptoms of a disease or for those identified with a risk marker to assess whether they have the disease or to follow its progress.

The primary purpose of cervical cancer screening is detection of precancerous changes and prevention of cancers.[17] The tests are screening tests and the results of the tests are graded by the screener using a prescribed grading system. If the test results declare 'no abnormality detected', the patient is usually recommended for a routine repeat examination unless there is something in the patient's clinical history which nonetheless warrants a recommendation of a repeat test at an earlier point than would otherwise routinely be the case. Where the laboratory finds the cells to be abnormal, the referring doctor is informed, leading to an earlier repeat screening or a colposcopy or other treatment. In the event of any ambiguity, the laboratory ought to report the cells as abnormal. No screening is 100% accurate. As a result, there is a greater tolerance for false negatives in screening, as opposed to in a diagnostic setting, before legal liability can arise. Where false negatives arise, the test result is negative although the disease is present. Contrarily, some results can be false positives where the result is positive, that is suggestive of cancer, but then no clinically significant disease is found on further testing.

Cancers developed between screening intervals are known as interval cancers. An interval cervical cancer is defined as

> a primary cervical cancer diagnosed in a woman after a negative screening test, but before the next invitation to screening is due, or within a period equal to a screening interval for a woman who has reached the upper age limit to attend screening.[18]

True interval cancers are those which showed normal or benign features in the previous smear tests. Cervical smear testing has resulted in the early diagnosis of cervical cancer in many women globally enabling those women to avail of

---

[15] *Freeney v Health Service Executive* [2020] IEHC 286.
[16] ibid para 101.
[17] Expert Reference Group, Interval Cancer Report, *CervicalCheck*, at p 5.
[18] International Agency for Research on Cancer, European Guidelines for Quality Assurance in Cervical Cancer Screening, Second Edition, Luxembourg, European Communities, 2008.

life saving treatment. The cervical smear testing programme has been heralded as a vital element of healthcare provided by the Health Service Executive.

SENSITIVITY AND SPECIFICITY IN CANCER SCREENING

The quality of a screening test is described in terms of:

- Sensitivity – how well the screening test shows who truly has a certain disease; and
- Specificity – how well the screening test shows who truly does not have the disease.

The goals of a screening test are to correctly identify everyone who has a certain disease (100% sensitivity) and to correctly identify everyone who does not have the disease (100% specificity).

Sensitivity is the indicator on the ability of screening to find cancer in the detectable preclinical phase. It refers to a test's ability to designate an individual with disease as positive. A highly sensitive test means that there are few false negative results and thus fewer cases of disease are missed. The specificity of a test is its ability to designate an individual who does not have a disease as negative. A highly specific test, therefore, means that there are few false positive results and a corresponding lesser amount of cases of disease being wrongly reported as being present. Radiological screening and histopathology (i.e., the examination of tissue for pathology) are examples of medical testing that benefit from a high degree of specificity, that is accuracy in determining if cancerous changes can be observed in the screening process. Cervical cancer screening and cytology screening (i.e., the examination of cells for pathology) are less definitive and suffer from a lower degree of specificity consequent upon their dependence on human observation of the sample cells, which is, in turn, affected by inter-observer variability.

A perfect test would correctly identify everyone with a disease with no mistakes. There would be no false negatives (when people who have the disease are missed by the test) and no false positives (when healthy people are incorrectly shown to have the disease). No screening test has 100% sensitivity and 100% specificity. There is always a trade-off between these two goals. A test that is very sensitive may pick up even the slightest abnormal finding. This means that while it will miss fewer cases of the disease, it will also mistake some people as having the disease when they do not (false positives). A test that is very specific, on the other hand, may have fewer false positive results but may miss more cases of the disease. The balance between sensitivity and specificity is, therefore, important for all screening.

As one can never achieve, nor be expected to achieve, 100% accuracy in any screening process, abnormalities will be missed which do not amount to negligence or breach of duty. Each particular case has to be analysed so as to truly determine not just if the abnormality existed at the time of the screening, but whether the abnormality was one which, in failing to detect it, by reason of its nature, a clinical breach of duty has occurred.

A screening programme carries out an evaluation of its performance by assessing interval cancers. Interval cancers can be found in between screening tests. They occur in every screening programme. This evaluation is done by way of an audit, for performance review purposes, by analysing the prevalence of interval cancers.

Hindsight bias

The concept of hindsight bias is predicated upon an expert having the knowledge of the diagnosis of a patient having cancer, after the original cancer screening process of that patient failed to detect an abnormality, when that expert sets about determining if there was a breach of duty in the original screening of that patient for cancer. With litigation arising from CervicalCheck, if the LBC slide was reviewed, after the patient was diagnosed with cervical cancer, as part of an audit of the entire screening and reporting process of a laboratory, knowledge of that expert of a change in the interpretation of the slide, following this review process, also gives rise to the suggestion that the expert's independence is undermined by hindsight bias. As Arkes HR succinctly states:

> The hindsight bias manifests in the tendency to exaggerate the extent to which a past event could have been predicted beforehand.[19]

Accordingly, when a screening test is being analysed with the knowledge that the person has been diagnosed subsequently with cancer, the question arises as to whether the review of that test is undermined by this knowledge. The controversial practice of 'blind' reviews has emerged, therefore, in response to hindsight bias by creating various conditions for the review of a screening test without disclosing to the reviewer that the patient in question was subsequently diagnosed with cancer. Findings of clinical negligence and breach of duty are, however, always reached from the perspective of hindsight. Nonetheless, in giving judgment in the High Court in *Morrissey and anor v Health Service Executive and ors*,[20] Cross J noted the potential hazard of hindsight bias in respect of any retrospective review of an LBC test. The adverse effects of hindsight bias were also subsequently alluded to by Hyland J in the case of

---

[19] Arkes HR, 'The Consequences of the Hindsight Bias in Medical Decision Making' (2013) 22(5) Current Directions in Psychological Science 356.
[20] *Morrissey and Morrissey v Health Service Executive, Quest Diagnostics Incorporated and MedLab Pathology Limited* [2019] IEHC 268.

Freeney v Health Service Executive[21] in the context of the evaluation of the interpretation of mammography in the course of screening for breast cancer.

BLIND REVIEW

The objective of a 'blind review' is to reproduce an environment as close as possible, if not even identical, to the original testing conditions. The same screening process takes place again and the screener is not meant to have any knowledge of what occurred in the prior screening process, or, if possible, as to whether there was even a prior screening process. There is significant controversy surrounding the value of blind reviews, how blind reviews should be administered, the effect of hindsight bias in the conduct of a blind review and whether a screener in cytology testing can ever truly be blind or entirely unaware of the prior screening process which is then being reviewed.

The concept of a 'blind review' is a fraught issue, therefore, in medical negligence litigation. Different sources have interpreted the concept in different ways. Commonly, in the context of litigation relating to CervicalCheck, a 'blind review' is thought to be a process where the screener does not know that the liquid-based cytology sample relates to a woman who was subsequently diagnosed with cervical cancer. According to the Expert Reference Group, Interval Cancer Report, CervicalCheck, which was commissioned by the Health Service Executive, when conducting a review of the invasive cancer slides in a 'blinded' fashion, reviewers are unaware of the cancer diagnosis.[22] To enable this blinding to take place, it is contended by those who wish to conduct a 'blind review' that the marking(s) placed upon the slide by the cytoscreener(s) who originally reviewed it must first be removed. The alternative view is that the removal of markings made by a cytoscreener is not justified because the original conditions of the screening process can never be properly replicated and the cytoscreener carrying out the review invariably knows that this is not the first time that the slide in question is being screened.

This issue was argued in *Wallace*[23] where an application was made by Clinical Pathology Laboratories Incorporated in that case and in a number of similar cases, for leave to remove the original markings of the cytoscreeners from the slide, so as to facilitate the conduct by it of a 'blind review'. It was argued that for the reviewing cytoscreeners to be blinded to the interpretation of the side by the original cytoscreeners, the latter's original markings from the slide must first be removed. Noonan J described the position as follows when giving the judgment on behalf of the Court of Appeal in *Wallace*:

---

[21] *Freeney v Health Service Executive* [2020] IEHC 286.
[22] Expert Reference Group, Interval Cancer Report, *CervicalCheck*, at p 26.
[23] *Vivienne Wallace v Health Service Executive and Sonic Healthcare (Ireland) Ltd and MedLab Pathology Ltd and Clinical Pathology Laboratories Incorporated* [2021] IECA 141.

There may be forms of blind review that can be undertaken without removing the markings, but the removal of the markings is an absolute pre-requisite for the form of blind review that Clinical Pathology Laboratories Ltd wishes to have carried out.[24]

Accordingly, the Court of Appeal appeared to tolerate that defendant's expansive view of what a 'blind review' requires. It was based upon the perspective that if a slide to be reviewed has original markings upon it, it is not a true reproduction of what was before the original screener and thereby frustrates the carrying out a truly 'blind' review.

Whereas the argument in support of blind review as the premier method of reproducing the original testing environment is a sound and logical one, there are potential hazards evident in any method of examination after the fact. The hazards of a 'blind review' have been identified and submitted to the Superior Courts on behalf of plaintiffs. One such hazard is that a 'blind review', as envisaged in *Wallace*, leads to an irreversible and arguably unwarranted destruction of physical evidence consequent on the requirement for any markings made by the original cytoscreener(s) being removed from the cytology slide. Once the markings are removed, the slide cannot be returned to its original state, although defendants usually submit that this can be overcome by way of prior digital imaging precisely replicating the condition of the original slide.

INTER-OBSERVER VARIABILITY

Inter-observer variability is the amount of variation between the results obtained by two or more observers examining the same material. The concept of inter-observer variability arises in this context from how different cytology screeners/experts can have a difference of opinion when reporting upon the same LBC slide. It was of continuous relevance in the course of the hearing at first instance of *Morrissey and anor v Health Service Executive and ors*[25] in respect of the original reporting, audit review reporting and subsequent expert reporting that were all intrinsic to the issues arising in that litigation. It should be distinguished from inter-observer variability which is the amount of variation one observer experiences when observing the same material more than once. This did not surface as an issue in the hearing of *Morrissey* as no witness gave evidence of a variation in his or her interpretation of an LBC slide arising from different examinations of it.

Before examining the recent case law in relation to these three concepts of a blind review, hindsight bias and inter-observer variability, it is important to

---

[24] ibid para 31.
[25] *Morrissey and Morrissey v Health Service Executive, Quest Diagnostics Incorporated and MedLab Pathology Limited* [2020] IESC 6.

note that the judgment of Cross J in *Morrissey* is relevant regarding the judicial leeway afforded to screening processes compared to diagnostic processes. The High Court found that there were abnormalities on the LBC slide screened by MedLab Pathology Limited but the abnormalities were not such, particularly when allowing for hindsight bias, upon which this party could be found to have been negligent in failing to detect. Such a finding is particularly significant because it contradicts the polemical and inaccurate rhetoric from some quarters that the Superior Courts demand 'absolute certainty' in the screening process. For instance, the Interval Cancer Report of CervicalCheck, produced by an Expert Reference Group in October 2020, seven months after the decision of the Supreme Court in *Morrissey*, entirely misstated this decision of the Supreme Court by claiming that:

> The Supreme Court ruling of 'absolute confidence' in the *Morrissey* case will inadvertently create the erroneous impression that all cytology must be 100% accurate. This is unachievable.[26]

The Supreme Court actually abandoned the term 'absolute confidence' in that judgment.[27] Furthermore, at page 8 of this report, the assertion is made that:

> since the cytology smear test is prone to significant observer variability, it cannot be considered a diagnostic test, nor can it provide absolute certainty that is rules out precancerous changes.

'Absolute certainty' has never been postulated by any court in this jurisdiction when considering the duty of care to be exercised when conducting a cancer screening service due to the well-accepted premise that screening processes have to be allowed a certain tolerance for false negatives, as clarified by Cross J in *Morrissey*.[28] False negatives and false positives can, therefore, both arise in an entirely non-negligent context because the standard of 'absolute certainty' in the accuracy of cancer screening is neither possible nor the standard of approach of the medical profession itself and, accordingly, it is not the what is expected when the standard of cancer screening falls to be evaluated by the Superior Courts. It is surprising that this report chose to employ the term 'absolute certainty' in making this assertion given that it has not been used in the judgments of the Superior Courts and is inconsistent with the acknowledgement in those judgments that a false negative can arise in a screening test in a non-negligent manner.

---

[26] Expert Reference Group, Interval Cancer Report, CervicalCheck, at p 43.
[27] This is explained in greater detail in the first chapter in this text entitled 'Has the duty of care for medical professionals been changed by the introduction of the test of 'the standard of approach' into the duty of care? by Julia Best and Oisín Quinn SC at p 3.
[28] *Morrissey and Morrissey v Health Service Executive, Quest Diagnostics Incorporated and MedLab Pathology Limited* [2019] IEHC 268.

Recent developments in case law

The purpose of the second part of this chapter is to explore the emergence of the 'blind review' in response to alleged hindsight bias of expert evidence and the issue of inter-observer variability in the evidence of experts in cancer screening arising from recent case law in this jurisdiction relating to cervical cancer screening. Prior to assessing this case law, one must begin by reviewing a protocol which has arisen for the examination of LBC slides between experts who are engaged by the parties who are involved in litigation which has arisen from CervicalCheck.

In December 2018, in the context of CervicalCheck litigation, which was then firmly established, in an attempt to deal with the controversial issues of the transfer of slides between the relevant parties and their respective experts, Cross J heard submissions from all parties for the purpose of devising a protocol that would apply in these situations. This process led to the formulation of a protocol entitled 'Final Protocol 25 January 2019' (the Protocol).

The Protocol establishes a process in which slides are to be made available to plaintiffs and, after examination, returned to the relevant laboratory. Furthermore, the Protocol provides for digital imaging of the slides prior to discharge. Clause 4 of the Protocol provides as follows:

> 4. Any existing markings, save for the cancer audit markings, are not to be removed or any new markings applied to the slide(s) without the prior approval of the court. Unless otherwise agreed between the parties in writing, the removal of the cancer audit markings can only occur following the review of the slide by the expert engaged by the requesting patient or legal representative of the patient or deceased patient and on the basis that, any removal of cancer audit markings only be undertaken by the relevant laboratory contracted to the HSE/NSS. It is acknowledged by the HSE/NSS that if a patient or their representative requests the removal of such markings, the HSE/NSS will procure their removal by the contracted laboratory as soon as practicable. Prior to the removal of any such markings, the laboratory in question will be required to image the slide(s) in accordance with paragraph 8 below.[29]

As the clause asserts, the cancer audit markings on any given slide may be removed without a court order subject to the terms specified therein. These are the marking that are placed on a slide in the course of it being reviewed as part of an audit process, after the patient in question has been diagnosed with cervical cancer. On the other hand, any other markings, such as the markings made by the cytoscreeners who originally screened it in the course of their employment with the laboratory in question, may not be removed save by order of the High Court.

---

[29] Final Protocol, 25 January 2019, at clause 4.

***Morrissey and Morrissey v Health Service Executive, Quest Diagnostics Incorporated and MedLab Pathology Limited* [2019] IEHC 268 (The High Court, Cross J, 3 May 2019)**

In the seminal case of *Morrissey and Morrissey v Health Service Executive, Quest Diagnostics Incorporated and MedLab Pathology Limited*,[30] Cross J had to consider the issue of blind reviews generally and in the context of the 'Guidelines for the Review of GYN Cytology Samples' (the Guidelines) issued by the American Society of Cytopathology. The Guidelines advised their members of an obligation in all cases for a 'blind review' as a prescriptive measure to counteract litigation. Moreover, in the absence of a 'blind review', the Guidelines stated that it was erroneous to impute any negligence to the screening done by a cytoscreener. In the United States, plaintiffs had argued in the courts that the Guidelines were an attempt to limit litigation and provide a robust defence for screeners accused of negligence and breach of duty in the screening process. Specifically, the Guidelines were criticised and rejected in the US Court of Appeals for the Eleventh Circuit in the case of *Adams v Laboratory Corporation of America*.[31]

In *Morrissey*,[32] Cross J held that the Guidelines do not set a legal standard that can be endorsed by the High Court in this jurisdiction. He said:

> I do not accept these guidelines as in any way setting a legal standard for the Courts to operate.[33]

When hearing this case at first instance, which proceeded over 36 trial days (separate to other days relating to interlocutory applications), Cross J examined evidence regarding blind review testing. In this context, the second of the Guidelines was particularly germane. It provides that:

> 2. Equivocal interpretive categories including atypical squamous cells (ASC) and atypical glandular cells (AGC) have poor inter- and intra-observer reproducibility. Therefore, most cases of ASC and AGC do not represent consistently identifiable abnormalities and a reasonable basis for allegations of practice below a reasonably prudent practitioner standard of care.

Moreover, one of the expert witnesses called to give evidence on behalf of Quest Diagnostics Incorporated referred to the high degree of inter-observer variability in respect of ASCUS and AGUS categories and stated that the categories are not used in the United States for proficiency audits or examinations of cytoscreeners. The two experts in cytoscreening, who were

---

[30] ibid.
[31] *Adams v Laboratory Corporation of America* No 13-10425 (11th Cir 2014).
[32] *Morrissey and Morrissey v Health Service Executive, Quest Diagnostics Incorporated and MedLab Pathology Limited* [2019] IEHC 268.
[33] ibid para 58.

called to give evidence on behalf of the plaintiff's case, did not conduct 'blind reviews' upon the slides in question and arrived at their conclusions based on their expertise and their analysis of each particular slide.

The judgment of Cross J is neutral in relation to the legitimacy and value of 'blind reviews'. The judgment of the Supreme Court, on appeal, does not alter the position. Both of the laboratories adduced evidence from 'blind reviews' which they conducted to suggest that neither of their respective slides was screened in a negligent manner. One laboratory (MedLab Pathology Limited) was successful with this argument and the other (Quest Diagnostics Incorporated) was unsuccessful. The former was found to be negligent in relation to the screening of the slide it reviewed for a different reason, namely that the slide did not have an adequate amount of cells to be tested and should not, therefore, have been screened and reported as showing no abnormality. Accordingly, the Superior Courts, when considering evidence relating to 'blind reviews', hindsight bias and inter-observer variability in the future, will have regard to all of the expert evidence in relation to these issues which is adduced at the trial and objectively assess that evidence prior to reaching a determination.

Morrissey and Morrissey v Health Service Executive, Quest Diagnostics Incorporated (Quest) *and MedLab Pathology Limited* (MedLab) [2020] IESC 6 (The Supreme Court, Clarke CJ, 19 March 2020)

The defendants sought leave to appeal directly to the Supreme Court and this leave was granted by that court. Essentially, the Supreme Court was confronted with five sets of legal issues to be determined. For the purposes of this chapter, we are concerned with the second and third legal issues which centred upon the contention made by both Quest and MedLab that the trial judge, Cross J, failed to engage properly with certain aspects of evidence in the case and that he consequently delivering an insufficiently reasoned judgment.

Specifically, Quest argued that there was a failure to engage with the evidence adduced of the blind review co-ordinated by the expert cytotechnologist, Mr Tim Feit, of an LBC slide of 2009. The blind review supposedly replicated the original screening conditions insofar as possible in order to assess how a reasonably competent cytoscreener would interpret a slide.

The procedure and result of the blind review of the 2009 slide, as recorded in the judgment of Cross J[34] is as follows:

> The 2009 slide was reviewed by eight cytoscreeners alongside nine other slides. The screeners were unaware of which slide was of interest, nor by who they were instructed. Six out of eight screeners concluded

---
[34] *Morrissey and Morrissey v Health Service Executive, Quest Diagnostics Incorporated and MedLab Pathology Limited* [2020] IESC 6.

that the 2009 slide was negative, and two screeners made findings of abnormalities.[35]

Quest acknowledged the legitimacy of Cross J's engagement with the hazards associated with blind reviews in general. Yet, the trial judge was said not to have engaged with the methodology or results of Quest's blind review. Moreover, the trial judge was alleged not to have explained how the results of the blind review could be consistent with his finding of negligence on the part of Quest in its screening of the slide in question. As a result, Quest submitted that the trial judge's approach to the blind review was flawed. Furthermore, it was submitted on behalf of Quest that the trial judge expressly refused to consider the evidence of Professor Roese, an expert in the concept of hindsight bias, thus failing to appreciate the need to mitigate hindsight bias in cytology review.

In response to this defendant's submission regarding the blind review and hindsight bias, counsel for the plaintiffs submitted that based on the evidence adduced, the trial judge was entitled to formulate his assessment of the appropriate weight to be given to the expert evidence provided by this defendant's expert witnesses.

Ultimately, the Supreme Court upheld the evidential findings of Cross J and his preference for the evidence given by the plaintiff's expert witnesses in relation to the screening of the slide of 2009. This meant that the relevant evidential findings of the High Court, which favoured expert evidence in relation to cytology screening which had no recourse to a blind review, were not overturned by the Supreme Court. Similarly, the rejection by the High Court of the criticism that their evidence was undermined by hindsight bias, was also not disturbed by the Supreme Court.

Vivienne Wallace v Health Service Executive and Sonic Healthcare (Ireland) Ltd and MedLab Pathology Limited and Clinical Pathology Laboratories Incorporated [2021] IECA 141 (*Wallace*)

The recent Court of Appeal decision in *Wallace* addresses the issue of whether the original markings of a cytotechnologist can be removed so as to facilitate a 'blind review' of a cervical cytology slide. An application for leave to do so, made on behalf of Clinical Pathology Laboratories Incorporated (CPL) in relation to seven cases which it was defending, was initially rejected by Cross J in the High Court on 19 January 2021. This refusal of the High Court to grant this permission was then the subject of an appeal hearing before the Court of Appeal. At that point, six of these cases remained alive, with one having since been settled, and *Wallace* was treated as the lead case in the determination of this appeal.

---

[35] ibid para 8.5.

The judgment of the Court of Appeal was given by Noonan J and was delivered on 11 May 2021.

Noonan J highlighted in this judgment that CPL wished to conduct blind reviews to eliminate the possibility of hindsight bias by experts when examining the plaintiff's slides. Counsel for the plaintiffs opposed the removal of markings to facilitate these blind reviews as this removal would result in an eradication of critically important original evidence. CPL submitted that there could be no specific prejudice to these plaintiffs by removing the markings on the relevant slides. It claimed that digital imaging of the slide would be undertaken, creating a permanent record of all markings on the slide prior to removal. It was not contested on behalf of these plaintiffs that this permanent record would be in any way deficient or compromised in terms of its evidential value when compared with the original slides before these markings, placed upon them by the cytoscreeners who first screened the slides, had been removed.

Considerable debate ensued in the course of this appeal hearing as to the interpretation of the Protocol. The Court of Appeal was not persuaded by the argument that the Protocol should be regarded as a contractual document.[36] Neither should it be applied in the same way as one would apply the provisions of a statute. The Court of Appeal held that the closest equivalent to it is that of a practice direction or a case management direction. More specifically, the objective of the Protocol is to better manage and regulate complex multi-party litigation on a large scale.[37] Accordingly, the judgment given by Noonan J conveys that an appeal court will be hesitant to interfere with a case management order made by a court of first instance.

The Court of Appeal did not uphold the reasoning of Cross J, at first instance, which had endorsed the submission of counsel for the plaintiff that CPL must provide 'special and exceptional' circumstances before an order pursuant to clause 4 of the Protocol could be made. Noonan J stated:

> I am not persuaded that there is any warrant for implying into the Protocol a requirement for a party to demonstrate special or exceptional circumstances before an order pursuant to Clause 4 can be made, as the trial judge held.[38]

The Court of Appeal held that a blind review order may be granted if an applicant produces appropriate admissible evidence and if the High Court is satisfied, following a balancing exercise, that the order would not specifically prejudice the plaintiff. At paragraphs 29 and 30 of his judgment, Noonan J

---

[36] *Vivienne Wallace v Health Service Executive and Sonic Healthcare (Ireland) Ltd and MedLab Pathology Ltd and Clinical Pathology Laboratories Incorporated* [2021] IECA 141 per Noonan J, para 21.
[37] ibid.
[38] ibid para 25.

established the test to be applied when considering an application to remove the original markings from a slide. There are two specific limbs to the test in determining whether the threshold has been reached for such an application to be successful. Firstly, CPL must prove that without an order granting the removal of the markings for the purposes of a blind review, it will suffer a 'litigious disadvantage' resulting in a real risk of prejudice. Secondly, the court must consider if there are any 'countervailing circumstances that militate against the making of the order', specifically taking into consideration 'any demonstrable prejudice to the plaintiff', whether actual or apprehended. As a result, the court is required to strike a balance in the interest of justice between the parties.

The Court of Appeal held that CPL failed to provide satisfactory evidence for its application to be successful on this occasion. It had only provided an affidavit from a solicitor in support of the application. Accordingly, the Court of Appeal held that the appropriate order to be made was to remit the application to the High Court, providing an opportunity for the High Court to reconsider the matter, in light of additional evidence that the parties may wish to adduce.

Vivienne Wallace v Health Service Executive, MedLab Pathology Limited, Sonic Healthcare (Ireland) Limited and Clinical Pathology Laboratories Incorporated [2021] IEHC 681 (The High Court, Judgment of Reynolds J, delivered on 26 October 2021)

When this issue was then remitted for further hearing before the High Court, it came before Reynolds J, who delivered a judgment on 26 October 2021. The renewed application brought by CPL sought the following relief:

> An Order granting liberty to remove all markings from the slide in respect of the smear test taken on the 14 September 2010 numbered ZA322603 in accordance with paragraph 4 of the Final Protocol of the 25 January 2019.[39]

It was submitted on its behalf that such relief was necessary to complete a blind review of the slide in question. CPL relied on the expert evidence of Ms Alison Cropper, a biomedical scientist and an expert in cytology screening, placed before the court by way of affidavit. Ms Cropper highlighted the significant risk of hindsight bias when a slide is being reviewed by a cytologist who has knowledge that the patient in question has been subsequently diagnosed with invasive cervical cancer.[40] It was submitted, as a matter of inevitably, that the expert cytologist reviewing the slide, with the markings of the original cytoscreeners thereon, is expected to find abnormalities in the slide. In other words, given that the original screening exercise is not replicated, hindsight

---

[39] *Wallace v Health Service Executive, MedLab Pathology Limited, Sonic Healthcare (Ireland) Limited and Clinical Pathology Laboratories Incorporated* [2021] IEHC 681, para 1.
[40] ibid, Reynolds J, para 28.

bias will taint the review. Ms Cropper noted at paragraph 10 of her affidavit, sworn on 14 July 2021, that:

> Reviewing a marked slide creates hindsight bias and is entirely different from screening an unmarked slide.[41]

Accordingly, Ms Cropper asserted that the only way to avoid hindsight bias is to have the slide reviewed in precisely the same condition as it was originally reviewed by the cytoscreener in 2010, absent of all markings. Furthermore, the solicitor acting for CPL also stated on affidavit that if the trial proceeded and CPL was not granted permission to remove the markings from the slide, it would be significantly prejudiced in the presentation of its defence.[42]

In giving judgment, Reynolds J accepted that CPL had established a real risk of being put at a litigious disadvantage should the application be refused. Being denied the opportunity to remove the markings from the slide would undermine the ability of CPL to replicate the original screening conditions resulting in the inherent risk of hindsight bias. Reynolds J was satisfied that there would be a real risk that the defence of CPL may be prejudiced if the application was not granted. Moreover, when considering compelling countervailing circumstances, Reynolds J was not satisfied that granting the relief sought would prejudice the plaintiff, particularly as there was no evidence to suggest that the digital photography of the slide, prior to the removal of the original markings thereon, would be evidentially compromised when compared to this slide without these marking removed therefrom. As a result, Reynolds J acceded to the application granting liberty to remove the markings from the slide for the purposes of conducting a blind review.[43]

Conclusion

The litigation which has arisen since 2018 in relation to CervicalCheck is characterised by an abundance of expert evidence, truncated proceedings and ambiguous grey areas. The Supreme Court decision in *Morrissey and anor v Health Service Executive and ors*[44] has established a clear statement of various legal principles to be applied to cervical cancer screening and to medical negligence litigation in general, thereby providing order to various areas of uncertainty.

Amidst the progression of this litigation, technology for cervical cancer screening is advancing. There is a correlation between more definitive testing

---

[41] ibid para 28.
[42] ibid para 30.
[43] ibid para 37.
[44] *Morrissey and Morrissey v Health Service Executive, Quest Diagnostics Incorporated and MedLab Pathology Limited* [2020] IESC 6.

and a higher degree of specificity. As a result, we can expect more definitive expert evidence being forthcoming as this litigation continues to unfold in the Superior Courts. In the meantime, the emergence of the process of blind reviews may bring some clarity to the contentious area of review of cervical cancer screening. The judgments of the Court of the Appeal and of Reynolds J in *Wallace* have confirmed the entitlement of the parties involved in this litigation to conduct blind reviews in anticipation of the hearing of these actions. The Superior Courts have now recognised the entitlement of the parties to remove original markings from a slide in order to conduct a blind review.

The issue of hindsight bias looks set to remain as an issue in these cases. One can anticipate that experts will continue to be asked to address their knowledge of a patient's diagnosis with cancer and, where applicable, of subsequent audit results, at the time that they have reviewed a contested slide. This will continue at least until the Superior Courts decide on the validity of such a proposition. Both the concept of hindsight bias and the process of blind reviews are objective issues that have general applicability to all cervical cancer screening cases. They are capable of judicial consideration and determination having heard expert evidence. A definite judgment from the Superior Courts in relation to the status of both would be a welcome development in the future. Separately, the issue of inter-observer variability appears to be incapable of general consideration as it is a subjective and intrinsic aspect of cytology screening. It is inevitable, therefore, that it will remain a key issue in these cases.

Difficult and complex as these concepts are, ultimately the Superior Courts' consideration of them remains an objective process having regard to the factual and expert evidence adduced at the trial of the action, tested against the six principles that define the duty of care as enunciated by Finlay CJ in *Dunne v National Maternity Hospital and another*.[45] This will remain so, although the judicial task of addressing the respective legitimacy of hindsight bias and the validity of blind reviews may become more streamlined in the future following further judicial pronouncements upon both.

---

[45] *Dunne (An Infant) v National Maternity Hospital and Jackson* [1989] IR 91.

CHAPTER IX

OPEN DISCLOSURE IN IRELAND: HOW WILL THE PROPOSED LEGISLATION IMPACT UPON MEDICAL PRACTITIONERS, PATIENTS AND MEDICAL NEGLIGENCE LITIGATION?

Sadhbh Brennan and Declan Buckley SC[1]

INTRODUCTION

The law in relation to open disclosure impacts on the relationship between medical practitioners and their patients. It dictates how and when disclosures and effective apologies should be delivered to patients, in circumstances where legal proceedings are a possibility. Traditionally, there have been difficulties in medical practitioners admitting to errors in this context. Recent and forthcoming legal reforms in this area, however, may bring about significant benefits for stakeholders – the medical practitioner whose actions or omissions brought about the notifiable event and the patient who has suffered as a consequence.

This chapter considers the objectives of open disclosure, it tracks the legislative developments which have occurred and which are still to occur and seeks to set out the merits and pitfalls of past practice and of recent and future reforms. Developments in this area are to be welcomed, particularly in light of major events which have occurred in recent times such as the CervicalCheck controversy. There will still, however, be major challenges in terms of the utilisation of the legislation in some instances, for example, the procedural requirements associated with the making of open disclosures may create practical difficulties, while the mandatory nature of the system provided for in the proposed legislation may result in some disclosures lacking sincerity.

---

[1] Sadhbh Brennan prepared this chapter having recently graduated with an LL.B degree from the School of Law at Trinity College Dublin. Declan Buckley SC is a member of the Inner Bar of Ireland.

Open disclosure – what and why

'To err is human, and human error is ubiquitous and inevitable, but so too is reluctance to confess error'.[2] The concept of open disclosure is founded on the idea that where medical error occurs, the patient, the practitioner and the entire healthcare system benefits from this error being disclosed to the relevant parties along with an apology and a record taken of the error. This concept seeks to create a culture of accountability and allows, therefore, practitioners to learn from their mistakes and the mistakes of others, while patients benefit from learning about adverse events sooner rather than later, and directly from the source. This in turn can increase trust and transparency in the health system.

Open disclosure policy was brought into the public focus in Ireland when the CervicalCheck controversy broke in 2018, and again more recently following the judgments in *Morrissey and anor v Health Service Executive and ors*.[3] It will be recalled that in *Morrissey* there was held to be a delay in communicating the outcome of an audit into the reporting of the first plaintiff's smear samples which prompted the then Taoiseach, Leo Varadkar TD, to state during a Dáil debate:

> There is no information about a patient that the patient should not know. No patient should ever feel stonewalled by the system. We should never fail to act out of fear of litigation or recrimination even if those fears are real.[4]

The controversy underlined the desirability of open disclosure within the health system with observations made during the ensuing Dáil debate that 'the introduction of mandatory open disclosure is a necessary and immediate step in rebuilding confidence in the healthcare service'.[5]

Open disclosure – a background

'It may surprise many that medical error accounts annually for more deaths than motor vehicle accidents, breast cancer or AIDS'.[6] Each profession has different attitudes, cultures and approaches to the making of a mistake or error.

---

[2] Marianne Paget, *The Unity of Mistakes: A Phenomenological Interpretation of Medical Work* (Philadelphia: Temple University Press 1988) at p 59.
[3] *Morrissey & anor v Health Service Executive & ors* [2019] IEHC 268. See also the judgment of the Supreme Court [2020] IESC 6.
[4] Dáil Debate 22 October 2019 Vol 988 No. 22 Leo Varadkar https://www.oireachtas.ie/en/debates/debate/dail/2019-10-22/5/.
[5] Dáil Debate 15 May 2018 Vol 969 No.1 Deputy Louise O'Reilly https://www.oireachtas.ie/en/debates/debate/dail/2018-05-15/34/.
[6] See L Kohn, J Corrigan and M Donaldson (eds), *To Err is Human: Building a Safer Health System* (Washington: National Academy Press 1999) at 1.

Apologising in a professional environment can be difficult: there is a stigma related to an apology that can be traced back to feelings of guilt and shame associated with the making of an error or mistake in the workplace. As David Hilfiker observed, the traditional culture of medicine promoted the highly unrealistic idea of an 'error-free practice'.[7]

The medical profession has been described as having a culture whereby 'mistakes have been neutralised, rationalised and even some-times trivialised'.[8] This fatalistic attitude is interconnected with the very nature of practising medicine – a profession where risk and fatality is inevitable.[9] It has been stated that '[p]ublic conceptions of doctors have also contributed to this unrealistic pursuit of human perfectibility; after all, we prefer to envisage an error-free rather than error-prone physician'.[10] As such, patient expectations can also contribute to this perception.

The desirability of shifting emphasis away from blame centric reviews of adverse events towards a more measured and instructive review of the event is at the heart of the concept of open disclosure. The aviation industry traditionally employs 'black box thinking' whereby every error is recorded and investigated to ensure that the cause of the error is known, and that a similar error does not occur in the future. Open disclosure within the aviation industry has been used and portrayed as a tool to combat errors using a system-based approach, as opposed to facilitating the levelling of blame on an individual level. The aim of open disclosure within the healthcare system is the same in that it is hoped to foster an environment whereby physicians can acknowledge error without fear of personal repercussions.

THE SPECTRUM OF APOLOGY AND OPEN DISCLOSURE LAWS

An overview of disclosure and apology laws identifies three similar but distinct mechanisms being apology laws, open disclosure and the duty of candour. In order to fully understand the effects of mandatory open disclosure, it is necessary to look at the full spectrum of laws in this area and to contrast the positives and negatives of each code.

Apology laws are the 'mildest' form of law, merely allowing that an apology made by certain healthcare practitioners cannot be used as evidence to establish proof of negligence at a tribunal or in a court. Such apology laws can

---

[7] David Hilfiker 'Facing Our Mistakes' (1984) 310 New Eng J Med 118.
[8] Oliver Quick, 'Outing medical errors: questions of trust and responsibility' (2006) 14 Med L Rev pp 22–43 at 28. This must, however, be looked at relatively: Quick commented that a bad pilot is easier to spot than a doctor making errors on singular patients.
[9] ibid.
[10] ibid 29. D Hilfiker (note 6) at 121 states that admitting and apologising for mistakes does not fit into the patient–physician relationship.

also sometimes provide protection from a refusal by an insurer to indemnify under an insurance policy where an apology has been made to a patient. Open disclosure laws can achieve more than apology laws. Patients can be provided with an apology, but also with 'accessible, frank and comprehensive information as to why and how treatment went wrong'.[11] It goes beyond just an apology: it is informational. If the disclosure is made in accordance with the legislation, it will generally not be admissible as evidence to prove negligence or wrongdoing. Irvine P, the former President of the High Court, states that '[o]ne of the major limitations of disclosure laws is the fact that the disclosure protected is voluntary and the decision as to whether or not to make any disclosure is left to the healthcare provider'.[12] Finally, there are duty of candour laws, which are similar to open disclosure, but with the distinction that disclosure is compulsory from the practitioner or the hospital to the patient when certain events take place. Duty of candour laws can also often provide for the mandatory reporting of the occurrence of such events to a regulator with oversight.

The laws which are currently in place in Ireland[13] are voluntary open disclosure laws, although there has been a move towards reforming the law to make open disclosure mandatory, which would bring the law more in line with duty of candour laws. The concept of a duty of candour is not an unfamiliar concept to medical practitioners as can be seen in the Medical Council's *Guide to Professional Conduct and Ethics*[14] which provides for a duty to support and promote open disclosure and a culture of candour and acknowledges that patients and their families are entitled to honest, open and prompt communication about adverse events.

Irvine P has observed that legislators started with an apology law, assuming that if they could stop the negative legal consequences of making an apology or disclosure to patients, practitioners would be more likely to apologise to patients.[15] Over time, it has become apparent, however, that these laws do not go far enough to foster transparency and to engage sufficiently with patients. In particular, in Ireland, the CervicalCheck controversy has prompted further discussion and proposals of new legislation[16] introducing more robust disclosure laws to reinforce public confidence in the healthcare system.

---

[11] Ms Justice Mary Irvine, President of the High Court and Laurenz Boss, 'Apologies, Disclosure and the Duty of Candour: A Discussion' (2019) 25(2) MLJI 69–74 at 69.
[12] ibid.
[13] The Civil Liability (Amendment) Act 2017 and the Civil Liability (Open Disclosure) (Prescribed Statements) Regulations 2018, SI 237/2018.
[14] Medical Council, *Guide to Professional Conduct and Ethics for Registered Medical Practitioners* (8th edn 2016) para 67, at p 43.
[15] See note 11 above, at 71.
[16] Patient Safety (Notifiable Patient Safety Incidents) Bill 2019.

THE CIVIL LIABILITY (AMENDMENT) ACT 2017 AND THE CIVIL LIABILITY (OPEN DISCLOSURE) (PRESCRIBED STATEMENTS) REGULATIONS 2018

The Civil Liability (Amendment) Act 2017 and the Civil Liability (Open Disclosure) (Prescribed Statements) Regulations 2018[17] set out the current law relating to open disclosure of an adverse event or 'patient safety incident'. Part 4 of the 2017 Act was commenced on 22 September 2018, which placed open disclosure on a legislative footing. Part 4 of the Act of 2017 provides for open disclosure and an apology to be made in relation to *patient safety incidents* as defined in s 8. Without prejudice to other provisions in the Act, s 10 of the 2017 Act provides that this open disclosure and an apology made at an open disclosure meeting shall not constitute an express or implied admission of fault or liability and shall not be admissible as evidence of fault or liability in medical negligence proceedings arising from the consequences of the patient safety incident. The section also provides that such an apology or open disclosure in accordance with the Act shall not invalidate or affect the cover provided by an insurance policy.

This provision sought to encourage open disclosure and the making of apologies to provide some legal protection to the medical practitioners by preventing the use of such statements in litigation. This protection does not, however, extend to any statements or communications made outside the formal open disclosure meeting. Section 16 of the Act outlines the meaning of an *open disclosure meeting*. The Civil Liability (Open Disclosure) (Prescribed Statements) Regulations 2018 outline the prescribed statements required to be provided in the open disclosure process.

The 2017 Act relates to voluntary open disclosure but in the wake of the CervicalCheck controversy in particular, reform has been urged to make open disclosure a mandatory practice. In the inquiry carried out by Professor Gabriel Scally into the CervicalCheck screening programme, his final report was interpreted as being critical of the open disclosure policy and practice in place as he believed there was no compelling requirement for clinicians to disclose adverse events and that instead disclosure had been left to their personal and professional judgment.[18] In June 2018, the Government established an expert group to give consideration to open disclosure. In the report, *Expert Group Report to Review the Law of Torts and the Current Systems for the Management of Clinical Negligence Claims*, dated 17 January 2020, which was published on 16 December 2020, this expert group noted that the relevant sections of the 2017 Act are not phrased in a mandatory way and stated that '[t]his is unsatisfactory'.[19]

---

[17] SI 237/2018.
[18] G Scally, *Scoping Inquiry into the CervicalCheck Screening Programme* (2018), available at https://www.gov.ie/en/publication/aa6159-dr-gabriel-scallys-scoping-inquiry-into-cervicalcheck/.
[19] *Expert Group Report to Review the Law of Torts and the Current Systems for the Management of Clinical Negligence Claims* dated 17 January 2020, at page 10. This

Proposed law reform: mandatory open disclosure

The proposed reform to the law, the Patient Safety (Notifiable Patient Safety Incidents) Bill 2019,[20] introduces a requirement for *mandatory* open disclosure of specific serious patient safety incidents, known as notifiable patient safety incidents, amongst other changes. Section 2 of the Bill provides that a 'notifiable incident' is an incident as specified in Schedule 1 to the Bill or as specified in regulations made under s 8 and the list can therefore be updated with other specified incidents. The incidents specified in Schedule 1 are those that cause death and the narrow list includes wrong site surgery, wrong patient surgery, wrong procedure, unintended retention of a foreign object in a patient, maternal and perinatal death and death due to surgical error, medical procedure or anaesthesia, medication error, blood transfusion amongst others. As these are notifiable incidents that may cause death they are obviously the most serious and extreme of patient safety incidents. Any updating to the list in regulations made under s 8 must meet a certain threshold of criteria in order to be designated as a notifiable incident requiring mandatory disclosure.

Madden and Tumelty have commented that '[g]iven the political imperative behind the legislation in Ireland, it is surprising that the definition of a "notifiable incident" in the 2019 Bill is relatively narrow'.[21] In their article considering the 2019 Bill, Madden and Tumelty also doubt whether certain scenarios under cancer screening programmes such as the diagnosis of an interval cancer would fall within the scope of a notifiable incident having regard to the criteria to be met.[22]

Section 5 of the Bill provides for the mandatory obligation to make an open disclosure of a notifiable incident. This proposed Bill would bring the law in Ireland more in line with a duty of candour as seen in England under the Health and Social Care Act (Regulated Activities) Regulations 2014 in that there will be an obligation on health service providers and practitioners to be transparent with patients and their families when there has been such an incident. The purpose of this Bill is to 'support a culture of patient safety, quality and learning in the delivery of health services, as well as openness, transparency and compassion'.[23] The Bill would ensure that where such an incident arises, the patient and their family are met with a system which is structured and consistent in providing them with open disclosure. The mandatory disclosure

---

report can be accessed at https://www.gov.ie/en/publication/ffb23-expert-group-report-to-review-the-law-of-torts-and-the-current-systems-for-the-management-of-clinical-negligence-claims/.

[20] The Patient Safety (Notifiable Patient Safety Incidents) Bill 2019, No 100 of 2019 initiated on 5 December 2019.
[21] Deirdre Madden and Mary-Elizabeth Tumelty, 'Open Disclosure of Patient Safety Incidents: Legislative Developments in Ireland' (2019) 25(2) MLJI 76–89 at 80.
[22] ibid.
[23] Summary Guide to the Patient Safety (Notifiable Patient Safety Incidents) Bill 2019 at p 3.

and notification systems will apply to both public and private health services, which is a welcome change from the current law whereby private hospitals, clinics and nursing homes under the regulatory remit of HIQA (the Health Information and Quality Authority) were excluded.

The proposed Bill is lengthy and technical, laying down narrow restrictions of the required procedure as to how and when[24] open disclosures can be made, what form they can take and the information that can be given within them. Similar to the Act of 2017, s 10 of the 2019 Bill provides that information provided or an apology made at a notifiable incident disclosure meeting shall not constitute an express or implied admission of fault or liability and shall not be admissible as evidence of fault or liability in a court in relation to that notifiable incident or a clinical negligence action. If the open disclosure is not provided under the conditions and procedure as set out in the Act, this legal protection cannot be afforded to the apology or information given to the patient, which may then be used as evidence of fault or liability against the practitioner. Part 7 of the 2019 Bill outlines the sanctions for non-compliance with the mandatory duty to disclose notifiable incidents.

The momentum of the proposed Bill appears to have stalled as the Oireachtas has not updated the status of the progression of this Bill since 28 July 2020 where it has remained before Dáil Eireann, Third Stage.[25] The realistic effects of the proposed mandatory open disclosure law as provided for in the 2019 Bill are considered in further detail below.

THE REALISTIC EFFECTS

Mandatory open disclosure: is it the correct approach?

There are arguments for and against mandatory disclosure laws, as opposed to voluntary disclosure laws. This section will analyse both sides of the argument to consider the advantages and disadvantages of the proposed reform and whether such apology and disclosure laws are effective. The arguments against mandatory disclosure are that it will foster an environment where disclosure is motivated by self-protection, and that this self-serving form of open disclosure will only report major issues, with the detail of information surrounding the error being lost.[26] It has also been argued that a voluntary system 'facilitates a gradual process'[27] which practitioners can adapt to in a more supportive

---

[24] Section 14 of the proposed Patient Safety (Notifiable Patient Safety Incidents) Bill 2019 provides for the time of making the open disclosure.
[25] The Patient Safety (Notifiable Patient Safety Incidents) Bill 2019, No 100 of 2019, initiated on 5 December 2019.
[26] Clodagh Geraghty, 'Advancing Patient Safety in Ireland: The American Model and Cultural Change' (2009) 15(1) MLJI 27–34 at 7, Michael Cohen, 'Why Error Reporting Systems should be voluntary' (2000) 320 BMJ 728–729.
[27] ibid.

environment. It is argued that this slower approach 'has the distinct advantage of being able to capture less severe harm, and near misses, where so much of the learning can emerge'.[28] The aviation industry which has long been acknowledged as a model reporting system, has been voluntary since 1976.[29]

While all of the above arguments are valid, the first is the most likely to have a tangible negative effect on medical negligence litigation. The proposed and current law provides for stringent and structured circumstances in which open disclosures can be made. In order for practitioners to avail of the protection the law offers from an admission of liability and the admissibility of evidence against them in court, the practitioners must abide by strict procedures. This may encourage practitioners, who are not voluntarily choosing to make a disclosure, to be defensive about the disclosure they make, and the way in which it is made out of fear of litigation. A defensive or seemingly incomplete or insincere disclosure may in actuality encourage patients to go down the litigation route in order to obtain a full apology or to have full information disclosed.

A second argument in respect of facilitating a gradual process, when coupled with the first, also has merit. If practitioners are given the space to make open disclosure voluntarily, they will perhaps be less likely to go about it in a way that has been motivated only by self-protection. It is well established, however, that there are certain circumstances in which a disclosure must be mandated, for reasons of patient safety and public interest. This need for mandatory disclosure in such circumstances will trump the problems with complexity within the law and worries of self-protecting disclosures. It might also be hoped that whilst there may be legally mandated open disclosure for serious incidents, if this becomes a habit and a culture within the practice of medicine it may trickle down to less serious incidents, which may then be reported voluntarily.

The arguments in favour of mandatory open disclosure have been identified by Irvine P as being that 'duty of candour legislation, although a very recent creation, appears to be the most comprehensive, and as a result the most effective'.[30] In order for a comprehensive mandatory disclosure regime to be effective, however, it will be necessary to have the requisite training and supports in place to make mandatory reporting practicable and successful.

Ultimately, these issues will come to light if the proposed Bill is passed and comes into effect. Insight into the potential consequences and effect of the proposed reform can for the moment only be gained by looking at the analysis from other jurisdictions with similar laws. Irvine P has also referred to a

---

[28] ibid.
[29] Caroline Clancy, 'New Patient Safety Organizations Lower Roadblocks to Medical Error Reporting' (2008) 23 Am J Med Qual 318.
[30] See note 11 above, at 74.

2019 study in the United States which showed that apologies did not have an effect on the risk of the practitioner being taken to court, or on the level of damages awarded by the court, or agreed in settlements.[31] As observed by Irvine P, reducing litigation is not the only objective of disclosure and apology laws to measure the effectiveness of the proposed Bill but also the objective of seeking to improve patient–doctor relationships and transparency in the healthcare system must be taken into account.

Apology: do it right or pay the price

An apology, if made correctly, can be therapeutic for both the giver of the apology and the recipient. It can reduce anger, promote healing and repair relationships.[32] Ross and Newman believe that an effective apology contains four elements: acknowledgement of harm, evidence of remorse, an offer of reparation for damage caused and the promise of behavioural change.[33] Other aspects that affect the sincerity of an apology can include the timing of the apology, a lack of defensiveness, evidence of reparative action and the lack of an ulterior motive for the apology.[34] It is difficult to ensure that an apology is conveyed correctly in order for it to have the desired effect. A poor apology can often be more damaging than no apology at all. Inadequate apologies can cause hurt, anger and mistrust.[35] Newman and Ross observe that

> Ineffective apologies are so common that the word *non-apology* has been created, defined as a statement that takes the form of an apology but does not constitute an acknowledgment or regret for what has caused offense or upset.[36]

It could be argued that the prescriptive nature of the current and proposed laws do not encourage sincere apologies.

The Health Service Executive defines open disclosure as:

> an open, consistent, compassionate and timely approach to communicating with patients and, where appropriate, their relevant person following patient safety incidents. It includes expressing regret for what has happened, keeping the patient informed and providing reassurance in relation to on-going care and treatment, learning and the steps being

---

[31] See note 11 above, at 71 and 74.
[32] Nina Ross and William Newman, 'The Role Of Apology Laws In Medical Malpractice' (2021) 49(3) J Am Acad Psychiatry Law at 1.
[33] ibid. See Susan Daicoff, 'Apology, Forgiveness, Reconciliation & Therapeutic Jurisprudence' (2013) 13 Pepperdine Dispute Resolution Law Journal, 131–180.
[34] ibid.
[35] Erin Ann O'Hara and Douglas Yarn, 'On Apology and Consilience' (2002) 77(1) Washington Law Review 21–92.
[36] See note 32 above, at 1.

taken by the health services provider to try to prevent a recurrence of the incident.[37]

Mandated disclosure

The manner in which the proposed 2019 Bill has been drafted could give rise to some criticism. Irvine P has observed that:

> Disclosure and apology legislation needs to set out its terms in an intuitive manner. If it does not, there is a risk that any conversation between healthcare professionals is stifled by a rigid form that makes what should be a genuine and sincere apology unduly artificial.[38]

An effective apology must not come across as fuelled by an ulterior motive or as being mandated. This is a risk that must be mitigated by the practitioners themselves by ensuring that the apology and information is conveyed in a sincere and meaningful manner. This will take refined interpersonal skills from the disclosing practitioner. The prescriptive nature of the proposed mandatory disclosure legislation may negatively impact on the quality and sincerity of the apologies given to individuals in comparison to apologies which are given voluntarily. However, a positive of the proposed reform is that a mandatory system will likely give patients in general more trust in the healthcare system; as they know that if something *does* go wrong in their case, they will be informed of it, if it is a notifiable incident. As outlined above, however, the 2019 Bill provides for a very narrow list of such notifiable incidents that require mandatory disclosure.

Stringent procedure or no protection

The Patient Safety (Notifiable Patient Safety Incidents) Bill 2019 and the Civil Liability (Amendment) Act 2017 both provide that open disclosure and an apology, made at an open disclosure meeting or at the proposed notifiable incident disclosure meeting, shall not constitute an express or implied admission of fault or liability and shall not be admissible as evidence of fault or liability in medical negligence proceedings. If a practitioner, however, in the course of making an open disclosure, discloses information or makes an apology in a way that does not ascribe to the procedure set out in the legislation, that admission will *not* be protected.

---

[37] See note 23 above.
[38] See note 11 above, at 72.

Open disclosure legislation, has, across several jurisdictions been classed as 'narrow and inaccessible'.[39] Irvine P expands on this, citing a US case, *Woronka v Sewall*[40] whereby a doctor who, during the course of delivering the plaintiff's baby, had caused second degree burns to the plaintiff in the application of a disinfectant solution. The doctor made an expression of regret to the plaintiff and her husband. The doctor admitted the cause of the incident and reassured the plaintiff and her husband that it would be rectified.[41] These comments were then used as the basis of the plaintiff's successful claim against the defendant doctor. A similar situation unfolded in *Greenwood v Harris*[42] where the defendant doctor discovered during the course of surgery on the plaintiff for a supposed tumour, that there was no tumour and that the plaintiff was in fact pregnant. The doctor had not been satisfied with a pre-operative blood test but had gone ahead with surgery nonetheless, resulting in this unfortunate outcome. After the incident, the doctor expressed deep regret for what he had done, and apologised to the plaintiff's husband. These comments were admissible in court as evidence of the defendant's liability. As Irvine P observes, these two cases demonstrate a situation where 'a doctor's well-intended and well-received disclosure or apology, rather absurdly, resulted in him or her incurring liability'.[43]

This 'narrowness', particularly in mandatory open disclosure laws, leaves practitioners very vulnerable to having their own well-meaning words used against them if they do not follow the legislative procedure meticulously when making an apology or acknowledgement of regret. Practitioners who are well-meaning and act out of compassion in the moment may, therefore, be punished for doing so under the current Irish law and the proposed reform under the 2019 Bill.

Research has shown that legislation which limits the scope of how a practitioner can or cannot with protection, explain and give information on what went wrong, and how they can or cannot apologise with protection from the legislation, may encourage patients to go to court as they may feel that they are entitled to information that they believe is being withheld. If practitioners must narrowly construe explanations of events and apologies in order to avail of the protection of the legislation, patients may be more likely to feel that information is being withheld and pursue litigation as an avenue to access this information.

---

[39] See note 11 above, at 71, where Ms Justice Mary Irvine, President of the High Court, cites McMichael et al, 'Sorry Is Never Enough: How State Apology Laws Fail to Reduce Medical Malpractice Liability Risk' (2019) 71 Stanford Law Review at 386–387.
[40] *Woronka v Sewall* 320 Mass 362 (http://masscases.com/cases/sjc/320/320mass362.html).
[41] It was stated that the doctor had exclaimed 'My God, what a mess; my God, what happened here ... It is a darn shame to have this happen'.
[42] *Greenwood v Harris* 362 P 2d 85 (Okla 1961) (https://casetext.com/case/greenwood-v-harris).
[43] See note 11 above, at 70.

It is probably worth wondering here that if, as in the two cases outlined above, practitioners make heartfelt disclosure in the spur of the moment and are brought to court with those disclosures admissible as evidence against them and, also, if patients are more likely to take practitioners to court where they feel that a full or effective apology hasn't been given on the grounds that the disclosure process was too procedural and impersonal, where is the middle ground? Ultimately, it will require time and effort to implement a policy and provide training alongside such legislation in order to allow practitioners deliver open disclosure in a way which will be beneficial to the patient whilst affording the practitioner the protections offered in the legislation. In analysing the legislative developments in Ireland, Madden and Tumelty have concluded that

> legislative measures will not bring about a change in culture and behaviours without additional education and training, strong leadership and support from professional regulatory bodies.[44]

The proposed legislation, if passed, will put a particularly heavy burden on practitioners and require the correct supports to be put in place to educate the practitioners on the law and procedures and to provide training in how to adhere to them.

Conclusion

The proposed move from voluntary open disclosure to mandatory open disclosure is a step forward for the Irish healthcare system. Despite some potential problems in the proposed law, such as the narrow definition of open disclosure which prescribes stringent procedural requirements in order for practitioners to be shielded from implied or express admissions of liability, it is an important piece of law that will hopefully have an overall positive effect on the healthcare system. It will, however, be necessary to keep any mandatory open disclosure regime under constant review and to have a robust policy plan and supports in place to complement the legislation in order to guarantee success from this proposed law.

The importance of such supports and training has been emphasised by Irvine P

> [w]here healthcare providers take training their staff seriously and, proverbially, put meat on the bones that is the legislation, disclosure, candour and apology laws can make a difference.[45]

---

[44] Deirdre Madden and Mary-Elizabeth Tumelty, 'Open Disclosure of Patient Safety Incidents: Legislative Developments in Ireland' (2019) 25(2) MLJI 76–89 at 76 and 85–86.

[45] See note 11 above, at 73.

Medical practitioners must be provided with guidance on how to deliver open disclosures that will both satisfy the patient and ensure that they are legally protected. The momentum of the proposed Bill appears to have stalled as the Oireachtas has not updated the status of the progression of this Bill since 28 July 2020 where it has remained before Dáil Eireann, Third Stage. It remains to be seen whether this Bill or an alternative amended Bill proposing mandatory open disclosure will be passed but in the meantime it appears that the status quo of voluntary open disclosure will remain for the foreseeable future.

Chapter X

IS MEDIATION PREFERABLE TO NEGOTIATION AS A MEANS OF ALTERNATIVE DISPUTE RESOLUTION IN WAYS THAT ARE SPECIFIC TO THE NATURE OF MEDICAL NEGLIGENCE LITIGATION?

Fionn O'Callaghan and Sara Moorhead SC[1]

INTRODUCTION

Mediation is now established in Ireland as the preferred means by which the parties in a medical negligence suit seek to settle the claim without recourse to a contested trial. In the past number of years, in medical negligence litigation commenced before the Irish High Court, the Health Service Executive has consistently availed of mediation, as opposed to pre-trial negotiation, as the primary method of dispute resolution in advance of the trial date. The purpose of this chapter is to explore whether mediation offers something to the resolution of a dispute in a medical negligence action which a negotiation between the parties does not offer. This chapter will suggest that it does and will offer the reasons why.

Prior the practice of mediation becoming so popular in the resolution of medical negligence litigation, by reason of its endorsement by the Health Service Executive and by the indemnifiers of medical professionals, these claims would largely be resolved through negotiation between counsel retained by the parties to these proceedings. Proceeding by way of negotiation still remains but it has now become a secondary method of pre-trial dispute resolution in medical negligence litigation. This transformation in how these claims are resolved raises the question as to what is offered by mediation for the potential resolution of these claims which is not offered by negotiation.

In recent years, a number of high-profile cases arising from the provision of CervicalCheck, the national population-based screening programme of women

---

[1] Fionn O'Callaghan prepared this chapter as a final year undergraduate student at the School of Law at Trinity College Dublin. Sara Moorhead SC is a member of the Inner Bar of Ireland.

for cervical cancer, have drawn the method of resolution of medical negligence litigation in Ireland into sharp focus in the public square. In particular, the media coverage of these cases has shed a revealing light on the procedural dimension of pursuing medical negligence litigation through the Irish courts, demonstrating the 'destructive emotional impact'[2] that often comes to bear on those speaking redress through the courts for clinical negligence. Indeed, a recent empirical study on medical negligence litigation in Ireland has reported 'significant shortcomings' in relation to those who have suffered medical wrongdoing are concerned[3] and argued that reform is necessary to a system that currently fosters 'protracted, contentious, emotionally draining and expensive legal battles'.[4] This has sparked a renewed focus on the importance of alternative dispute resolution (ADR) in medical negligence cases, such as negotiation and mediation.

Indeed, the prospect of mediation and negotiation as viable alternatives to litigation in the context of medical negligence has been widely endorsed by members of the judiciary such as by former President of the High Court, Mr Justice Peter Kelly and by the Law Reform Commission.[5]

THE LEGISLATIVE FRAMEWORK OF MEDIATION

The Mediation Act 2017, which was enacted by the Oireachtas in light of the European Mediation Directive 2008[6] and when adopting a number of recommendations from the Law Reform Commission,[7] defines mediation as:

> a confidential facilitative and voluntary process in which parties to a dispute, with the assistance of a mediator, attempt to reach a mutually acceptable agreement to resolve the dispute.[8]

Pre-trial negotiation, by contrast, entails the direct engagement of counsel representing each party in the absence of an independent mediator in order to reach an agreed settlement. Thus, mediation gives rise to the additional expense of paying for the professional fees of a mediator. Moreover, in practice, mediation tends to take considerably longer than a negotiation on the day, or indeed days, that it is conducted, as often a mediation in a medical negligence action may continue into a second day or longer still.

---

[2] See Mary Tumelty, 'Medical Negligence Litigation and Apologies: An Empirical Examination' (2020) European Journal of Health Law, 27(4), 386–403.
[3] ibid.
[4] ibid.
[5] See LRC CP 50-2008.
[6] (2008/52/EC).
[7] Law Reform Commission, *Alternative dispute resolution: Mediation and Conciliation* (2008).
[8] Mediation Act 2017, s 2.

Yet, notwithstanding the additional costs incurred by mediation and the greater time which its process may demand, it has been gaining increasing traction in this jurisdiction as a means of ADR, particularly in the context of clinical negligence actions. In March 2017, the Irish Government established a Review Group to examine the administration of civil justice in the Republic of Ireland, with a focus on encouraging ADR. The Review Group reported that ADR mechanisms, such as mediation, were a 'particular focus of civil procedural reform in Ireland'.[9] Following its enactment, commentators have praised the Mediation Act 2017 and its practical facilitation of mediation through the associated amendments to the Rules of the Superior Courts.[10]

The Mediation Act 2017 came into force on 1 January 2018 and adopted a number of recommendations from the Law Reform Commission Report of 2010 entitled 'Alternative dispute resolution: Mediation and Conciliation'. In accordance with its definition in s 2 of this Act, mediation is a confidential and voluntary process in which an independent and neutral mediator assists two or more parties to a dispute towards achieving a negotiated settlement of it. In so doing, the parties always retain control of the decision as to whether to settle or not and upon what terms.

Section 14(1) of the Mediation Act 2017 provides that a practising solicitor shall, prior to issuing proceedings on behalf of a client, advise the client to consider mediation and explain the benefit of it and its voluntary nature. Furthermore, s 14(2) of this Act provides that if a practising solicitor is acting on behalf of a client who intends to institute proceedings, the originating document by which proceedings are instituted shall be accompanied by a statutory declaration made by the solicitor evidencing (if such be the case) that the solicitor performed the obligations imposed upon him or her under ss (1) in relation to the client and the proceedings to which the declaration relates.

Mediation has been encouraged for a number of reasons, the main ones being that it can lead to the early resolution of a dispute, the ensuing reduction of legal costs and stress for parties involved in court proceedings and the more efficient administration of cases. All of these undoubted advantages apply, however, to the process of negotiation as well. The question remains as to what mediation has to offer, in the specific context of medical negligence litigation, which makes it a more attractive option for the resolution of these proceedings than a negotiation between the parties would otherwise be.

---

[9] Review of the Administration of Civil Justice: Review Group Report, at p 124.
[10] See Hutchinson and Cheevers, 'Encouraging Alternative Methods of Dispute Resolution' [2018] Civil Justice Review, Sutherland School of Law, University College Dublin.

All of the benefits of negotiation remain within the context of mediation

In answering this question, it needs to be borne in mind, from the outset, that negotiation and mediation are not 'either/or' forms of dispute resolution. Instead, a more accurate understanding of the relationship between the two is to understand negotiation as being incorporated within mediation, a lesser which is included in the greater.

In practice, this means that in the course of a mediation of a medical negligence action, a mediator may shrewdly decide to simply facilitate counsel who are retained by both parties to simply speak directly to each other in his or her presence or absence. Often, a frank conversation between counsel, which the mediator simply observes or not, can be decisive in progressing a mediation towards a resolution. For this to occur, the mediator must understand his or her role, which is not to bring about a resolution of the dispute between the parties but rather to facilitate the parties to bring about this resolution between themselves.

Accordingly, a mediator who places himself or herself as the sole conduit between the parties has divested the process of an essential instrument in the resolution of the dispute, that is the benefit of a direct negotiation between the counsel retained by both parties, which can be simply facilitated and potentially observed by the mediator as it occurs. A mediator may be aware that the counsel retained by both parties have an excellent professional relationship. Accordingly, it would be inimical to the interests of all parties involved in the mediation if the mediator blocked a direct and open dialogue between them which may prove to be a bridge that leads to the resolution of the dispute. So, in the first instance, mediation does not entail losing the benefits of a negotiation. Rather, it retains, in full, the benefits of a negotiation which an effective mediator will continuously be open to draw upon as the process of mediation is unfolding. In fact, when the parties are close to reaching a settlement but one final step is needed on both sides to achieve this, a mediator may wisely decide to bring the parties' counsel together at this critical point, for what may be their first and only direct meeting, so as to effect the settlement between their respective clients.

The benefit of the supervisory intervention of the courts

We turn then to consider specific benefits of mediation which are not available in the process of negotiation. While mediation is based on the voluntary participation of the parties involved, one of its most distinctive features is that, unlike with a negotiation, an application can be made to the court to 'invite' the parties to engage in mediation pursuant to s 16 of the Mediation Act 2017.

The use of the term 'invite' was not how the supervisory intervention of the courts, enabling them to bring parties to a dispute into the mediation process, was originally established by the Oireachtas. The role of mediation in personal injuries litigation was first placed on a statutory footing in this jurisdiction through s 15 of the Civil Liability and Courts Act 2004. It provides that:

> 15. (1) Upon the request of any party to a personal injuries action, the court may –
>
> (a) at any time before the trial of such action, and
> (b) if it considers that the holding of a meeting pursuant to a direction under this subsection would assist in reaching a settlement in the action, direct that the parties to the action meet to discuss and attempt to settle the action, and a meeting held pursuant to a direction under this subsection is in this Act referred to as a 'mediation conference'.
>
> (2) Where the court gives a direction under subsection (1), each party to the personal injuries action concerned shall comply with that direction.

The strong and normative wording used in this section is notable. It conferred upon the courts the capacity to direct the parties to enter into a mediation conference if requested by one of the parties to make such an order. It further provided that each party shall then comply with this direction of the court. Corbett highlighted the fundamental problem which this created when he rightly observed that:

> By choosing an approach whereby the power to initiate mediation rests with one of the parties, irrespective of the views of the other side, the legislature has created a significant power imbalance in the relationship between the parties, which will cause grave difficulties for the mediation process.[11]

The very nature of mediation as a voluntary process was contradicted by this legislative provision. Accordingly, in its report of 2010, the Law Reform Commission addressed the issue of the courts having the capacity to compel parties to engage in mediation which seemed to go against the voluntary nature of processes such as mediation and conciliation. The Commission highlighted that where a court compels parties to enter into mediation to which they object, it would be likely to increase costs on both parties. The Commission

---

[11] Corbett, 'Mediations in Actions for Personal Injury: Is it Good to Talk?' in Binchy and Craven, *Civil Liability and Courts Act 2004: Implications for Personal Injuries Litigation* (FirstLaw, 2005) at p 103.

also defended the fundamental principle that the process of mediation remains voluntary despite the courts having the power to direct the parties to engage.[12]

Many of the recommendations of the Law Reform Commission were adopted and implemented in the Mediation Act 2017. Section 22 of the 2017 Act amended s 15(1) of the Civil Liability and Courts Act 2004 by providing:

> Section 15 (1) of the Civil Liability and Courts Act 2004 is amended by the insertion of 'or upon its own initiative' after 'party to a personal injuries action'.

This amendment enables the courts, of their own volition, rather than having to await an application from one of the parties to a personal injuries action, to issue a direction for parties to engage in mediation in such proceedings. The normative wording of s 15 of the 2004 Act, which provides that a court can 'direct' the parties in a personal injuries action to engage in mediation, can be contrasted with s 16 of the Mediation Act 2017 which significantly dilutes the authority conferred upon the courts to oblige the parties to engage in mediation. It provides that:

> 16. (1) A court may, on the application of a party involved in proceedings, or of its own motion where it considers it appropriate having regard to all the circumstances of the case:
>
> (a) invite the parties to the proceedings to consider mediation as a means of attempting to resolve the dispute the subject of the proceedings;
> (b) provide the parties to the proceedings with information about the benefits of mediation to settle the dispute the subject of the proceedings.

The wording of this section is substantially different to that of s 15 of the Civil Liability and Courts Act 2004. With this section, the court does not direct the parties to engage in mediation but can merely 'invite' them to do so. This approach is consistent with the nature of mediation as a voluntary process and not one in which the parties are coerced or pressurised to engage.

Nonetheless, the Mediation Act 2017 amended s 15 of the Civil Liability and Courts Act 2004 and did not repeal it. This means that in the specific context of medical negligence litigation, it remains open to one of the parties to apply to the courts to direct the other party to engage in mediation notwithstanding the entirely inconsistent nature of this relief and with the essentially voluntary nature of engagement by parties in mediation. In practice, s 15 of the Act of 2004 is rarely invoked. There are situations, however, in medical negligence litigation where it has a highly important value. If a plaintiff is terminally ill and the defendant is not engaging in the active resolution of the dispute,

---

[12] LRC 98-2010 at 4.69.

the claim for general damages will be lost when the plaintiff is deceased. In these exceptional and tragic circumstances, the potential for the plaintiff's legal representatives to make an application to the High Court to 'direct' the defendant to engage in mediation can be of critical importance, particularly where the defendant is reluctant to engage in mediation.

THE IMPACT OF THE MEDIATOR

The most obvious advantage of mediation as a means of ADR in the clinical negligence context, in comparison with a straightforward negotiation, is the impact of the mediator themselves. Whilst a mediator's primary role is to be an impartial, neutral facilitator, who assists the parties in achieving a negotiated settlement of a dispute, he or she may, at the request of the parties, make proposals as to how a dispute might be resolved. It is the decision of the parties alone, however, whether they will accept any such proposals. A mediator may bring a fresh perspective to a dispute that may otherwise prove to be intractable between the parties' existing legal representatives and offer another non-judgmental voice in the process of settling a clinical negligence dispute.

There are a whole range of circumstances in which the independence of the mediator can assist this process. A party may be reluctant to accept the advice given by the legal representatives who have been engaged. The view of the mediator may provide a frankness and a clarity which would otherwise not be available and which can lead to the expectations of that party in relation to the resolution of the dispute becoming more realistic.

A mediator can only convey an impression of one disputing party to another which is truthful and thereby dissolve false perceptions held by a party which are blocking a resolution of the dispute. Equally, a party may need to be really heard and validated by someone with extensive legal experience beyond the legal representatives who have been engaged. A mediator can provide this external validation of the wrong which has been suffered by a party which would otherwise be sought from a trial judge. A mediator is also entirely non-judgmental. He or she offers a space to explore all sorts of options for resolving a dispute with one party, or between the parties, without them being closed down in a premature or accusatory manner. Finally, an experienced mediator will know the legal representatives acting for all of the parties. This is a vital asset so as to ensure that the particular concerns of these representatives are met and that human characteristics or behaviours, which we all share, which can frustrate the resolution of a claim are also challenged when it is appropriate to do so.

THE MEDIATION PROCESS IS CONFIDENTIAL

It is a fundamental term of every mediation agreement between the parties in a medical negligence action that the documents shared between the parties in this process, together with what is represented on their behalf during it, remain entirely confidential. Even after the process results in a resolution of the dispute, the mediation agreement will usually provide that the confidentiality of what was said and what occurred during the process remain entirely confidential. This is in marked contrast to the negotiation process. A negotiation between the parties is conducted on a 'without prejudice' basis, meaning that what is stated by the parties during the negotiation cannot be disclosed in the course of the proceedings at trial. There is no impediment, however, to the parties disclosing what occurred in the negotiation to other parties who have no involvement in the dispute.

The process of mediation lends an added element of confidentiality to the process of settling clinical negligence claims which the process of negotiation cannot provide. This is a vital benefit of mediation as opposed to pre-trial negotiation in such litigation as often sensitive information concerning a patient's medical history is at issue, which the plaintiff would understandably wish to remain entirely private. Similarly, an allegation of clinical negligence may be made against a medical practitioner or a hospital which the defendant in question would also wish to remain as private as possible. Mediation offers this assurance of privacy in the discussions between the parties which are seeking to resolve the dispute. The protective surrounding of confidentiality also has the corresponding effect of enabling the parties to be more open about what their respective positions are and which can often be instrumental in establishing the momentum between them which enables the matter to be resolved.

The possibility for more direct engagement and the answering of questions

One of the ironies which arises from this benefit of the confidentiality of mediation is that a plaintiff can often obtain a clearer and more definitive answer in relation to the medical care which is complained of than by proceeding with a fully contested trial. The glaring and pressurised environment of a contested trial obviously leads to a defendant being concerned about making admissions or offering explanations which undermine the defence of the claim. In turn, this prevents a plaintiff from discovering what happened in the provision of clinical care which has given rise to the claim.

While it is not the purpose of the mediation process to be a fact-finding exercise, many plaintiffs in clinical negligence claims are understandably eager to know the precise circumstances of what occurred in the care provided to them which has given rise to their claims. The mediation process, with the benefit of confidentiality, offers the context for such explanations to be forthcoming. This can often have a hugely ameliorative effect upon a plaintiff who has felt that his or her care has not been central when it otherwise should have been. A plaintiff may also realise in the course of a mediation that the clinical care complained of is highly complex and the level of criticism which has been made of the medical practitioner or hospital in question is not warranted.

The independence of the mediator can also play a critical role in discerning what are the real issues for a plaintiff in understanding the medical care which is being complained of. The mediator is also uniquely positioned to elicit an answer from a defendant in response to a critical query from a plaintiff, about the clinical care provided, in a manner which is non-threatening and which does not undermine the position of that defendant in the subsequent defence of the claim should the mediation not lead to a resolution of the proceedings.

THE FACILITATION OF QUALIFIED DISCLOSURE OF EXPERTS' REPORTS

The mediation process works best when the parties have made full disclosure of their respective experts' reports. It often occurs, however, that the parties have not made an exchange of their respective experts' reports or have only exchanged the reports of corresponding experts on what is termed a 'like for like' basis. This deficiency in disclosure cannot be cured in a conventional negotiation process. With a mediation, however, a party can give a non-disclosed expert report to the mediator and allow it to be used by the mediator to advance that party's position while not permitting a copy of that report to be disclosed to the other side.

The particular role of mediation in overcoming a deficit of disclosure of experts' reports between the parties was brought into focus by the decision of the Court of Appeal on 1 April 2022 in *O'Flynn v Health Service Executive, MedLab Pathology Limited, Sonic Healthcare (Ireland) Limited and Clinical Pathology Laboratories Limited*. In that case, as the matter proceeded to trial, there was a fundamental dispute between the plaintiff and Clinical Pathology Laboratories Incorporated in relation to the right of this defendant to obtain all of the experts' reports obtained on behalf of the plaintiff's claim, while this defendant reserved the right to obtain further experts' reports. The divergence between the parties in their respective understanding of their obligations to make disclosure of experts' reports led to the issue being ventilated before Cross J and then, on appeal, before the Court of Appeal.

The judgment of the Court of Appeal, which was given on behalf of the Court by Noonan J, establishes that Order 39 Rules 45–51 of the Rules of the Superior Courts 1986, which derive from s 45 of the Courts and Court Officers Act 1995 and SI 391/1998 (Rules of the Superior Courts (No 6) (Disclosure of Reports and Statements) 1998), are far from straightforward in terms of the obligations which they place upon parties to make disclosure of their respective experts' reports in proceedings relating to clinical negligence. Noonan J made the following observation about this statutory regime at paragraph 80 of his judgment:

It is difficult to avoid the conclusion that there are significant shortcomings in the disclosure regime introduced by S.I. 391, as this case casts in stark relief. As the 25th anniversary of the disclosure rules approaches, they would, I think, benefit from recalibration to take account of the issues thrown up by this and previous cases which consider them. It may indeed by necessary to revisit s. 45 itself.

Noonan J then had to proceed in the next paragraph of his judgment to set out in nine paragraphs the specific steps which the parties needed to take in order to ensure proper and fair compliance with the disclosure obligations as they applied in that case. Given this ongoing complexity in the interpretation and application of these disclosure obligations in medical negligence proceedings, the role of the mediation process in allowing experts' reports to be ventilated and relied upon by the parties, while not formally disclosing them, is likely to be understood more for the value which it offers unless and until these obligations are the subject of reform in the manner which has been suggested by the Court of Appeal.

STOPPING THE PROVISIONS OF THE STATUTES OF LIMITATIONS

Section 18 of the Mediation Act 2017 deals with the effect of mediation upon the application of limitation and prescription periods. It provides as follows:

> 18. (1) In reckoning a period of time for the purposes of a limitation period specified by the Statutes of Limitations, the period beginning on the day on which an agreement to mediate is signed and ending on the day which is 30 days after either -
>
> (a) a mediation settlement is signed by the parties and the mediator, or
> (b) the mediation is terminated, whichever first occurs, shall be disregarded.
>
> (2) The mediator in a mediation shall inform the parties in writing of the date on which the mediation ends.

With claims for damages arising from clinical negligence, the current limitation period is of two years from the date of the accrual of the cause of action, following the amendment of the Statutes of Limitations by s 7 of the Civil Liability and Courts Act 2004. If the parties enter into a signed mediation agreement and the mediation does not succeed in resolving the proceedings, this limitation period is suspended until 30 days after the mediation is terminated, with the mediator informing the parties in writing of the date upon which it has ended. The effect of this statutory provision is that the mediation agreement mirrors a practice in commercial disputes which is to enter into a 'standstill agreement' which allows the parties to negotiate or otherwise appraise their respective positions while agreeing not to use the period of time during which this takes place to criticise the other party's claim. Once again, this ability of mediation to pause the application of the Statute of Limitations is a highly significant benefit of mediation, which arises by statute in a clinical negligence action. For the same benefit to arise in the context of a negotiation, it would require the parties to enter into a separate 'standstill agreement' which is not an approach which has any existing currency in clinical negligence proceedings before the Irish Superior Courts. It should also be noted that Order 56A, Rule 9 of the Rules of the Superior Courts 1986, as amended, further provides that where proceedings are referred to mediation, the time for taking any step in the proceedings shall, unless the court orders otherwise, be calculated as if time did not run during the period of any adjournment to facilitate the mediation.

The implications for costs of an unreasonable refusal to engage in mediation

Section 21 of the Mediation Act 2017 provides as follows:

> 21. In awarding costs in respect of proceedings referred to in section 16, a court may, where it considers it just, have regard to –
>
> (a) any unreasonable refusal or failure by a party to the proceedings to consider using mediation, and
> (b) any unreasonable refusal or failure by a party to the proceedings to attend mediation, following an invitation to do so under section 16(1).

Section 169(1)(g) of the Legal Services Regulation Act 2015 is also of significance in this context. The section endorses the fundamental principle concerning the awards of costs by the courts which is that costs follow the event, or, as stated therein, a party who is entirely successful in civil proceedings is entitled to an award of costs against a party who is not successful in those proceedings, unless the court orders otherwise, having regard to the particular nature and circumstances of the case, and the conduct of the proceedings by the parties, including whether the parties were invited by the court to settle the claim (whether by mediation or otherwise) and the court considers that one or more than one of the parties was or were unreasonable in refusing to engage in the settlement discussions or in mediation.

Order 99 Rule 3(1) of the Rules of the Superior Courts 1986, as amended, is also prescriptive in relation to the application by the Superior Courts of this statutory provision. It provides that the High Court, in considering the awarding of the costs or any action or step in any proceedings, and the Supreme Court and Court of Appeal in considering the awarding of the costs of any appeal or step in any appeal, in respect of a claim or counterclaim, shall have regard to the matters set out in s 169(1) of the 2015 Act, where applicable.

One of the implications of these statutory provisions is that when a party to an action is anxious to settle the claim and the other party is not willing to engage in a pre-trial negotiation, that party can employ the costs implications of an unreasonable refusal to settle the claim, whether by mediation or otherwise, to persuade the other party to so engage. To so rely upon these statutory provisions requires that party who is seeking to have the claim resolved to first seek to have the court invite the parties to engage in mediation. Once the court has issued this invitation, the unreasonable refusal of the other party to engage in mediation will then be a factor in determining how costs are to be awarded at the conclusion of a contested trial and independent of the actual outcome thereof.

As a successful party in an action can potentially be penalised for having unreasonably refused an invitation from the court to mediate the dispute, this is a highly significant benefit of the mediation process which can aid a party to a clinical negligence claim who wishes to have it resolved. It is also of note in this regard that s 17(1) of the Mediation Act 2017 provides that when a court invites the parties to engage in mediation, where they so engage and subsequently apply to the court to re-enter the proceedings, but where the mediation did not take place, the mediator shall prepare and submit to the court a written report which shall set out a statement of the reasons as to why it did not take place. Section 17(2) of this Act of 2017 further provides that except where otherwise agreed or directed by the court, a copy of a report prepared under ss (1) shall be given to the parties at least seven days prior to its submission to the court. The potential implications of this report can, therefore, provide the necessary incentive to a party, who is unwilling to engage in the pre-trial resolution of the claim, to proceed to duly do so.

Conclusion

While this chapter offers a brief overview of the particular benefits of mediation in the context of clinical negligence claims, which are not provided by a conventional negotiation process between the parties, it is important to conclude by emphasising the humanity of the exercise of the mediation process rather than its legality. This emphasis is particularly important for all parties involved in a clinical negligence claim. Litigation is highly stressful for plaintiffs in such claims, but it is also very stressful for defendants and can have various reputational consequences for medical practitioners and the administrators of hospitals and the staff employed therein.

With this centrally in mind, it is also essential to emphasise that the mediator listens to both sides and accurately conveys the sentiment between them in a manner which is in absolute accordance with the requirements of confidentiality. It is important that the mediator conveys the sentiment on both sides. The mediator will often spend more time with the plaintiff than with the defendant in the mediation of a clinical negligence action but if, for instance, a doctor wishes to have his or her position conveyed to the plaintiff, it is of fundamental importance that the mediator does so. At the end of the mediation process, whether successful or unsuccessful, the parties should be in a better position to understand the case and where each of them is coming from. Accordingly, irrespective of the added benefits of the mediation process, over that of negotiation, the engagement in mediation, even if not successful, always inevitably helps to narrow and clarify the issues between the parties and ensure the more efficient use of the court's time should the matter proceed to trial thereafter.

PART F
DAMAGES

CHAPTER XI

POST-*MORRISSEY*: HOBSON'S CHOICE FOR TERMINALLY ILL PLAINTIFFS AND THEIR STATUTORY DEPENDANTS?

Kate McCullough and Oonah McCrann SC[1]

INTRODUCTION

The recent Supreme Court decision in *Morrissey and anor v Health Service Executive and ors*[2] bears important implications for injured persons and their dependants as regards the damages they may recover under common law and statute. The Supreme Court applied the rule in *Baker v Bolton*[3] to hold that in an ordinary negligence action, one cannot recover damages for the cost of having to provide care for dependants that will be required after the death of the injured person. The court also effectively confirmed that once a personal injuries claim has been resolved during the lifetime of a victim of negligence, as for instance where it has come to final judgment, been settled or become statute barred, the victim's dependants are precluded from bringing a claim pursuant to Part IV of the Civil Liability Act 1961 principally for loss of services. While Clarke CJ, in giving judgment on behalf of a unanimous Supreme Court, declared that the issue 'await[ed] a final determination',[4] meaning that the matter requires further and final judicial determination, the tenor of the judgment suggests that the rule is as is stated above.

In the course of submissions, the point was raised that it follows that if Mrs Morrissey's husband were precluded from recovering for the prospective loss of free services arising as a result of the imminent death of his wife, he would in theory *never* be allowed to recover for that loss by virtue of the existence of the personal injury proceedings before the court. As it happens, Mr Morrissey was not personally prejudiced by the Supreme Court's determination in this respect since the State, driven by political considerations, had at that point pledged to pay the full sum of damages, awarded to both he and his now-deceased wife at first instance in the High Court, regardless of the conclusion

---

[1] Kate McCullough prepared this chapter as a final year undergraduate student at the School of Law and of Political Science at Trinity College Dublin. Oonah McCrann SC is a member of the Inner Bar of Ireland.
[2] *Morrissey & Morrissey v Health Service Executive, Quest Diagnostics Incorporated and MedLab Pathology Limited* [2020] IESC 43.
[3] *Baker v Bolton* [1808] 170 ER 1033.
[4] See note 2 above, at para 15.21.

the Supreme Court reached. Nevertheless, the Supreme Court's determination is significant as a matter of first principles and for other claimants who are terminally ill by reason of alleged negligence and breach of duty and who have statutory dependants.

In practice, it means that an individual facing imminent death as a result of negligence and breach of duty is forced to make a tactical decision to ensure that their dependants will be provided for into the future. They must decide if they wish to pursue a personal injuries claim in respect of their loss of earnings and *'lost years'* thereafter on the one hand, or on the other hand, refrain from taking such an action so as to afford their dependants the opportunity to pursue a claim pursuant to s 48 of the Civil Liability Act 1961 for, *inter alia*, loss of the free services of the deceased parent or relative, and possibly risk the suit becoming statute barred. In choosing not to pursue a personal injuries action, the terminally ill claimant loses the opportunity to recover for their own pain and suffering or any costs incurred in financing the care and support they need to manage their illness during their final years. Equally, the claim after their death will not have the advantage of their own evidence. Furthermore, the ruling may have a discriminatory impact on the dying plaintiff who has worked as an unpaid full time parent and/or homemaker and cannot, therefore, make a 'lost years' claim, based as it is on the earnings that this plaintiff would have earned but for the injury caused to them by reason of the negligence and breach of duty complained of. It is worth noting that in general, special damages will be larger in Civil Liability Act claims both because of the very fact that one can pursue a claim for the loss of the free services that the deceased relative had provided, but also because of the specific way in which each head of damage is calculated.[5]

This dilemma for a terminally ill claimant is particularly pronounced in the area of medical negligence litigation. Such claims often arise in the context of cancer misdiagnosis cases where a claimant alleges that their life has been greatly foreshortened by a failure to detect the existence of the cancer and to prevent the earlier and potentially entirely successful treatment thereof. Such claimants, while in a state of acute anxiety knowing that their death is imminent, must make an invidious choice between (a) maintaining a personal injuries claim while they are alive but potentially precluding a claim for loss of their free services, after their death, or (b) foregoing such a claim, and their claim for general damages, which will often be at the upper limit, so as to protect the entitlement of their statutory dependants to bring a claim after their death, pursuant to the Civil Liability Act.

The kernel of this problem derives from s 48 of the 1961 Act. Section 48(1) provides:

---

[5] *Murray v Shuter* [1975] COA (Civil Division), [1976] QB 972; *Thompson v Arnold* [2007] EWHC 1875 (QB), [2007] 8 WLUK 65, at para 28.

> Where the death of a person is caused by the wrongful act of another such as would have entitled the party injured, but for his death, to maintain an action and recover damages in respect thereof, the person who would have been so liable shall be liable to an action for damages for the benefit of the dependants of the deceased.

Section 48(2) further provides:

> Only one action in damages may be brought against the same person in respect of the death.

If the terminally ill claimant has brought a claim arising from the negligence and breach of duty to finality before dying, does this mean that their statutory dependants cannot then maintain an action after this claimant's death for the loss of the free services of care they would otherwise have provided, given that this claimant was not entitled to include such a claim in the proceedings which had been brought and finalised during their lifetime?

While draft legislation is under discussion to amend the 1961 Act, there is no certainty that this will come to fruition. Thus, the courts and practitioners must look at other approaches. One possibility is that the courts determine that there exists a distinct common law cause of action for wrongful death, as espoused by various academics.[6] Alternatively, the courts might interpret s 48 in a way that ensures that a previous personal injuries action does not bar dependants from bringing a claim pursuant to Part IV of Civil Liability Act 1961. Unfortunately, the Supreme Court seems to have implicitly accepted that neither is permitted, meaning the aforementioned arguments will be difficult, although not impossible, to advance in court.

A further possibility is that the courts will determine that s 48 of the 1961 Act is unconstitutional. The constitutionality of the section was not considered by the Supreme Court in *Morrissey*. As such, this approach still has some chance of success in future litigation. Yet, in practical terms, interim awards of damages seem the best way to deal with the issue in the years to come. However, the High Court's 'inherent jurisdiction'[7] to adjourn a trial and grant an interim award of damages has not yet been the subject matter of a written judgment in the context of a dying plaintiff in Ireland.[8]

---

[6] E.g., John P M White, *Irish Law of Damages for Personal Injuries and Death* (2nd edn, Butterworths, Ireland 1989), at para 7.4.12.
[7] *Miley v Birthistle* [2016] IEHC 196, [2016] 4 JIC 1904; *Hegarty (A Minor Suing by his Mother and Next Friend Jacinta Collins) v Health Service Executive* [2019] IEHC 788.
[8] Such an award has been granted in the context of catastrophic injuries where there is uncertainty as to the future care needs of the victim.

THE MORRISSEYS' CASE

The late Mrs Ruth Morrissey was terminally ill from cervical cancer when she began a personal injuries suit along with her husband. She had undergone screening with the National Cervical Screening Programme, CervicalCheck, once in 2009 and again in 2012. At both points, her smear test came back negative. The first test had been read by Quest Diagnostics Incorporated and the second had been read by MedLab Pathology Limited, having both received her liquid-based cytology samples from the Health Service Executive, as the providers of this national cervical screening programme.

In 2014, after experiencing symptoms, Mrs Morrissey was referred for further testing which revealed the existence of cervical cancer. Following this, her 2009 and 2012 results were audited. Both of these auditing processes found that her two samples had been incorrectly read. Controversially, the results of the audits were not made available to Mrs Morrissey until mid-2018.

Mrs and Mr Morrissey issued proceedings in the High Court, against the Health Service Executive, Quest Diagnostics Incorporated and MedLab Pathology Limited (MedLab), in that order. In 2019, Cross J gave judgment in favour of the Morrisseys against all three defendants. Each defendant then sought leave to appeal on various points. For present purposes, only a specific damages-related appeal brought by MedLab is relevant. In the course of this appeal, MedLab argued that the damages for loss of the free services of Mr Morrissey's wife, which he would sustain subsequent to her death, were wrongly awarded to him. It was submitted that this head of damages is only recoverable in a wrongful death claim made pursuant to the provisions of Part IV of the Civil Liability Act 1961. The Supreme Court, while acknowledging that its decision would give rise to certain anomalies, allowed Medlab's appeal on this point.[9]

HISTORICAL BACKGROUND

This decision follows from the continued force of an old common law rule that the death of a person cannot give rise to a claim for damages. In *Baker v Bolton* (1808), the plaintiff and his wife had been on top of the defendant's stage coach travelling from Portsmouth to London when it overturned. The plaintiff's wife died a month later from her injuries. Lord Ellenborough held that the jury was only permitted to take into account the injuries sustained by the plaintiff himself as well as the loss of his wife's society and the mental distress he had suffered up until the point of her death since 'in a civil court, the death of a human being could not be complained of as an injury'.[10]

---

[9] *Morrissey and Morrissey v Health Service Executive, Quest Diagnostics Incorporated and MedLab Pathology Limited* [2020] IESC 43, at para 15.28.
[10] *Baker v Bolton* [1808] 170 ER 1033.

At the level of principle, it seems clear that an injury should not be unactionable merely because it was so serious as to cause death.[11] As such, the *Baker* rule has been subject to much criticism since its inception in 1808. It ensures that at common law, it is 'better to kill than to maim' from the perspective of a tortfeasor.[12] Some argue that the rule can be explained by the maxim *actio personalis moritur cum persona*, which provides that 'a personal right of action dies with the person'.[13] That maxim is of limited utility since the claim at issue in *Baker* was not personal, but one taken by the husband of the deceased.[14] Others seek to explain the rule through the felony merger doctrine, which holds that a master's private right of action against someone who causes the death of his servant is 'drowned' by the offence to the crown. It appears that the doctrine, however, is addressed only to killings that amounted to felonies.[15] Since the death at issue in *Baker* was not felonious, the doctrine, which is in any event confined to history, does not provide much by way of explanation.

Thus, while it seems that the rule is 'one ... originally created for some legal reason which in the mutation of things has crumbled away',[16] it is now entrenched in the common law. Perhaps more importantly, it forms the basis of a significant corpus of legislation in various common law jurisdictions.[17] So, while one could discuss the peculiarity of the rule and its lack of doctrinal basis at length, such discussion is futile for present purposes.

The Impact of the Civil Liability Act 1961

In 1846, legislation afforded a new statutory right of action to certain relatives of the deceased.[18] 'Lord Campbell's Act' or the Fatal Accidents Act 1846, now re-enacted in Ireland in Part IV of the Civil Liability Act 1961, mitigated the harsh effects of the common law rule. It allowed dependants of a deceased person to recover 'earnings' and 'services' dependency damages. These include cover for the cost of providing care and other costs that are incurred as a result of the victim's death. In *Morrissey*, the Supreme Court concluded that the passage of the 1961 Act, despite having ameliorated the harsh effects of the

---

[11] *Osborn v Gillett* [1873] Ex 88, [1873] LR 8, Lord Bramwell; John P M White, *Irish Law of Damages for Personal Injuries and Death* (2nd edn, Butterworths Ireland 1989).
[12] H R Preston, 'A Bit of Legal History' (1896) 2(1) Virginia Law Register 3, at pp 5–7; John Munkman, *Damages for Personal Injuries and Death* (10th edn, Butterworths Law 1996), at p 130; Tadhg Dorgan and Peter McKenna, *Damages* (2nd edn, Round Hall 2015), at p 167; *Osborn v Gillett* [1873] Ex 88, [1873] LR 8, Lord Bramwell.
[13] John Munkman, *Damages for Personal Injuries and Death* (10th edn Butterworths Law 1996), at p 130.
[14] HR Preston, 'A Bit of Legal History' (1896) 2(1) Virginia Law Register 3, at p 5.
[15] Anthony Gray, '*Barclay v Penberthy*, The Rule in *Baker v Bolton* and the Action for Loss of Services: A New Recipe Required' (2014) 40(3) Monash University Law Review 920; HR Preston, 'A Bit of Legal History' (1896) 2(1) Virginia Law Register 3, 4.
[16] ibid 8.
[17] ibid.
[18] Fatal Accidents Act 1846.

common law rule in a variety of circumstances, did not abolish it. As such, the court found that there can be no recovery in respect of damage caused by the death or prospective death of a person outside the special circumstances for which the Act provides. Mr Morrissey contended that if he was not entitled to this head of damages as the law stood, the anomalies that arose and the resulting injustice to him and the couple's young daughter required a 'reasonable evolution of ... jurisprudence'.[19] The Supreme Court felt that this was something it could not do. Similar to the older English case of *Osborn v Gillett*,[20] in which the court held that it was 'not at liberty to disregard the law ... established so long ago and expressly recognised by the legislature, nor in effect to add by the decision of this Court another clause to Lord Campbell's Act',[21] Clarke CJ expressed the view that it is the prerogative of the Oireachtas to legislate if they wish to make a fundamental alteration to the law. The court concluded that it is not appropriate for the courts to develop the common law so 'radically' through what it perceives to be a 'piecemeal approach'.[22] As a consequence, Mr Morrissey did not recover for the loss of services he was inevitably going to incur following the death of his wife.

The 'lost years' doctrine

Arguably, such a purist view of the *Baker v Bolton* rule is unjustified in the first place, given that exceptions to the historical position have already been 'fashioned'[23] by the courts, namely through the 'lost years' doctrine, which allows a plaintiff who has suffered a shortened life expectancy by reason of a tortious act to recover for their 'lost years' in a personal injury action brought before their death (the 'lost years' being the period during which they would have lived but for their injuries and the income they would have earned during those years less the sum that would have been spent maintaining them).[24] In *Pickett v British Rail Engineering Ltd*,[25] the House of Lords accepted the principle in England. It was accepted in this jurisdiction in *Doherty v Bowaters Irish Wallboard Mills Ltd*,[26] where Walsh J set out that 'the period or length of time by which the expectation of life has been reduced must also be taken into account'.[27] Given that the lost years doctrine *already* violates the *Baker v Bolton* principle by allowing injured persons to recover for losses they will

---

[19] *Morrissey & anor v Health Service Executive, Quest Diagnostics Incorporated and MedLab Pathology Limited* [2020] IESC 43, at para 15.3.
[20] *Osborn v Gillett* [1873] Ex 88, [1873] LR 8.
[21] ibid para 93, Piggott B.
[22] *Morrissey and Morrissey v Health Service Executive, Quest Diagnostics Incorporated and MedLab Pathology Limited* [2020] IESC 43, at para 15.25.
[23] ibid para 15.6.
[24] Bryan M E McMahon and William Binchy, *Law of Torts* (4th edn, Bloomsbury Professional 2015), para 44.144.
[25] *Pickett v British Rail Engineering* [1978] UKHL 4; [1980] AC 136.
[26] *Doherty v Bowaters Irish Wallboard Mills Ltd* [1968] IR 277.
[27] ibid para 285. See also Bryan M E McMahon and William Binchy, *Law of Torts* (4th edn Bloomsbury Professional 2015), at para 44.144.

incur after death, it is not altogether clear why the courts view recovery for loss of services during the same time as being too radical a change to make through case law.

THE REQUIREMENT FOR AN ACTIONABLE SUIT AT THE TIME OF DEATH

Although the Supreme Court in *Morrissey* did not explicitly decide this point,[28] the decision appears to proceed on the premise that, by pursuing a personal injuries action to judgment or settlement, the victim's dependants are precluded from pursuing a Part IV Civil Liability Act claim.[29] Precedent broadly supports this conclusion. In *Mahon v Burke*,[30] the deceased had brought an action based upon negligence against the defendant which settled before his death. In a circuit appeal before the High Court, Lavan J ruled that the dependants were disentitled to bring a wrongful death action pursuant to the provisions of the Civil Liability Act 1961 given that no cause of action existed at the time of death as the deceased had already compromised it. In *Hewitt v Health Service Executive*,[31] the Court of Appeal considered a slightly different situation. The plaintiff sought to bring an action under the Act in respect of the death of his wife. His wife's personal injuries claim had, however, become statute barred, and thus, her dependants were barred from bringing a wrongful death suit pursuant to the Act.[32]

Various commentators suggest that the statutory wrongful death suit is entirely independent from the personal injuries action arising out of the same negligence.[33] White reasons that it therefore follows that it is not necessary that the wrong to the deceased be actionable at the time of death. He submits that the 'supposed requirement of an actionable wrong vested in the deceased at the time of his death is ... not an inevitable conclusion from the wording of the statute' and that 'the dependents' action ought to be unaffected ... where there is no risk of imposing double liability upon the defendant'.[34] In *Morrissey*, counsel for the plaintiffs cited the US decision of *Sea-Land Services Inc v Gaudet* as authority for the proposition that judgment in, or compromise of, a personal injuries action does not bar a dependency claim. In *Gaudet*,[35] the Court of Appeal cited the earlier case of *Moragne v States Marine Lines Inc*[36]

---

[28] *Morrissey and Morrissey v Health Service Executive, Quest Diagnostics Incorporated and MedLab Pathology Limited* [2020] IESC 43, at para 15.21.
[29] This seems to be the general thrust of the decision of Clarke CJ in *Morrissey and Morrissey v Health Service Executive, Quest Diagnostics Incorporated and MedLab Pathology Limited* [2020] IESC 43, at paras 15.23 to 15.25.
[30] *Mahon v Burke* [1991] 2 IR 495; [1991] ILRM 59.
[31] *Hewitt v Health Service Executive* [2016] IECA 194, [2016] 2 IR 649.
[32] ibid.
[33] John P M White, *Irish Law of Damages for Personal Injuries and Death* (2nd edn, Butterworths Ireland 1989), para 7.4.16.
[34] ibid para 8.3.06.
[35] *Sea-Land Services Inc v Gaudet* 414 US 573 (1974) 72-1019.
[36] *Moragne v States Marine Lines Inc* 398 US 375 (1970) 1772.

in which the US Supreme Court recognised a federal non-statutory maritime wrongful death remedy which was not extinguished by the earlier personal injuries claim. Brennan J held that 'Moragne States-Marine Lines ... created a true wrongful death remedy that is founded upon the death itself, and is independent of any action the decedent may have had for his own personal injuries'.[37] It is relevant, however, that those claims were brought in a maritime context, which is an area in which there had not been legislative intervention. On that basis, one could argue that such claims are distinct from those at issue in cases like *Mahon* and *Hewitt*.

The better view is that expressed by Lord Blackburn in *The Vera Cruz*.[38] He felt that while the statutory cause of action is 'in every way new',[39] it is a 'condition precedent'[40] that the injured person would have been able to maintain a claim had she survived. Similarly in *Hewitt*, Hogan J held that while the cause of action is separate from that which might have been maintained by the wife, the two claims are inter-related. Hogan J held that to maintain an action under the 1961 Act, one must be able to show that the deceased would have succeeded in her action but for her death, or at the very least would have been entitled to bring such an action.[41] It is also worth noting that an ordinary construction of s 48(1) of the Civil Liability Act indicates that in order for dependants to bring a claim under it, there has to have been an actionable suit at the time of the victim's death. The legislature's use of the past conditional tense, 'would have entitled', is significant.[42]

'A REASONABLE EVOLUTION OF THE JURISPRUDENCE'[43] – A COMMON LAW CAUSE OF ACTION FOR WRONGFUL DEATH?

White argues there is still a need for a common law cause of action since he views the 1961 Act as being 'seriously deficient'.[44] In theory, such a common law cause of action could in principle be accommodated through the reference

---

[37] *Sea-Land Services Inc v Gaudet* 414 US 573 (1974) 72-1019, 578, 583.
[38] *The Vera Cruz* (No 1) (1884) 10 App Case 59.
[39] John Munkman, *Damages for Personal Injuries and Death* (10th edn, Butterworths Law 1996), 131–132; *The Vera Cruz* (No 1) (1884) 10 App Case 59, Lord Blackburn.
[40] ibid.
[41] *Hewitt v Health Service Executive* [2016] IECA 194, [2016] 2 IR 649.
[42] Section 48(1) of the Civil Liability Act 1961 sets out that '[w]here the death of a person is caused by the wrongful act of another such as would have entitled the party injured, but for his death, to maintain an action and recover damages in respect thereof, the person who would have been so liable shall be liable to an action for damages for the benefit of the dependants of the deceased'.
[43] *Morrissey and Morrissey v Health Service Executive, Quest Diagnostics Incorporated and MedLab Pathology Limited* [2020] IESC 43, at para 15.3.
[44] John P M White, *Irish Law of Damages for Personal Injuries and Death* (2nd edn, Butterworths Ireland 1989), at para 7.4.02.

of Clarke CJ reference to a 'reasonable evolution of [the] jurisprudence'.[45] This action could potentially be available to dependants notwithstanding the fact that a personal injuries suit arising from the same negligence was not actionable immediately prior to the death of the victim.[46] The rationale behind the refusal to recognise such a cause of action may lie in the fact that damages for injury, during someone's lifetime, seek to make the individual whole again and no award of damages can undo death.[47] At a doctrinal level, this argument lacks teeth, even when account is taken of the practical difficulties of defining the class of beneficiaries who could recover.

THE IRISH CONSTITUTION

Various arguments could be advanced as to why the interpretation given to s 48 of the Civil Liability Act 1961 in *Morrissey* is unconstitutional. One of those most likely to succeed, at least at a level of principle, centres upon Article 42A.1 of the Irish Constitution, which is addressed specifically to children. It provides that '[t]he State recognises and affirms the natural and imprescriptible rights of all children and shall, as far as practicable, by its laws protect and vindicate those rights'. A reasonable argument could be advanced that children of victims of negligence causing death have a constitutional right to recover for loss of the care, company and society of their parent and that tort law should intervene to protect that personal right where statute has not adequately done so.

Constitutional torts have been recognised in this jurisdiction on a number of occasions, pursuant to which the Irish Constitution can be relied upon to found a claim in tort that is not otherwise available at common law.[48] In *Grant v Roche Products (Ireland) Ltd*,[49] which came before the Supreme Court, Hardiman J noted that '[t]here is ... authority, both judicial and academic, for the proposition that the law of tort is at least in certain circumstances, an important tool for the vindication of constitutional rights'.[50] Although the context was distinct, this case is at least authority for the proposition that tort law is an instrument through which constitutional rights can be vindicated.

It is also important to note that the Supreme Court has qualified the constitutional protection afforded to the child on a number of occasions. For

---

[45] *Morrissey and Morrissey v Health Service Executive, Quest Diagnostics Incorporated and MedLab Pathology Limited* [2020] IESC 43, at para 15.3.
[46] ibid.
[47] John P M White, *Irish Law of Damages for Personal Injuries and Death* (2nd edn, Butterworths Ireland 1989), at para 7.4.03.
[48] Bryan M E McMahon and William Binchy, *Law of Torts* (4th edn, Bloomsbury Professional 2015), at para 1.52; See for example *Meskell v CIE* [1973] IR 211; *Hayes v Ireland* [1987] ILRM 651; *Sullivan v Boylan* [2013] 1 IR 510.
[49] *Grant v Roche Products (Ireland) Ltd & ors* [2008] IESC, [2008] 4 IR 679.
[50] ibid, Hardiman J, para 79.

instance, in *AO & DL v The Minister for Justice, Equality and Law Reform*,[51] the Supreme Court clarified that the right of a child to the care, company and society of their parent is not absolute. Moreover, the Superior Courts are generally slow to invoke constitutional torts. In *Blehein v Minister for Health and Children*,[52] Charleton J recognised the existence of constitutional torts in Ireland but 'cautioned' that they should only be used in 'rare instances of the inadequacy of existing tort law to uphold rights that were declared by the constitution'.[53] He noted that judicial 'restraint and the duty not to legislate requires any such resort to be only where it is absolutely necessary'.[54]

A SHORT TERM SOLUTION – INTERIM AWARDS OF DAMAGES

While the ideal resolution is statutory intervention, the Superior Courts might fashion some alternative in the interim. One possibility is the awarding of interim damages pending final determination of the issue under Part IV of the Civil Liability Act 1961. In the English case of *Thompson v Arnold*,[55] the English High Court recognised the distinction between damages claimed under a personal injury action during a victim's lifetime and a Fatal Accidents dependency claim.[56] Langstaff J observed that the latter is likely to be more advantageous. This is true for a number of reasons. Firstly, the amount of the damages awarded under the 'lost years' doctrine tends to be less financially generous than those awarded under a claim for loss of earnings.[57] Secondly, any sum left unspent after the victim's death, which had been awarded to them pursuant to the 'lost years' doctrine, will be dealt with as part of their estate or according to the rules of intestacy. This may disadvantage dependants when one considers that, by contrast, dependants are the direct beneficiaries of a dependency claim.

Interim payments, equal or almost equal to a lifetime award, have been described as a 'well-recognised'[58] way to overcome the issue where liability has already been conceded. In *Thompson*, the English Court of Appeal decision of *Murray v Shuter*[59] was cited as an authority, in which case Stephenson LJ found that a judge may order an adjournment of a trial, which was ready and due to

---

[51] *AO & DL v The Minister for Justice, Equality and Law Reform* [2003] 1 IR 1.
[52] *Blehein v Minister for Health and Children* [2018] IESC 40.
[53] *Blehein v Minister for Health and Children* [2018] IESC 40, Charleton J, at para 6.
[54] ibid, Charleton J, para 15.
[55] *Thompson v Arnold* [2007] EWHC 1875.
[56] ibid.
[57] Where a man and woman lived together, the 'lost years' have in recent years tended to amount to 50% of the victim's future earnings whereas the calculations for a fatal claim dependency award generally start at 75% of same; *Thompson v Arnold* [2007] EWHC 1875, Langstaff J, at para 24.
[58] ibid, Langstaff J, para 28.
[59] *Murray v Shuter* [1976] QB 972.

be heard so that the dependents of a plaintiff could recover the more 'generous financial compensation likely to be awarded under the Fatal Accidents Act'.[60]

In England, there is provision for making interim awards of damages under the Civil Procedure Rules 25.6 to 25.9. While there is no equivalent jurisdiction in Ireland, the High Court has accepted Order 36 Rule 34 of the Superior Courts[61] as being sufficiently broad to allow a court to adjourn a case and make an interim award of damages pending a final assessment of the claim.[62] In his assessment in *Miley v Birthistle*, Barr J also alluded to the court's 'inherent jurisdiction' to grant such awards where liability has been conceded.[63]

DID THE 2017 LEGISLATIVE PROVISION FOR PERIODIC PAYMENT ORDERS (PPOs) ALTER THE COURTS' INHERENT JURISDICTION TO GRANT INTERIM AWARDS OF DAMAGES?

Before the legislative introduction of periodic payment orders (PPOs) in 2017, the State Claims Agency developed a practice in cases where liability was not an issue of making interim payments of damages in catastrophic injury cases. This was generally done where there was uncertainty as to the level of care that would be needed into the future for victims of negligence. The Irish legislative provision for PPOs, set out in an amendment to the Civil Liability Act 1961, has been described by the High Court as unsatisfactory. In *Hegarty v Health Service Executive*,[64] Murphy J expressed the view that it would almost inevitably result in systematic under-compensation of plaintiffs since it only requires referral to the Harmonised Index of Consumer Prices with no discretion or deviation permitted by the court.[65] Given that the cost of care is usually the most substantial component in any calculation of future needs, if there is to be an accurate assessment, the annual amounts afforded to plaintiffs for future home care needs must be linked to a wage-based index.[66]

In the High Court, Murphy J concluded that the 2017 amendment did not 'automatically remove, replace, or adapt the pre-existing jurisdiction of the Court'[67] to make interim awards of damages. She felt that the relevant section of the Act made it clear that the power conferred on the court to make a PPO is

---

[60] *Thompson v Arnold* [2007] EWHC 1875, at para 28.
[61] Order 36 Rule 34 of the Rules of the Superior Courts 1986, as amended, provides that 'the judge may, if he thinks it expedient for the interests of justice, postpone or adjourn a trial for such time, and upon which terms, if any, as he shall think fit'.
[62] *Miley v Birthistle* [2016] IEHC 196, [2016] 4 JIC 1904, Barr J.
[63] ibid.
[64] *Hegarty (A Minor Suing by his Mother and Next Friend Jacinta Collins) v Health Service Executive* [2019] IEHC 788.
[65] ibid para 72.
[66] ibid para 63.
[67] ibid para 56.

discretionary.[68] As such, the court made the determination that the legislative introduction of PPOs only sought to 'supplement the Court's existing jurisdiction rather than ... oust or replace it'.[69] Based on this determination as well as the perceived deficiencies of the new legislative scheme for PPOs, the court approved an interim award of damages, 'including a payment in satisfaction of a plaintiff's claim for general damages, as well as losses incurred to the date of settlement, in addition to the costs of care for a specified period'.[70] While this is useful in that it is an example of the High Court making use of its 'inherent jurisdiction' to grant interim awards notwithstanding the new legislative provision for PPOs, it is not clear whether it would operate in precisely the same way in situations where the concern is related not to uncertainty about future care needs, but reserving to dependants the opportunity to sue post-death. Nor is it certain that if a victim was to initiate a claim and achieve an interim award of damages, her dependants would subsequently be able to demonstrate that, at the time of her death, she 'would have been' entitled to bring a claim so as bring the dependants' suit within the parameters of s 48 of the Civil Liability Act 1961.

A PERMANENT RESOLUTION – STATUTORY INTERVENTION

In terms of statutory intervention, there are a number of possibilities. First, it is conceivable that an alteration to s 48 of the 1961 Act could remove the requirement for there to have been an actionable suit immediately prior to the death of the victim – i.e., where a personal injuries claim had been pursued to judgment or settlement or had become statute barred, the dependants of the deceased would still be able to bring a claim under s 48 of the 1961 Act. This might involve the removal of the more problematic portion of s 48(1). It could stipulate that:

> where the death of a person is caused by the wrongful act of another, the person who would have been so liable shall be liable to an action for damages for the benefit of the dependants of the deceased.[71]

---

[68] ibid para 58; s 51(1) of the Civil Liability (Amendment) Act 2017 sets out that where a court awards damages for personal injuries to a plaintiff who has suffered catastrophic injury, the court may order that the whole or part of such damages ... be paid by a defendant in the proceedings in the form of a periodic payment.

[69] *Hegarty (A Minor Suing by his Mother and Next Friend Jacinta Collins) v Health Service Executive* [2019] IEHC 788, at para 57; Murphy J also cited *McEnery v Sheahan* [2019] IESC 64 as authority for this conclusion in which case the Supreme Court restated that legislative change does not automatically change the Court's jurisdiction absent clear evidence to that effect. See also *AM v Health Service Executive* [2019] IESC 3, in which the Supreme Court held that its wardship jurisdiction was not automatically ousted by provisions of the Mental Health Act 2001.

[70] *Hegarty (A Minor Suing by his Mother and Next Friend Jacinta Collins) v Health Service Executive* [2019] IEHC 788, at para 42.

[71] This involves removing the phrase 'such as would have entitled the party injured, but for his death, to maintain an action and recover damages in respect thereof' from the section, which was identified by the Supreme Court in *Morrissey* as giving rise to the present difficulty.

Such an amendment could be accompanied by an additional subsection proscribing double recovery of damages such that an individual cannot recover for the same head of damages in a personal injuries action and in a suit maintained pursuant to Part IV of the Civil Liability Act 1961.

Another alternative is the inclusion of a proviso at the beginning of s 48 to remove uncertainty as to the proper interpretation of s 48. This would involve a stipulation that s 48(1) is not to be understood as barring a claim pursuant to Part IV of the Civil Liability Act 1961 where a personal injuries claim has already been pursued to finality. This would also require the inclusion of a provision prohibiting double recovery. While this would remove some of the anomalies presented by the decision in *Morrissey*, it could create new ones. Specifically, it could give rise to potential for injustice from the perspective of defendants. For instance, it would expose defendants to a wrongful death suit even where an unsuccessful personal injuries claim has already been brought against them during the injured person's lifetime and thus violate the principles of *res judicata* and issue estoppel.

A further alternative is a legislative provision allowing victims of negligence and their dependants to recover for loss of free services in personal injuries claims, being the exact head of damages which Mr Morrissey was prohibited from recovering in the Supreme Court. Such a provision would introduce a further exception to the common law rule established in *Baker v Bolton* so as to ameliorate its harsh effects even beyond what is currently provided for in the Civil Liability Act 1961.

CONCLUSION

The Supreme Court decision in *Morrissey* made clear that while the Civil Liability Act 1961 ameliorated the harsh effects of the old common law rule, it did not go far enough. The reality is that s 48 (2) of this Act is limited in its scope. While other understandings can *reasonably* be advanced,[72] its proper interpretation is one which requires there to have been an actionable suit immediately prior to the death of victims of negligence so as to give dependants a cause of action under the legislation. This forces victims to make a tactical decision as to whether they wish to pursue a personal injuries claim during their lifetime in order to ensure their dependents are taken care of into the future. Interim awards of damages *may* offer a solution in the short term. It is not, however, clear if and how they will operate in practice in this context. Thus, the optimal solution may be legislation. This chapter has suggested certain statutory amendments which could resolve the issues engendered by *Morrissey*. Some of these alternatives may give rise to problems from the perspective of defendants. Nonetheless, given that there is such major difficulty in

---

[72] Indeed, they were advanced by counsel for the plaintiffs before the Supreme Court in *Morrissey* by reference to the US cases of *Gaudet* and *Moragne*. Such an interpretation is also espoused by various academics as discussed above.

'attempting to produce an internally logical and coherent regime to compensate those who may have suffered financial loss as a result of death or reduced life expectancy',[73] the potential for these problems should not deter the Oireachtas from acting. Equally, potential difficulty should not automatically deter the courts from resolving the issue at the judicial level, either by recognising a common law cause of action for wrongful death or re-interpreting s 48 of the Civil Liability Act 1961 as not requiring there to have been an actionable suit at the time of death, even if that involves effectively overruling a unanimous decision of the Supreme Court. The judicial responsibility to defend the personal rights of individuals cannot be understated and at some point, as once famously stated by the former Associate Justice of the US Supreme Court, Benjamin N Cardozo:

> History or custom or social utility or some compelling sense of justice or sometimes perhaps a semi-intuitive apprehension of the pervading spirit of our law must come to the rescue of the anxious judge and tell him where to go.

---

[73] *Morrissey and Morrissey v Health Service Executive, Quest Diagnostics Incorporated and MedLab Pathology Limited* [2020] IESC 43, at para 15.16.

CHAPTER XII

DO THE PERSONAL INJURIES GUIDELINES OF THE JUDICIAL COUNCIL ESTABLISH A STATUTORY CAP UPON GENERAL DAMAGES AND, IF SO, ARE THEY CONSTITUTIONALLY SUSPECT IN DOING SO?

Lauren Keane and Derry O'Donovan SC[1]

The Personal Injuries Guidelines (the Guidelines) were adopted by the Judicial Council on 6 March 2021 pursuant to s 7 of the Judicial Council Act 2019. Their enactment into law was effected by s 30 of the Family Leave and Miscellaneous Provisions Act 2021, which amended ss 99 and 100 of the 2019 Act, which in turn amended s 22 of the Civil Liability and Courts Act 2004. They commenced on 24 April 2021.

One of the many issues which arises from their enactment into law is whether they now set an unprecedented statutory cap on general damages at €550,000. If so, this would not appear to be in accordance with the preceding fluid and changing nature of this cap, which heretofore was exclusively a matter of judicial discretion, having not been specified in the Book of Quantum, which immediately before the coming into operation of s 99 of the Act of 2019, stands published by the Personal Injuries Assessment Board under the Personal Injuries Assessment Board Act 2003. As stated in the Law Reform Commission's Report on *Capping Damages in Personal Injuries Actions*,[2] the cap on general damages was understood to be a judicial matter which 'has been raised from time to time so that it currently (August 2020) stands at €500,000'[3] following the decision of the Supreme Court on 19 March 2020 in *Morrissey and anor v Health Service Executive and ors*.

The question arises, therefore, as to whether the legislation implementing the Guidelines is open to constitutional challenge by reason of the legislature

---

[1] Lauren Keane prepared this chapter as a final year undergraduate law student at the School of Law at Trinity College Dublin. Derry O'Donovan SC is a member of the Inner Bar of Ireland.
[2] Law Reform Commission Report, *Capping Damages in Personal Injuries Actions* (LRS 126-2020).
[3] ibid para 2.33.

having fettered the exclusive jurisdiction and discretion of the judiciary to raise the cap on general damages in an appropriate case and/or by impeding the right of access of citizens to the courts and to the vindication of their rights therein. At the very least, the Guidelines raise a concern as to whether there is now a legislative restriction upon the autonomy of the Superior Courts as provided for by the Constitution of Ireland in relation to fixing the limit for the assessment of general damages in a personal injuries action. The personal and constitutional rights of the citizen to bodily integrity and access to the courts would also appear to be called into question by a restriction, imposed by statute, which caps the level of damages that the Superior Courts can award for compensation for catastrophic injuries.

This issue is of particular relevance in the context of medical negligence litigation. With increasing frequency, cases are coming before the Superior Courts in which claimants are seeking general damages for the maximum amount possible in law by reason of them facing impending and certain death in the foreseeable future by reason of an error in the clinical diagnosis of cancer or otherwise. Accordingly, it is of central importance in such litigation to determine the extent of which the cap of €550,000, as prescribed by the Guidelines, is definitively applicable to this litigation or whether it could be subjected to a successful constitutional challenge.

In order to properly examine the constitutionality of the Guidelines in this specific respect, it is helpful to commence from the foundational principle of general damages. Upholding the *restitutio in integrum* principle, the purpose of an award of general damages, that is an award for pain and suffering or loss of amenity, is to put the injured person in the same position, as far as money can do, as if the injury involved had not happened. Although damages are, in theory at least, restitutional, the difficulty inherent in calculating them is that the loss is non-financial. Thus, when one subjects damages for pain and suffering to a 'cap', one is placing a financial limit upon a personal harm and loss which is not monetary in nature. Accordingly, when assessing general damages, a court awards a sum which, by convention and experience, society considers to be fair and just compensation for the injury complained of.

JUDGE-MADE UPPER LIMIT ON GENERAL DAMAGES

Beginning in the 1980s, the courts developed an upper limit or 'cap' on general damages for the most catastrophic type of injury such as quadriplegia. The Supreme Court in *Sinnott v Quinnsworth* set this cap at IR£150,000,[4] a figure that was raised to €500,000 by this court in the most recent decision of

---

[4] *Sinnott v Quinnsworth Ltd* [1984] ILRM 523.

Morrissey and another v Health Service Executive and others,[5] to take account of inflation and other economic factors.

Distinction between 'cap' and 'non-cap' cases?

The application of the cap itself has been subject to intense debate following comments by the Supreme Court, in the case of *Gough v Neary* [2003] IESC 39, that it only applies in cases with large special damages. In that case, Geoghegan J commented that:

> In my view, there is no compulsory 'cap' if there is no 'omnibus sum' or in other words if the special damages are low. On the other hand that does not mean that the 'cap' figure cannot be taken into account in a general way in assessing the appropriate general damages in a non-cap case.[6]

If the upper limit or 'cap' first enunciated by the Supreme Court in *Sinnott* applied to cases where special damages were low that would, as Geoghegan J noted, certainly be an extension of the original rule. In the absence of any express statement in *Morrissey* that casts doubt on comments such as those of Geoghegan J in the *Gough* case, together with a consistent thread of judgments of the High Court over the past twenty years relating to the applicability of a cap upon general damages, the preferred view is that the upper limit or 'cap' has only continued to apply in cases where both the special damages and the general damages awards are very high, that is in what have been termed as 'omnibus' or 'totality' cases.[7] At the same time, as also noted by Geoghegan J in *Gough v Neary*, while the upper limit or 'cap' does not apply, as such, in cases where special damages are low, this does not mean that the 'cap' figure cannot be taken into account in a general way when assessing the appropriate general damages in such cases when special damages are low. The significance of this distinction between 'cap' and 'non-cap' cases in the specific context of medical negligence litigation will be returned to at the conclusion of this chapter.

Proportionality

With that clarification, we can then consider the courts' method of calculating general damages by applying the principle of proportionality. Proportionality requires an award to be fair to both parties so that 'there is a rational relationship between awards of damages in personal injuries cases'.[8] This concept of proportionality in awards of damages for personal injuries thus falls to be considered in two particular respects, first against the yardstick of the cap for the most serious injuries and where on the spectrum of damages

---

[5] *Morrissey and another v Health Service Executive and others* [2020] IESC 6.
[6] *Gough v Neary* [2003] IESC 39.
[7] *McKeown v Crosby* [2020] IECA 242.
[8] *MN v SM* [2005] IESC 17, at para 44.

the injury under consideration fits.[9] Secondly, the award must be considered in light of awards given by courts for comparable injuries.

This desire for a proportionate mechanism led the Court of Appeal to develop a three-point scale of injuries related to the assessment of damages. This was set out in *Nolan v Wirenski* where the Court of Appeal stated that

> minor injuries attract appropriately modest damages, middling injuries moderate damages and more severe injuries damages of a level which are clearly distinguishable in terms of quantum from those that fall into the other lesser categories.[10]

In two judgments from the Court of Appeal in 2016, the court pronounced that while an award must, therefore, be 'proportionate within the scheme of awards for personal injuries generally',[11] that is not to say that the judicial limit or cap is a maximum or '[t]hat there have not been cases where that sum has occasionally been exceeded'.[12] It is important and desirable, however, that the trial judge explains how a particular figure for damages is arrived at, since otherwise the appellate court is left in the dark about the trial judge's approach and whether it ought to be regarded as correct or not.[13]

These statements of the Court of Appeal then led to an interesting assertion by Clarke CJ when giving the sole judgment of the Supreme Court in *Morrissey and anor v Health Service Executive and ors*,[14] when he set out the manner in which the 'cap' should be altered in future. He stated:

> it does not seem to me that a first instance judge should alter the limit even when that judge feels that circumstances have changed sufficiently to justify a departure from a previous limit set by appellate courts. Rather, as applied in a situation where a first instance judge is bound by precedent set by a higher court, it should be open to a first instance judge, while awarding damages at the limit previously fixed, to set out a reasoned basis for supporting that a higher limit might be appropriate in the prevailing circumstances and, thus, to leave it to an appellate court, most likely the Court of Appeal to consider whether such an increased limit is appropriate. It is, of course, open to a party who wishes to seek to persuade the courts that a different limit should be applied, to lead whatever evidence they might consider appropriate to that end. It would then be open to a trial judge, in giving reasons for suggesting a change in the limit, to set out whatever evidence was considered persuasive. Such an approach would pay appropriate respect to the experience of

---

[9] Noted by Irvine J (as she then was) in *Shannon v O'Sullivan* [2016] IECA 93.
[10] *Nolan v Wirenski* [2016] 1 IR 461, at para 44.
[11] *Shannon v O'Sullivan* [2016] IECA 93, at para 32; *Nolan v Wirenski* [2016] 1 IR 461, at para 31.
[12] *Shannon v O'Sullivan* [2016] IECA 93, at para 36.
[13] *Nolan v Wirenski* [2016] 1 IR 461.
[14] *Morrissey and another v Health Service Executive and others* [2020] IESC 6.

trial judges but also ensure consistency by ensuring that any changes are made in only one place, i.e. the Court of Appeal.[15]

The additional significance of this statement by Clarke CJ is that the judicial discretion on the limit for damages is of such magnitude that the Court of Appeal is not bound by the limit which has last been judicially set by the Supreme Court in *Morrissey* of €500,000. The application of the Guidelines must proceed in a manner which is constitutional. Consistent with this, it would then appear that the upper limit on general damages in the Guidelines can be departed from by the Superior Courts in the way this judgment suggests. Provided there are reasons given for this departure, it would then be up to the Court of Appeal to ensure the proportionality of the award.

THE PERSONAL INJURIES GUIDELINES: A STATUTORY CAP ON GENERAL DAMAGES?

As noted earlier, the Personal Injuries Guidelines of the Judicial Council are now established in law by statute. Section 22 of the Civil Liability and Courts Act 2004, as significantly amended by s 99 of the Judicial Council Act 2019, provides that:

> The court shall, in assessing damages in a personal injuries action –
>
> (a) have regard to the personal injuries Guidelines, and
> (b) where it departs from those Guidelines, state the reasons for such departure in giving its decision.

Accordingly, while the court retains its independence and discretion when it comes to making an award of general damages, it is mandatory for the court to make its assessment having regard to the Guidelines. This is subject always to the proviso that where it chooses to depart from the Guidelines it should detail, in its judgment, the considerations which warranted that departure. Arising from these developments, the courts will no longer be required to have regard to the Book of Quantum in their assessment of damages.

The Guidelines also set out the general principles which should be employed by a court when making an award. They provide that any award of damages for personal injury must be fair and reasonable for both the claimant and defendant. Further, awards must be proportionate to the injuries sustained and to the awards of damages commonly made in other cases involving greater or lesser magnitude.[16] It is clear, therefore that in preparing the Guidelines, the

---

[15] ibid para 14.25.
[16] See note 4 at p 5. Regarding the importance of principle of proportionality, the Guidelines expressly cite the judgment of Denham CJ in *MN v SM* [2005] IESC 30; [2005] 4 IR 461 and Clarke CJ in *Morrissey and another v Health Service Executive and others* [2020] IESC 6.

Judicial Committee which did so was ever cognisant that the proportionality principle, both in regard to the injuries sustained in an individual case and in regard to the level of awards made in other cases, must be satisfied.[17] To that end, the Committee set the cap on damages for the highest level of award for catastrophic injury at €550,000, taking guidance from the level of top awards provided in suitable comparator countries, as well as undertaking an economic analysis regarding the appropriate level of the highest award to be provided for general damages having regard to the present condition of the Irish economy. The Committee concluded that the level of award for catastrophic injury cited in *Morrissey and anor v Health Service Executive and ors*[18] was appropriate and was not out of alignment with other jurisdictions with a similar standard of living to that enjoyed in this State.[19]

A key consideration in relation to the constitutionality of the Guidelines is whether the cap it sets out is mandatory or presumptive in nature. The Guidelines note that while it is 'mandatory' for a trial judge 'to have regard to the Guidelines',[20] should he or she consider that the justice of the case warrants an award above the level of damages proposed for that or a similar injury in the Guidelines, the trial judge retains discretion to state the considerations which brought about that departure.[21] The question then arises as to what the phrase 'have regard to' entails.

This has been considered by the court in a number of cases.[22] There are certain steps which the trial judge must follow. The trial judge:

1) must not ignore the Guidelines and proceed as if they did not exist;
2) must inform himself or herself fully of, and give reasonable consideration to, such Guidelines with a view to accommodating their objectives;
3) is not, however, required rigidly or 'slavishly' to comply with the Guidelines and may depart from them for bona fide reasons.[23]

Following this analysis, the permissive nature of the phrase 'have regard to' and the discretion retained by the trial judge clearly strengthens the status of the Guidelines by comparison with the approach to the Book of Quantum. The effect is that the courts must apply the Guidelines or else explain why not, being a form of 'comply or explain' test that nonetheless has been careful to ensure that a court retains the ability to make an award that is consistent with the proportionality principle articulated in the case law. While this new 'comply

---

[17] *Personal Injuries Guidelines Committee Report*, at para 37.
[18] *Morrissey and another v Health Service Executive and others* [2020] IESC 6.
[19] *Personal Injuries Guidelines Committee Report*, December 2020, paras 82 and 110.
[20] Section 99 of the Judicial Council Act 2019, amending s 22 of the Civil Liability and Courts Act 2004.
[21] See note 4 at p 6.
[22] *McEvoy v Meath County Council* [2003] 1 IR 208, 220–224.
[23] See n 1, 54.

or explain' regime imposes some limit on judicial discretion, it also retains a key element of judicial independence.[24] The Guidelines, therefore, provide for a presumptive cap on general damages, a cap that the court 'must have regard to' when making an award, but one which it can depart from provided there are reasons given in the judgment. The question then arises as to whether the Guidelines are constitutionally suspect, having regard to proportionality in the constitutional context and the separation of powers.

ARE THE PERSONAL INJURIES GUIDELINES CONSTITUTIONALLY SUSPECT IN ESTABLISHING A STATUTORY CAP ON GENERAL DAMAGES?

Does the cap on damages in the Guidelines infringe constitutional rights?

The first question to ask is whether the Guidelines infringe certain constitutional rights and if so, would it be a permissible restriction on those rights? In its report entitled *Capping Damages in Personal Injuries Actions*,[25] the Law Reform Commission observed that once a constitutional right is engaged, the capping legislation may place limits on the constitutional right so long as these limits can satisfy certain tests that have been identified by the courts. The tests to be satisfied include firstly, the proportionality test which was first set out by the Supreme Court in *Heaney v Ireland*[26] and secondly, the rationality test, which was originally formulated by the Supreme Court in *Tuohy v Courtney*.[27]

The constitutional right of the citizen to bodily integrity

The right to bodily integrity (an unspecified right under Article 40.3.1 of the Constitution of Ireland 1937) must be considered because tort law and its remedies, including damages, have been identified as a means by which the State meets its constitutional obligation to safeguard this right.[28] As noted by the Law Reform Commission, the Constitution imposes the following standards in terms of common law causes of action:

> First, the law must be just (*Sweeney v Duggan*); the law must be basically effective (*Blehein v Minister for Health*); and if the plaintiff cannot establish liability under a common law tort (such as negligence or malfeasance of public office) because the facts of his or her case do not meet the elements of the common law cause of action, the existence of the tort will usually meet the standard of a 'basically effective' remedy, so that no separate claim for breach of a constitutional right will, usually, arise (*MC v The Clinical Director of the Central Mental Hospital*).[29]

---

[24] ibid 55.
[25] See n 1.
[26] *Heaney v Ireland* [1994] 3 IR 593.
[27] *Tuohy v Courtney* [1994] 3 IR 1.
[28] See note 1, at p 57.
[29] See note 1, at p 62.

It should also be noted that Article 40.3.2 of the Constitution provides that the State shall, in particular, by its laws protect as best it may from unjust attack and, in the case of injustice done, vindicate the life, person, good name and property rights of every citizen. Ultimately though, the constitutional viability of the capping legislation centres upon whether it is capable of adequately vindicating the constitutional right to bodily integrity. The statement in *Sweeney v Duggan*[30] that Article 40.3.2 of the Constitution offers 'no more than a guarantee of a just law of negligence' supports the contention that capping legislation that takes the form of a mandatory cap would be unconstitutional, on the basis that, inherent in a 'just law of negligence' is the capacity for the plaintiff to obtain a just remedy. This necessarily entails that the courts maintain jurisdiction to award proportionate compensation that bears a rational relationship to the harm caused.

Nevertheless, it is reassuring to understand that the Guidelines go to considerable lengths to emphasise that the longstanding principle of proportionality continues to apply, so that compensation for pain and suffering should be proportionate to the severity of the injury suffered.[31] In addition, the cap is not mandatory but rather it is mandatory for the trial judge to have regard to the Guidelines which provide for a cap of €550,000, which further supports the constitutionality of the current position.

The constitutional right to litigate and to an effective remedy

The right to litigate and the correlative right to an effective remedy (Article 40.3.2 of the Constitution of Ireland 1937) must also be satisfied in the application of the Guidelines. Consistent with case law, the Personal Injuries Commission has defined these rights as:

> the right to achieve by action in the courts the appropriate remedy upon proof of an actionable wrong causing damages or loss as recognised by law.[32]

In essence, the courts must

> ensure the remedies available to a litigant are effective to protect the right at issue and that our procedural law (including all legislation restricting or regulating access to the courts) respects basic fairness of procedures and is neither arbitrary nor unfair.[33]

---

[30] *Sweeney v Duggan* [1997] 2 IR 531.
[31] Maura McNally SC, '*Qui Bono?*' The Bar Review 2021, 26 (2), 57.
[32] Personal Injuries Commission, First Report of the Personal Injuries Commission (2017), at page 17.
[33] *S v Minister for Justice, Equality and Reform* [2011] IEHC 31, at paragraph 27.

Restriction on rights: proportionality and rationality

In the context of personal rights, including the right to bodily integrity, Article 40.3.1 of the Constitution of Ireland 1937 obliges the State only to vindicate those personal rights 'as far as practicable'. In addition, pursuant to Article 40.3.2, the State is required, by its laws, to vindicate the life, person, good name and property rights of every citizen from 'unjust attack'. As a result, the issue then becomes as to what extent a curtailment of these constitutional rights can be constitutionally permissible? In this regard, the courts have employed two standards, namely, the proportionality test and the rationality test.

Proportionality

Proportionality, in the ordinary sense of the word, is the key principle in assessing the constitutional viability of legislation capping awards for general damages. The test of proportionality was considered by the Supreme Court in *Heaney v Ireland*[34] where it was established that it must satisfy four elements:

1) The objective of the provision must be of sufficient importance to warrant overriding a constitutionally protected right (sufficient importance);
2) The measure should be rationally connected to the objective and not be arbitrary, unfair or based on irrational considerations (rational connection);
3) The measure should impair the right(s) as little as possible (minimum impairment);
4) The measure must be such that its effects on rights are proportional to the objective (overall proportionality).

The first two elements of the proportionality test, sufficient importance and rational connection, can be taken together and require consideration of the policy objectives that the legislation seeks to achieve. The sufficient importance element refers to the importance of the objective that the legislation seeks to achieve and is not generally applied by the courts in a rigorous manner. In addition, the rational connection element of the test requires that there be a rational connection between the measure and the objective, with the additional requirement that the measure chosen should not be arbitrary or unfair in achieving the relevant objective.

An objective of legislation that places a cap on awards of general damages is to control insurance costs. As the State is often a defendant in personal injuries claims, another objective is to achieve savings in these claims which could be used for other areas of public expenditure. The courts have endorsed the principle that, in the assessment of damages for personal injuries, regard must be had to the social good. This includes how the level of awards for damages may impact on insurance costs, taxation or other State services. For example,

---
[34] [1994] 3 IR 593.

the Supreme Court in *Kearney v McQuillan and North Eastern Health Board (No 2)* stated that:

> [e]ach award of damages for personal injuries in the courts may be reflected in increased insurance costs, taxation, or, perhaps, a reduction in some social service.[35]

It is arguable, therefore, that legislation which provides for the capping of general damages satisfies the rational connection test where it may, though not necessarily must, result in a less adverse impact on taxation and other publicly financed resources resulting in increased finances availability for social services.

One then turns to consider the 'minimum impairment' and 'overall proportionality' elements of the fourfold test of proportionality as enunciated by the Supreme Court in *Heaney v Ireland*.

In relation to the former, it is critical to stress again that while it is mandatory for the trial judge to 'have regard to' the cap on general damages in the Guidelines, he or she retains the discretion to depart from them provided the reasons for doing so are set out in the judgment. By allowing for an uplift on general damages beyond €550,000, this essentially makes this cap presumptive and minimises the impairment of the citizens' constitutional rights.

In order to satisfy the final element of the fourfold test, namely 'overall proportionality', one must weigh the objectives against the extent to which a constitutional right is restricted and determine whether an overall balance has been achieved. The objectives of the Guidelines included ensuring that awards of general damages are proportionate to the injury suffered by the plaintiff and to regulate the cost of insurance. When these are balanced against the presumptive nature of the cap and when the level of awards and their categorisation is consistent with suitable comparator countries' means, it suggests that the cap is proportionate and is unlikely to be impugned as disproportionately interfering with the constitutional rights of a claimant.

Rationality

The rationality test, established by the Supreme Court in *Tuohy v Courtney*,[36] was defined as follows:

> The Court is satisfied that in a challenge to the constitutional validity of any statute in the enactment of which the Oireachtas has been engaged in such a balancing function, the role of the Courts is not to impose their view of the correct or desirable balance in substitution for the view of

---

[35] *Kearney v McQuillan and North Eastern Health Board (No 2)* [2012] IESC 43, at para 28.
[36] *Tuohy v Courtney* [1994] 3 IR 1.

the legislature as displayed in their legislation but rather to determine from an objective stance whether the balance contained in the impugned legislation is so contrary to reason and fairness as to constitute an unjust attack on some individual's constitutional rights.[37]

This test applies to legislation that seeks to balance competing constitutional rights, so that, in the present instance, a court must balance the plaintiff's constitutional rights to bodily integrity (Article 40.3.1) and to litigate (Article 40.3.2) with the defendant's right to property (Article 40.3.2). In essence, the capping legislation must not be so contrary to reason and fairness as to constitute an unjust attack on an individual's constitutional rights. In that regard, the Supreme Court held in *King v Minister for the Environment (No 2)*,[38] in connection with the enactment of legislation concerning eligibility to stand as a general election candidate, that 'the Oireachtas must be considered to have a reasonable degree of discretion ... provided that the categories of persons concerned are so determined in a manner which is rational and not arbitrary'.[39] Under the *Tuohy* test, the courts are reluctant to interfere with the discretion of the Oireachtas. Against this background, the Guidelines draw well-defined categories that distinguish between minor, moderate, severe and catastrophic injuries. Since these are comparable to the three-point scale that is often employed by the courts[40] and as a trial judge is only mandated to have regard to the cap on general damages in the Guidelines, it is unlikely that they would fail an application of the *Tuohy* rationality test.

Does the cap on general damages in the Guidelines wrongly interfere with the autonomy and discretion of the Superior Courts to make awards?

In answering this question, one has to determine whether the upper limit on general damages in the Guidelines is subject to judicial discretion, that is whether it is in essence a judicial benchmark rather than a statutory cap. If one answers this question in the affirmative, a further issue arises as to whether the statutory implementation of these Guidelines has wrongly fettered this discretion.

Article 34.1 of the Constitution of Ireland 1937 provides that justice shall be administered in courts established by law by judges appointed in the manner provided by the Constitution. Accordingly, any restriction of judicial discretion by the legislature, in considering the limit of an award for general damages in personal injuries actions, may be perceived as interfering with judicial independence as enshrined in the Irish Constitution. The accuracy of this perception has to be tested, however, against the following factors.

---

[37] *Tuohy v Courtney* [1994] 3 IR 1, at p 47.
[38] *King v Minister for the Environment (No 2)* [2006] IESC 61, [2007] 1 IR 296.
[39] *King v Minister for the Environment (No 2)* [2006] IESC 61, [2007] 1 IR 296, at p 317.
[40] *Nolan v Wirenski* [2016] IECA 56, [2016] 1 IR 461.

Firstly, the Guidelines were formulated by the judiciary.[41] Those charged with determining the appropriate level of damages in personal injuries litigation adjusted and endorsed this upper limit of €550,000 for the assessment of general damages. Secondly, the Guidelines apply some of the principles established in case law. In relation to the cap on general damages, the Guidelines actually enhanced the limit of €500,000 as prescribed by the Supreme Court in *Morrissey and anor v Health Service Executive and ors*. Thirdly, the power remains vested in the Superior Courts, having considered the limit prescribed by the Guidelines, to then abandon it in the manner as directed by Clarke CJ in his judgment in *Morrissey* as referred to earlier and by giving proper reasons for doing so in the judgment. As a result, the discretion of the judiciary in relation to adjusting a cap on general damages is retained. Where exceptional circumstances arise that, in the court's view, justify granting an award of damages in excess of €550,000, it remains within the court's discretion to do so, provided they give reasons in the judgment.

Accordingly, the corollary of preserving the discretion of the Superior Courts is that the limit on general damages in the Guidelines is essentially a notional 'cap' for the most serious of injuries, set at €550,000, which can be departed from provided there are reasons given for doing so by the court in question. The Guidelines do not implement a strict statutory cap upon general damages. As a result, they are not constitutionally suspect on this ground. Furthermore, this notional cap of €550,000 for awards of general damages is consistent with the fourfold test for proportionality as enunciated by the Supreme Court in *Heaney v Ireland*. When assessing proportionality, it is of critical significance that the Superior Courts will be able to depart from this cap in particular cases, subject to an obligation to state the reasons for why they do so.

In essence, the suggestion that the Guidelines create a cap of €550,000 on general damages for pain and suffering is conceptual and is not to be interpreted strictly or fixed in practice. The procedure for assessing appropriate damages for personal injuries will still begin with the trial judge in the High Court assessing the injury, having due regard to the notional cap as set out in the Guidelines of €550,000. The Court of Appeal retains the discretion to adjust this upper limit or cap where appropriate in accordance with the procedure as set out in the judgment of Clarke CJ in *Morrissey*. The Guidelines do not, therefore, establish a strict cap upon general damages and they cannot then be viewed as constitutionally suspect on this ground.

---

[41] The members of the Personal Injuries Guidelines Committee were Ms Justice Mary Irvine, Chairperson and President of the High Court, Mr Justice Séamus Noonan, Mr Justice Michael MacGrath, Mr Justice Senan Allen, Judge Jacqueline Linnane, Judge Séan O'Donnabháin and Judge Brian O'Shea.

The specific relevance of the distinction between 'cap' and 'non-cap' cases in the context of medical negligence litigation

Finally, it is important to return to the debate concerning the application of a cap on general damages which followed after the decision of the Supreme Court in the case of *Gough v Neary* and, in particular, the judgment given by Geoghegan J therein. In his judgment, Geoghegan J suggested, having reviewed key earlier decisions of the High Court and the Supreme Court, that the cap only applied in cases where a large sum for special damages was being claimed. In such cases, the award for general damages could be calibrated on the basis of an upper limit so that the totality of the amount awarded would not be excessive. Geoghegan J stated:

> I have always understood that the principle of the 'cap' first enunciated in *Sinnott v. Quinnsworth Limited* [1984] ILRM 523 applied only to very substantial damages cases where there was a high element of special damages particularly loss of earnings.[42]

Geoghegan J proceeded to clarify that in the judgment of O'Higgins CJ in *Sinnott*, the former Chief Justice formed the view that a limit of IR£150,000 should be applied 'in a case of this nature' and that 'the words that precede that opinion make it perfectly clear that he is talking of a case where all the future needs etc. of the plaintiff had been covered by special damages'. This led Geoghegan J to confirm that in his view there is no compulsory 'cap' if there is no 'omnibus sum' or in other words if the special damages are low. He did also balance this view significantly, however, by stating that this does not mean that the 'cap' figure cannot be taken into account in a general way in assessing the appropriate general damages in a non-cap case.[43]

In medical negligence litigation, a particularly tragic set of circumstances can arise when a relatively young person is facing an impending death because of a pre-cancer or an early cancer not having been detected, diagnosed or otherwise treated in a timely manner, such as to give rise to a breach of duty in the clinical care provided to that person. Since the decision of the Supreme Court in *Morrissey*, the situation of a young mother, with children, who is dying by reason of a clinical breach of duty in the care of her condition, is additionally fraught because a claim for the loss of the free services of this mother cannot be advanced by her, for the benefit of her children, in her own claim for damages for personal injury before she dies. Added to this, the judgment of the Supreme Court leaves open the question as to whether her children can maintain a subsequent claim for the loss of her free services after her death, pursuant to Part IV of the Civil Liability Act 1961 as amended, as s 48(2) of that Act provides that only one action may be brought against the same person in respect of her death.

---

[42] *Gough v Neary* [2003] IESC 39.
[43] ibid.

In such a case, if the mother in question was engaged in the full-time care of her children and does not have a loss of earnings claim and if she also has a modest claim for future care needs as her life expectancy is drastically foreshortened, a compelling case can be made that this is a 'non-cap' situation in determining general damages and that the limit of €550,000, as prescribed by the Guidelines does not apply. In accordance with the judgment of Clarke CJ in *Morrissey*, if the trial judge in the High Court is persuaded of this argument, the correct procedure would then be for the trial judge to set out a reasoned basis as to why a higher limit might be appropriate in the prevailing circumstances and, thus, to leave it to an appellate court, most likely the Court of Appeal, to consider whether such an increased limit is appropriate. The plaintiff would have first led whatever evidence considered appropriate to that end. The trial judge, having expressly stated that he or she has had due regard to the cap as prescribed by the Guidelines, would then give reasons for suggesting a change in the limit, having set out whatever evidence was considered persuasive. Such an approach also confirms that the limit of €550,000 in the Guidelines is notional and that it is entirely foreseeable that the Superior Courts will grant awards for general damages in excess of it in due course. Once they proceed to do so, it will also underline that the Guidelines are not constitutionally suspect in so far as they prescribe a cap of €550,000 upon awards of general damages in personal injuries litigation, as this cap is notional and nothing more than that.

Conclusion

The conclusions which have been drawn in this chapter are now substantially reflected in the decision of Meenan J in *Bridget Delaney v The Personal Injuries Assessment Board, The Judicial Council, Ireland and The Attorney General*.[44] Whilst it should be acknowledged from the outset that this decision of the High Court is currently under appeal, there were a number of significant findings made by Meenan J, which, at the very least, establish that any challenge to the constitutionality of the Guidelines, whether by reference to the 'cap' on general damages, or otherwise, faces significant countervailing arguments.

In this case, the applicant has challenged the legal basis for the drawing up and passing of the Guidelines. She has maintained that the Personal Injuries Assessment Board erred in law in assessing the value of her injuries under the Guidelines and not the Book of Quantum. In a detailed judgment, the principal findings of Meenan J were as follows:

(i) There are well established principles for the awarding of general damages. These principles provide that the level of damages is not only a matter between a plaintiff and a defendant, but also for society in general. Economic social and commercial conditions have to be taken into account in fixing levels of awards;

---

[44] *Bridget Delaney v The Personal Injuries Assessment Board, The Judicial Council, Ireland and The Attorney General* [2022] IEHC 321.

The Limit on General Damages 217

(ii) Section 90 of the Judicial Council Act 2019 sets out clearly the principles and policies that were to be applied and followed by the Committee (The Personal Injuries Guidelines Committee of the Judicial Council) in drawing up the guidelines;

(iii) In drawing up the Guidelines the Committee methodically followed the principles and policies as directed by the Oireachtas in the said Act. The committee also took expert evidence, both economic and legal, as was provided for;

(iv) The Committee was not mandated to reduce the level of awards for less serious injuries no more than it was mandated to increase the level of awards for catastrophic injuries. The reduction of awards in the Guidelines was a result of the committee applying the provisions of the Act of 2019, as it was obliged to do;

(v) The Committee was entitled to fix levels of awards having regard to the level of awards in other jurisdictions. Both the Act of 2019 and the Supreme Court provided for this;

(vi) The statutory requirement that a court in assessing damages and personal injuries action shall have regard to the Guidelines is not an encroachment on judicial independence as there is provision for a court to depart from the Guidelines on given reasons these reasons have to be rational, cogent and justifiable;

(vii) Judicial independence, together with expertise and experience in the awarding of damages, meant the judiciary was an appropriate body to draft and adopt the Guidelines. The Act of 2019 also made specific provision to preserve judicial independence in s 93 thereof;

(viii) The applicant's constitutional rights of property, bodily integrity and equality do not encompass a right to a particular sum of damages but, rather, a right to have her damages assessed in accordance with well-established legal principles. The effect of the application of these principles is that the level of damages varies over time;

(ix) In assessing her claim the Personal Injuries Assessment Board acted in accordance with the relevant provisions of the Personal Injuries Assessment Board Act (as amended).

These findings of Meenan J speak for themselves. One can particularly see in them a clear statement of two particular propositions which have underlined the observations made in this chapter at paragraphs (vi) and (viii) above respectively. Firstly, as there is provision for a court to depart from the Guidelines for given reasons, which are rational, cogent and justifiable, judicial independence is, therefore, arguably fully preserved in the judicial application of them. Secondly, the constitutional rights of a plaintiff to maintain a claim for damages for personal injuries do not encompass a right to a particular sum of damages but rather a right to have that claim adjudicated in accordance with the principles established in law which pertain to that claim. These are two critical contentions which will undoubtedly be central to the hearing of the appeal in this case and to further litigation and debate in relation to the issues that will inevitably arise concerning the constitutionality of the Guidelines.

INDEX

Abnormality 9, 76, 141, 145, 147, 150, 152–154, 156
Abortion 76, 80, 82, 86, 87
Absolute certainty 10, 16, 150
Absolute confidence test 3, 7–11, 13–15, 150
A & B v Eastern Health Board 86
Ackner, Lord 59, 61
A'Court v Cross 121
Actio personalis moritur cum persona 193
Acute hepatitis 62
Adams v Laboratory Corporation of America 152
Alcock, Robert 59, 60, 71
Alcock v Chief Constable of South Yorkshire Police 58–59, 61, 70–73
Alternative dispute resolution (ADR) 174, 175, 179
'Alternative dispute resolution: Mediation and Conciliation' 175, 177
American Society of Cytopathology 7, 152
Aneurysm 66
Antenatal care 41
Antenatal screening stage 76
AO & DL v The Minister for Justice, Equality and Law Reform 198
Apology laws 161–162, 167
Arkes, HR 147
Asbestos exposure 51, 95, 96
Atkins, Lord 55
Atypical glandular cells (AGC) 152
Atypical squamous cells (ASC) 152
Auditing process 141
Auld, Mr Justice 60, 61, 65

Bailey v Ministry of Defence 97
Baker v Bolton 189, 192–194, 201
Barker v Corus UK Ltd 96
Barr, Mr Justice 128, 199
Battersby v American Oil Company Limited 130
Benefits offset test 84
Best, Chief Justice 121
Best v Wellcome Foundation Ltd 98
Bingham, Lord 96

Blackburn, Lord 196
Blehein v Minister for Health and Children 198, 209
Blind reviews 141, 142, 144, 147–149, 151–158
Bolam v Friern Hospital Management Committee 8, 11, 26–28, 37, 41–44
Bolitho v City and Hackney Health Authority 8, 11
Bolton v Blackrock Clinic 29, 30
Bonnington Castings Ltd v Wardlaw 94
Book of Quantum 203, 207, 208, 216
BowelScreen 144
Bradfield, Owen M. 84
Brain damage 4, 62–64, 97, 98
Breach of duty 7, 9, 23, 31, 33, 61, 62, 66, 69, 71, 77, 92, 94–96, 98, 103, 108, 110, 113, 122, 124, 132, 133, 136, 147, 152, 190, 191, 215
Breast cancer screening 145, 148
BreastCheck 14, 15, 144
Brennan, Mr Justice 196
Brereton v The Governors of the National Maternity Hospital 126
Bridge, Lord 58
Bridget Delaney v The Personal Injuries Assessment Board, The Judicial Council, Ireland and The Attorney General 216
Broadley v Guy Clapham & Co 117
Brooke, LJ 83, 114
Bullying 127, 130
'But for' test 91–93, 95–103
Byrne v Ryan 80–82, 85

Caesarean section 41, 44, 46
Cancer 141–143, 145, 147 *see also* Cervical cancer
  audit markings 151, 155–157
  diagnosis 141, 143, 145, 147, 150, 158
  interval 145, 147, 164
  misdiagnosis cases 190
Cancer screening test 145, 147, 150, 151, 164
  sensitivity and specificity in 146–147
Canning-Kishver v Sandwell and West Birmingham Hospital 97

Canterbury v Spence 34, 37
Capping Damages in Personal Injuries Actions 203, 209
Cardozo, Benjamin N. 202
Cattanach v Melchior 81, 85
Causation 91, 131–133, 136, 137 *see also specific cases*
  'but for' test and its development 91–93, 103
  cause in fact 91
  cause in law 91
  factual 91–93, 98, 103
  loss of chance 92, 99–102
  material contribution test 91–99
Cerebral palsy 92
Cervical cancer 7, 141, 144, 147, 148, 156, 174, 192
  diagnosis and treatment 144, 148
  interval 145
  screening 144–146, 157, 158
CervicalCheck 16, 141, 142, 144–148, 150, 151, 157, 159, 160, 162, 163, 173–174, 192
Cervical smear tests 54, 144–146, 192
Chamberlain, Mr Justice 69–71
Charleton, Mr Justice 110–112, 114, 115, 117–119, 123, 198
Chester v Afshar 37, 42–43, 100–101
Child-rearing costs 78–81, 83, 84
Child-rearing damages 79, 81, 83–85
Chronic neuropathic pain 29, 30
Circuit Court 57, 82
Civil law courts 81
Civil Liability Act (1961) 53, 193–194, 196, 199
  Part IV 189, 191–193, 195, 198, 201, 215
  s 2 81
  s 48 190, 191, 197, 200–202
  s 48(1) 190–191, 196, 200, 201
  s 48(2) 191, 201, 215
Civil Liability (Amendment) Act (2017) 163–165, 168
  Part 4 163
  s 8 163
  s 10 163
  s 16 163
Civil Liability and Courts Act (2004) 107, 131
  s 7 109, 182
  s 7(a) 122
  s 10 124
  s 15 177, 178
  s 15(1) 178
  s 22 203, 207
Civil Liability (Open Disclosure) (Prescribed Statements) Regulations (2018) 163–165

Civil Procedure Rules 25.6-25.9 199
Civil rights 128
Clarke, CJ, 3, 6, 10–12, 14, 15, 142, 153–154, 189, 194, 197, 206, 207, 214, 216
Classic litmus test 93
Clinical Pathology Laboratories Incorporated (CPL) 148, 149, 154–157, 181
Close proximate relationship test 53
Clyde, Lord 79
Code of Conduct for the Bar of Ireland 135
  Rule 5.9 131
Congenital abnormality 76, 85
Constitution of Ireland (1937) 197–198, 204
  Article 34.1 213
  Article 40.3.1 209, 211, 213
  Article 40.3.2 210, 211, 213
  Article 42A.1 197
  Eighth Amendment 86, 87
  Fourteenth Amendment 86
  Thirteenth Amendment 86
Corbett, Val 177
Countervailing circumstances 129, 156, 157
Courtney v Our Lady's Hospital & ors 53–54, 57
Courts and Court Officers Act (1995)
  s 45 181
Cropper, Alison 156, 157
Cross, Mr Justice Kevin 3, 4, 7–11, 54, 55, 57, 73, 127, 133–135, 147, 150–155, 181, 192
Cuddy v Mays 51
Cunningham v Neary 117
Curran v Cadbury Ireland Limited 57
Cytology screening 8, 141, 146, 148, 154, 158
  litigation 8, 9, 11, 13, 141, 143
  markings 143

Dáil debate 160
Dáil Eireann 165, 171
Damages
  actionable suit at time of death 195–196
  Baker v Bolton 192–194
  Civil Liability Act (1961) 193–194
  common law cause of action 191, 196–197, 202, 209
  interim awards 191, 198–201
  Irish Constitution 197–198
  'lost years' doctrine 194–195, 198
  Morrisseys' case 192
  overview of claims 189–191
  periodic payment orders (PPOs) 199–200
  statutory intervention 200–201
  wrongful death claim 191, 192, 195, 196

Index 221

Daniels and anor v Heskin 25, 26
Darjohn Developments Limited (in liquidation) v IBRC Limited 130
Davies, Mr Justice 72
Denham, CJ 49, 50, 53
Dental implant surgery 29, 30
Dermatitis 94
Devlin v National Maternity Hospital 53, 57, 73
Diabetic RetinaScreen 144
Digital imaging 149, 151, 155, 157
Diplopia (double vision) 36, 37
Distributive justice 79, 81, 83, 84
Dobbie v Medway HA 117
Doctor centred approach 37, 38, 45
'Doctor knows best' approach 19
Doctor–patient relationship 43, 47, 167
Doherty v Bowaters Irish Wallboard Mills Ltd 194
Donaldson, MR 115
Donoghue v Stevenson 55, 87
Downes v TLC Nursing Home 126, 134
Dunne (An Infant) v National Maternity Hospital & another 3–6, 8, 15, 20, 26, 30, 142, 158
  principles 4–13, 20–23, 25, 29–32
  standard of professional care for medical practitioners 20
Duty of candour laws 161, 162, 164, 166
Duty of care 4–6, 8, 9, 13, 16, 24, 46, 50, 51, 55, 58, 69, 70, 73, 77, 87, 103, 142, 150, 158
Duty of disclosure 26, 31, 32, 36, 46, 47
Dyson, Lord 65, 66

Edmund-Davies, Lord 58
Egan, Mr Justice 25, 29, 33, 50
Elective surgery 23, 24, 30–32, 35, 39
Ellahi v The Governor of Midlands Prison and others 126, 134
Ellenborough, Lord 192
Ellis v Wallsend District Hospital 34
Emeh v Kensington and Chelsea and Westminster Area Health Authority 77–79, 82
England 10, 13, 19, 26, 36, 37, 55, 81, 164, 199
English Court of Appeal 8, 77, 82–84, 198
English High Court 77, 198
English law 94, 101, 102
European Convention on Human Rights Article 6 128
European Mediation Directive (2008) 174
Evidence 4, 12, 21, 24, 28, 33–36
  credible witness 37

expert 13, 14, 22, 127, 131, 133, 136, 141, 143, 144, 151–154, 157, 158
medical 92–93, 128, 130, 132
oral 25
physical 149
unequivocal 44
Evidential gap 94, 95
Evidential uncertainty 92
Ex parte application 133
Expert Group Report to Review the Law of Torts and the Current Systems for the Management of Clinical Negligence Claims 163
Expert medical report 110, 121, 123, 124, 126, 131–133, 135–137
Expert Reference Group 16, 148, 150
Ex tempore judgment 127

factual causation 91–93, 98, 103, 158
Fairchild v Glenhaven Funeral Services Ltd 95–101
Family Leave and Miscellaneous Provisions Act (2021)
  s 30 203
Fassoulas v Ramey 83
Fatal Accidents Act (1846) 193, 194, 198, 199
Feit, Tim 153
Felony merger doctrine 193
Fennelly, Justice 101, 102
Final Protocol 25 January 2019 156
  Clause 4 151, 155
Finlay, CJ 20–23, 25, 28, 30, 31, 158
Finlay Geoghegan, Ms Justice 3–5, 12, 29, 51, 86, 111–114, 116, 118, 205, 215
Finnegan, Mr Justice 36
Fitzpatrick v White 36–41, 45, 47
Fletcher v The Commissioners for Public Works 51, 57, 73, 81
Forbes v Wandsworth Health Authority 116, 117
Freeney v Health Service Executive 4, 14–16, 145, 148

Galli-Atkinson v Seghal 63
Geoghegan v Harris 29–40
Gibson, Peter 61, 62, 66, 71
Gill, Lord 80, 81
Glencar Explorations Plc v Mayo County Council (No. 2) 55
Goddard, Lord 130
Goff, Mr Justice 68
'Good Medical Practice in Seeking Informed Consent to Treatment' 46
Gough v Neary 112, 114, 116, 205, 215
Grant v Roche Products (Ireland) Ltd 197
Green v Hardiman 110, 111, 116, 123

Greenwood v Harris 169
Gregg v Scott 98, 100, 101, 102
Guidelines for the Review of GYN Cytology Samples 152
Guide to Professional Conduct and Ethics 162

Hale, Lady 43, 44, 83, 84, 100, 101
Halford v Brookes 115
Hallett, Mr Justice 64
Hamilton, CJ, 29, 50, 54–57
Harassment 127, 130
Hardiman, Mr Justice 197
Harford v Electricity Supply Board 56
Harmonised Index of Consumer Prices 199
Harrison, Brian 59
Haughton, Mr Justice 127, 129, 134–137
Hay v O'Grady 39
Health and Social Care Act (Regulated Activities) Regulations (2014) 164
Health Information and Quality Authority (HIQA) 165
Health Service Executive (HSE) 7, 10, 11, 14, 132, 144, 146, 148, 151, 167, 173, 192
Healy v Buckley 39–41, 45
Heaney v Ireland 209, 211, 212, 214
Hederman, Mr Justice 23–25
Hegarty v Health Service Executive 199
Heil v Rankin 83
Hewitt v Health Service Executive 195, 196
High Court Central Office 124
High Court of Australia 37, 43, 76
Hilfiker, David 161
Hindsight bias 141–144, 147–148, 151, 153–158
Histopathology 146
Hoffmann, Lord 96–98, 100, 102
Hogan, Mr Justice 196
Hope, Lord 79
Hurley Ahern and anor v Moore & Southern Health Board 85
Hyland, Ms Justice 14, 15, 126, 147
Hypoxic injury 68
Hysterectomy 67

Individual rights 19
'Infallible threshold guidance' 92, 103
Informed consent 19–47
  content and timing of warning to reasonable patient 38–39
  developments in Ireland 39–40
  Dunne principles and its application 20–23, 25, 29–32
  Fitzpatrick v White 36–38
  Geoghegan v Harris 29–35
  implications in Ireland 44–47
  inquisitive patient doctrine 35–36
  Montgomery v Lanarkshire Health Board 41–43
  negligence principles applied to obligation 23–25
  overview 19–20
  patient choice 25–28
  reasonable patient test 29
  standard of professional care for medical practitioners 20
  UK Supreme Court judgment 43–44
Inherent defects provision 30–32
Inherent jurisdiction 191, 200
Inquisitive patient doctrine 35–36
Institute of Obstetricians and Gynaecologists (IOG) 10
Insurance costs 211, 212
Insurance policy 162, 163
Internal cranial haemorrhaging 132
Inter-observer variability 141–144, 146, 149–153, 158
Interval Cancer Report 16, 148, 150
Intra-observer variability 152
Irish Court of Appeal 39–41, 45, 56, 57, 59, 62, 63, 65–67, 69, 70, 72, 73, 97, 110, 121, 126–129, 132, 134–137, 142, 143, 148, 149, 154–156, 158, 181–183, 195, 206, 207, 214, 216
Irish Government 175
Irish High Court 3, 4, 6, 14–16, 22, 29, 30, 36, 39, 40, 49, 51, 53, 54, 56, 60, 64, 69, 80, 81, 85, 110, 124–127, 129, 132–136, 143, 147, 154, 155, 173, 179, 183, 190, 192, 195, 199, 200, 205, 214–216
  absolute confidence test in 7–10
  judgment in *Morrissey and Morrissey v Health Service Executive, Quest Diagnostics Incorporated and MedLab Pathology Limited* 7–10, 152–153
  judgment in *Vivienne Wallace v Health Service Executive and Sonic Healthcare (Ireland) Ltd and MedLab Pathology Ltd and Clinical Pathology Laboratories Incorporated* 156–157
Irish law 8, 11, 20, 36, 45–47, 102, 169
  on informed consent 45–47
  inquisitive patient in 36
  legal standard in 8
Irish Law of Torts (McMahon and Binchy) 26–29
Irish Superior Courts 14, 16, 76, 121–122, 137, 149, 150, 153, 158, 183, 198, 204, 207, 214, 216
Irish Supreme Court 3–6, 15, 16, 22, 28–31, 36, 38–40, 45, 47, 50, 53, 55, 57,

Index 223

70, 72, 73, 81, 87, 92, 98, 99, 101, 102, 110, 111, 114, 123–124, 135, 142, 150, 153–154, 157, 183, 189–195, 197, 198, 201–207, 209, 211–215, 217
IRM v Minister for Justice, Equality, Ireland and the Attorney General 87
Irvine, P 162, 166–170

John v Central Manchester Children's University Hospitals NHS Foundation Trust 97
Judicial Committee 208
Judicial Council Act (2019)
   s 7 203
   s 90 217
   s 99 203, 207
   s 100 203
Judicial Council of Ireland 82, 203, 207, 217
Jupp, Justice 77

Keane, CJ 51, 57
Kearney v McQuillan and North Eastern Health Board (No 2) 212
Kearns, Mr Justice 29–39, 52, 98, 99, 102
Kelly, P 80–82, 174
Kelly v Hennessy 50–57, 72, 73
Kerr, Lord 43–45, 77
King v Minister for the Environment (No 2) 213
Kirby, Mr Justice 37
'Known complication' 28, 30, 38

Langstaff, Mr Justice 198
Laparoscopic sterilisation procedure 82, 85
Latham, LJ 63
Lavan, Mr Justice 195
Law Reform Commission 174, 177–178, 203, 209
Law Reform Commission Report (2010) 175, 177
Legal principles 6, 7, 15, 16, 21, 35, 40, 102, 157, 217
Legal Services Regulation Act (2015)
   s 169(1)(g) 183
Legislative reform, in 1991 108, 109
Liquid based cytology (LBC) testing 144, 147, 149–151
Liverpool Women's Hospital NHS Foundation Trust v Ronayne 67, 69, 71
Lord Campbell's Act *see* Fatal Accidents Act (1846)
Loss of chance approach 92, 99–103
'Lost years' doctrine 190, 194–195, 198

Macken, Ms Justice 36
Macmillan, Lord 87

Madden, Deirdre 164, 170
Maguire, CJ 25
Mahon v Burke 195, 196
Mammography 145, 148
Mangan v Dockery & ors 135
Master of the High Court 125
Master of the Rolls 71, 72
Material cause approach 99
Material contribution test 91–99, 103
   Irish perspective 98–99
   in medical cases 96–98
   overview 93–96
Material facts 27, 28, 45
Materiality 28, 30–33, 38, 43, 45, 94
Material risks 26, 30, 32, 33, 36, 38, 43, 46
McCarthy, Mr Justice 25–29, 33
McFarlane v Tayside Health Board 77–84
McGhee v National Coal Board 94–96, 98, 99
McKechnie, Mr Justice 135
McKenna, Peter 12
McLoughlin v O'Brian 58, 62, 71
McMahon, Mr Justice 57
McMurdo, P 85
MC v The Clinical Director of the Central Mental Hospital 209
Media frenzy 9, 10
Mediation 173–185
   confidentiality 179–180, 184
   direct engagement and definitive answer 180–181, 185
   disclosure of experts' reports 181–182
   and impact of mediator 179
   legislative framework 174–175
   limitation period by Statutes of Limitations 182–183
   in personal injuries litigation 177, 178
   relationship with negotiation 176, 180, 183–185
   supervisory intervention of courts 176–179
   unreasonable refusal and awards of costs by courts 183–184
   as voluntary process 174–178
Mediation Act (2017) 174, 175
   s 2 175
   s 14(1) 175
   s 14(2) 175
   s 16 176, 178
   s 16(1) 178
   s 17(1) 184
   s 17(2) 184
   s 18 182
   s 18(1) 182
   s 21 183
   s 22 178

Medical Council of Ireland 46, 47, 162
Medical error 159, 160
Medical Independent 10
Medical negligence litigation *see also individual entries*
  allegations 4, 5, 12, 15, 20
  causation of damage in 28, 32–35, 42, 45
  claim for damages for personal injuries 55
  in cytology screening 8
  deficits in advice of treatment 19, 22
  development of 'but for' test in 103
  in diagnosis/treatment 5, 20, 21
  duty of care *see* Duty of care
  law on 4, 5, 10, 11
  legal standard of 7, 8, 10, 15
  legal test for 3, 8, 14
  against medical administrators 21
  in performance of surgery 22
  vs. professional negligence claims 136
Medical practitioners 4, 6, 31, 32, 35
  conduct 5, 20, 21
  duty of care *see* Duty of care
  guilty 5
  standard of professional care for 20, 23
Medical profession/professionals 3, 4, 11, 12, 14–16, 31, 67, 76, 79, 137, 150, 161, 173
Medical treatment 5, 20, 21, 23, 24, 31, 32
  law on consent to 40
  patient's consent on 43, 47
Medico-legal issues 75
MedLab Pathology Limited 7, 9, 150, 153, 192
Meenan, Mr Justice 216, 217
Meningitis 53
Mesothelioma 51, 95, 96
Miley v Birthistle 199
Millet, Lord 79, 81
Montgomery v Lanarkshire Health Board 19, 40–47
Moragne v States Marine Lines Inc 195
Morrissey, Ruth 192
Morrissey and Morrissey v Health Service Executive, Quest Diagnostics Incorporated and MedLab Pathology Limited 8, 10, 12, 14–16, 54, 57, 73, 142, 147, 149, 150, 157, 160, 189, 191, 193, 195, 197, 201, 203, 205–208, 214–216
  factual background 6–7
  High Court judgment 7–10, 152–153
  Supreme Court judgment 3, 10–14, 153–154
Mullaly v Bus Éireann 49
Murphy, Cliona 10
Murphy and Cullen v ARF Management Limited 126, 134

Murphy, Mr Justice 127, 133, 199
Murphy v Health Service Executive 121, 126, 127, 129, 132–134, 136
Murray v Shuter 198

National Cervical Screening Programme 3, 7, 144, 192
National Health Service 97
National Screening Service 16, 144
Neonatal mortality 41
Nerve damage 30, 35, 100, 101
Nervous shock 49–73
  Alcock v Chief Constable of South Yorkshire Police 58–59, 61, 70–73
  category of relationships to claim damages 52–53
  Courtney v Our Lady's Hospital & ors 53–54, 57
  Cuddy v Mays 51
  Curran v Cadbury Ireland Limited 57
  Devlin v National Maternity Hospital 53, 57, 73
  Donoghue v Stevenson 55
  Fletcher v Commissioners of Public Works 51, 57, 73
  Galli-Atkinson v Seghal 63
  Glencar Explorations Plc v Mayo County Council (No. 2) 55
  Harford v Electricity Supply Board 56
  Kelly v Hennessy 50–57, 72, 73
  limits in law to liability 53, 58, 71, 73
  Liverpool Women's Hospital NHS Foundation Trust v Ronayne 67, 69, 71
  McLoughlin v O'Brian 58, 62, 71
  Mullaly v Bus Éireann 49
  negligent infliction of damage 63, 64, 66–67
  North Glamorgan NHS Trust v Walters 62–67, 69–71
  Paul (A Child) v Royal Wolverhampton NHS Trust 69–70, 72, 73
  Polmear v Royal Cornwall Hospital NHS Trust 70, 72, 73
  Purchase v Ahmed 68–70, 72, 73
  recover damages for 49, 50, 52–54, 56, 61, 65, 68, 71
  Re (A Child) v Calderdale and Huddersfield NHS Foundation Trust 68
  Ruth Morrissey and Paul Morrissey v Health Service Executive, Quest Diagnostics Incorporated and MedLab Pathology Limited 54
  Sheehan v Bus Éireann/Irish Bus and Vincent Dower 57

Index

Shorter v Surrey and Sussex Healthcare NHS Trust 66
Sion v Hampstead Health Authority 61–62, 66, 71
Taylor v A Novo (UK) Ltd 65, 69–71, 73
Taylor v Somerset Health Authority 60–61, 65, 66, 70
White v Lidl UK 63–64, 71
Wild v Southend University Hospital NHS Foundation Trust 67–68
New Cross Hospital 69
Newman, William 167
Nolan v The Board of Management of St Mary's Diocesan School 127
Nolan v Wirenski 206
Non-negligent errors 11
Noonan, Mr Justice 56, 57, 127–129, 148, 155–156, 181, 182
North Glamorgan NHS Trust v Walters 62–67, 69–71
Notifiable patient safety incidents 164

Objective approach 33–35, 40, 45
O'Donnell, Mr Justice 110, 111, 118, 136
O'Donovan, Mr Justice 53
O'Donovan v Cork County Council 4
O'Flaherty, Mr Justice 23–25, 28–30, 37, 98
O'Flynn v Health Service Executive, MedLab Pathology Limited, Sonic Healthcare (Ireland) Limited and Clinical Pathology Laboratories Limited 181
O'Higgins, CJ 215
Oireachtas 165, 171, 174, 177, 194, 202, 212, 213, 217
Oliver, Lord 59, 60, 71
'Omnibus' cases 205
O'Neill, Mr Justice 54
Open disclosure policy 159–171
  apologies to patients 159–161
  apology, disclosure and duty of candour laws 161–162, 165, 167, 170
  availing protection of legislation 169–170
  in aviation industry 161, 166
  Civil Liability (Amendment) Act (2017) 163–165
  Civil Liability (Open Disclosure) (Prescribed Statements) Regulations (2018) 163–165
  concept of 160, 161
  effective and ineffective apologies 167, 168, 170
  Greenwood v Harris 169
  HSE definition of 167–168
  impact on medical practitioners 159, 160
  legislative developments 159
  mandatory disclosure and laws 164–170
  narrowness and inaccessible 168–170
  Patient Safety (Notifiable Patient Safety Incidents) Bill (2019) 164, 165, 168, 169, 171
  voluntary open disclosure laws 162, 163, 166, 170
  Woronka v Sewall 169
Orchialgia 22, 28
'Ordinary and aware' plaintiff 117, 118
Ordinary care 5, 11, 20, 24
Osborn v Gillett 194
O'Sullivan v Ireland, The Attorney General & ors 110, 111, 114–119, 123, 136
Overarching principle 11, 12
Owen, Philip 41

Pancreatitis 97
Parkinson v St James & Seacroft University Hospital NHS Trust 82–85
Patient centred approach 37, 38, 45, 47
Patient choice 25–28
Patient Safety (Notifiable Patient Safety Incidents) Bill (2019) 168, 169, 171
  Part 7 165
  Schedule 1 164
  s 2 164
  s 5 164
  s 10 165
Patient safety incident 163, 164
Paul (A Child) v Royal Wolverhampton NHS Trust 69–70, 72, 73
Pearce v United Bristol Healthcare NHS Trust 37, 43
Peart, Mr Justice 102
Pemberton, William 59
Penney, Palmer and Cannon v East Kent Health Authority 8–10, 12–13
Periodic payment orders (PPOs) 199–200
Peritonitis 67
Personal autonomy 19
Personal injuries 50, 64, 65, 68, 81, 96, 101, 107–110, 119, 122, 124, 126, 127, 130–133, 135, 137, 189, 190, 192, 194–196, 198, 200, 201, 211, 213–217
Personal Injuries Assessment Board 127, 131, 203, 216, 217
Personal Injuries Assessment Board Act (2003) 203, 217
Personal Injuries Guidelines 82, 203, 204, 207–209
Personal Injuries Guidelines and statutory cap on general damages 209–214
  autonomy and discretion of Superior Courts 213–214

infringe constitutional rights 209
proportionality 211–212
rationality test 212–213
right to bodily integrity 209–211, 213, 217
right to litigate and correlative right to effective remedy 210
The Personal Injuries Guidelines Committee 217
Personal rights 193, 197, 202, 211
Phelan, Vicky 7
Philips, Lord 100
Philp v Ryan 101, 102
Physical injury 50, 53, 55, 56, 59
Picken, Mr Justice 98
Pickett v British Rail Engineering Ltd 194
Polmear v Royal Cornwall Hospital NHS Trust 70, 72, 73
Postcoital bleeding 54
Post-traumatic stress disorder 49, 53, 56, 65, 68
Prejudice 128–129, 131, 133, 134, 155–157
Prenatal foetus testing 75, 86, 87
Prescribed grading system 145
Pre-trial negotiation 173, 174, 180, 184
Procedural sterilisation 75, 81, 82, 87
Professional negligence 4, 7, 10, 11, 13–15, 20, 131, 133, 135, 136
Property rights 210, 211, 213, 217
Prostate cancer 101
Prostatitis 101
Proximate cause of injury 92, 93, 98, 99
Psychiatric illness 50, 51, 56, 58, 59, 65, 67, 68
Psychiatric injury 54–57, 61–65, 67–70, 72, 73
Public policy 51, 55, 73, 77, 79, 81
Purchase v Ahmed 68–70, 72, 73
Purdy v Lenihan 92, 93

Queen's Bench Division 26
Quest Diagnostics Incorporated 7, 9–11, 152–154, 192
Quinn v Mid Western Health Board and anor 98, 99, 102

Radiological screening 146
Reasonable care 20, 43
Reasonable patient test 29, 32–35, 37, 40, 45, 47
  content of warning 38
  timing of warning 39
Reed, Lord 43–45
Reibl v Hughes 23, 29, 34, 37
Reid, Lord 94
Reproductive technology 75

Res judicata 201
Restitutio in integrum principle 204
Re (A Child) v Calderdale and Huddersfield NHS Foundation Trust 68
Review Group 175
Reynolds, Ms Justice 156–158
Roche v Peilow 20, 31, 32
Roese, Professor 154
Rogers, VW Horton, 81
Rogers v Whitaker 37, 38, 43
Rosenburg v Percival 37
Ross, Nina 167
Rules of the Superior Courts (RSC, 1986) 175
  Ord 1A 124
  Ord 8 121, 124–126, 128, 130–134, 136
  Ord 8, r 1 125
  Ord 8, r 1(1) 125
  Ord 8, r 1(3) 125
  Ord 8, r 1(4) 125–127, 130, 133, 134, 137
  Ord 36, r 34 199
  Ord 39, rr 45–51 181
  Ord 56A, r 9 183
  Ord 99 r 3(1) 183
Ruth Morrissey and Paul Morrissey v Health Service Executive, Quest Diagnostics Incorporated and MedLab Pathology Limited 54
Ryan, Mr Justice 85

Scally, Gabriel 163
Scarman, Lord 43, 45, 58
Scotland 81
Scottish Court of Session 42, 44
Sea-Land Services Inc v Gaudet 195
Self-determination 26, 27, 37, 43
Self-protection 165, 166
Septicaemia 67
Sexual capacity 25, 27, 28
Sexual impotence 28
Sheehan v Bus Éireann/Irish Bus and Vincent Dower 57
Shorter v Surrey and Sussex Healthcare NHS Trust 66
Shoulder dystocia 41, 42, 44
SI 391/1998 (Rules of the Superior Courts (No 6) (Disclosure of Reports and Statements) 1998) 181, 182
Sidaway v Governors of the Bethlehem Royal Hospital 27, 36, 37, 41–43, 45
Sine qua non test *see* 'But for' test
Sinnott v Quinnsworth Limited 204, 205, 215
Sion v Hampstead Health Authority 61–62, 66, 71
Slynn, Lord 78, 79
Smear tests
  cervical 3, 7, 8

Index 227

cytology 16
Smith LJ 116
Spargo v North Essex District Health Authority 114
'Special circumstances' test 95, 99, 125–131, 134–136, 155, 194
Specialisation and skill 5, 20, 21
'Standard of approach' 3, 4, 10–16
Standard of care 3, 4, 6–8, 11, 13, 14, 20, 23, 24, 142, 152
Standard operating procedure 15
State Claims Agency 199
Statute of Limitations (1957) 122
  s 11(2)(b) 107, 108
Statute of Limitations (Amendment) Act (1991) 107, 108
  s 2 110–113, 115–119, 122
  s 2(1) 108, 111, 115, 116, 118, 119
  s 2(1)(a) 113
  s 2(1)(b) 113
  s 2(1)(c) 110, 111, 113–115
  s 2(1)(d) 113
  s 2(1)(e) 113
  s 2(2) 109, 112
  s 2(3) 109
  s 3 108, 110, 113, 115–118
  s 3(1) 122
  s 6 108
Statutory cap on general damages 203–204
  'cap' *vs.* 'non-cap' cases 204–207, 215–216
  Personal Injuries Guidelines and *see* Personal Injuries Guidelines and statutory cap on general damages
  proportionality 205–207, 210
Staughton, LJ 61
Stephenson, LJ 198
Steyn, Lord 37, 79, 83
Strasser, Mark 80
Stroke 132, 133
Subarachnoid haemorrhage 66
Subjective approach 33, 34, 40, 45–47
Supreme Court of Canada 23, 34, 103
Supreme Court of Florida 83
Sweeney v Duggan 209, 210
Swift, Mr Justice 66, 67

Tan, S 12
Taxation 211, 212
Taylor & Anor v A Novo (UK) Limited 65, 69–71, 73
Taylor v Somerset Health Authority 60–61, 65, 66, 70
Technical assault and battery 22
Thake v Maurice 77, 78
Thompson v Arnold 198

Time limit for medical negligence 107–121
  commencement and service of proceedings 121
  'date of knowledge' determination 111–115, 122, 123
  'date of knowledge' to claims of 108, 110–111
  delays in obtaining expert opinion 136–137
  Irish Court of Appeal judgment 134–136
  Murphy v Health Service Executive 132–134
  Ord 8 of Rules of the Superior Courts (1986) 121, 124–126
  Ord 8 Rule 1(4) of Rules of the Superior Courts (1986) 126–127
  s 2(1)(c) of Statute of Limitations (Amendment) Act 1991 113–115
  s 2 of Statute of Limitations (Amendment) Act 1991 115–118, 122
  s 3(1) of Statute of Limitations (Amendment) Act 1991 122
  s 3 of Statute of Limitations (Amendment) Act 1991 115–118
  s 7(a) of Civil Liability and Courts Act (2004) 122
  shortening for personal injuries actions 131–132
  'special circumstances' test 125–131
  Statute of Limitations (1957) 122
Tomlinson, LJ 67
Tort law 77, 86, 87, 101, 197, 198, 209
'Totality' cases *see* 'Omnibus' cases
Travel and Information Amendments 87
Tubal ligation 75, 80
Tumelty, Mary-Elizabeth 164, 170
Tuohy v Courtney 209, 212, 213
Two-tier test 126, 134

Udale v Bloomsbury Area Health Authority 77–79
UK House of Lords 27, 36, 37, 58, 59, 61, 71, 72, 77–80, 83, 94, 95, 96, 98, 100–102, 194
Underhill, LJ 71, 72
United Kingdom 13, 34, 49, 57, 58, 60, 72, 73, 76–78, 80–82, 85, 114
United Kingdom Supreme Court 19, 40, 41, 43–47, 72, 73
United States 81, 152, 168
United States Supreme Court 196, 202
University Hospital Mayo 132
US Court of Appeals 34
US Court of Appeals for the Eleventh Circuit 152

Vaginal delivery 41, 44
Varadkar TD, Leo 160
Vasectomy 22–25, 28, 75, 77, 78
The Vera Cruz (No 1) (1884) 196
Viral gastric bug 53
Vivienne Wallace v Health Service Executive and Sonic Healthcare (Ireland) Ltd and MedLab Pathology Ltd and Clinical Pathology Laboratories Incorporated 142, 143, 148, 149
  Court of Appeal judgment 154–156
  High Court judgment 156–157
Vos MR, Geoffrey 70

Waite, LJ 62
Wales 13, 19, 26, 36, 37, 81
Waller, LJ 97
Walsh v Family Planning Services Ltd 21–22, 24–30, 33, 36–38, 47

Ward, LJ 62, 63, 66, 67
Warning of risks 19, 21–26, 28, 30–33, 38, 42
White, Mr Justice 37
White, John P M 196
White v Lidl UK 63–64, 71
Wilberforce, Lord 58, 62, 63, 94
Wild v Southend University Hospital NHS Foundation Trust 67–68
Wilsher v Essex Area Health Authority 95–97, 99
Wilson, Dr Given 145
Woolf, Lord 8, 10, 37, 43, 83
Wootton v J Docter Ltd 97
Woronka v Sewall 169
Wrongful conception claim 75–76 *see also specific cases*
  of disabled child 82–87
  of healthy child 76–82